D0539137

The Sailing Week-End Book

The Sailing Week-End Book

Paul Heiney
and Libby Purves

There was once an old sailor my grandfather knew,
Who had so many things which he wanted to do
That, whenever he thought it was time to begin,
He couldn't, because of the state he was in.

A A Milne

Illustrated by Trevor Ridley

Acknowledgements

The authors wish to thank the following for their help and advice with various sections of this book:

The Cruising Association, and the National Maritime Museum, for their excellent reference libraries; the Island Cruising Club, the Humber Keel and Sloop Preservation Society; Jeremy Burnett; Michael Hunt of Anglia TV; Spencer Herapath and the Royal Yacht Squadron; the Corporation of Trinity House and the Starboard crew of THV *Winston Churchill*; The Commissioners of Northern Lights; Patrick Purves; the Britannia Royal Naval College, Dartmouth; Everard Lines; Red Funnel Line; the Wildfowl Trust and Juliet Bailey; and other friends and chance acquaintances too numerous to name, without whose advice, suggestions, and experience we, and the book, would be far poorer.

The authors and publishers of *The Sailing Week-End Book* are most grateful to the authors, publishers and agents for permission to reproduce their work in the anthology between pages 149 and 175, and short items on other pages. Title page quotation from Now We Are Six, by courtesy Methuen Children's Books.

ISBN 0 85177 346 X

Published in Great Britain 1985 by
Nautical Books
an imprint of Conway Maritime Press Ltd.,
24 Bride Lane, Fleet Street, London EC4Y 8DR.

Filmset by Trevor Ridley Creative Services, Southend-on-Sea.

Printed in Great Britain by The Bath Press.

Contents

Introduction 7
A Cruise in Our Company 10
Keep Your Fingers Crossed 20
Ships That Pass 1 22
Red Sky at Night 43
How Big is She? 51
Other People at Sea 54
Ships That Pass 2 64
Distance-Judging at Sea 71
Looming Lights 76
Fare Ye Well and Adieu 87
Pipe Aboard! 93
The Captain's Log 101
Ships That Pass 3 106
Yo Ho Ho 113
Geese, Gulls, and Gannets 118
Flag-Upmanship 138
Dressing Up and Dressing-Down 146
Past and Present Pleasures 149
Ships That Pass 4 176
The Lower Deck 182
Well-Whipped Ropes' Ends 189

to

CHRISTOPHER THORNHILL
and *Kathleen*

Introduction

It was in the years before the Second War that the publishers Seeley Service & Co produced their famous library of 'Week-End Books'. The *Countryman's*, the *Angler's*, the *Gardener's*, the *Foxhunter's* and others — each a miscellany of information, jokes, opinions, and snatches of prose and verse around the central subject. People gave them for birthdays, bought them cunningly to convert new enthusiasts, borrowed and lent them, re-bound the sagging covers with care and left them thoughtfully alongside the jug of flowers and the bedside lamp in the guest-room. All that we mean by 'week-end' was summed up between their covers — private enthusiasm, gifted amateurishness, a leisurely and unforced interest in everything to do with the beloved pursuit. The 'Week-End Books' were a very British phenomenon.

We think — but we are biased — that the best of the lot was the *Yachtsman's Week-End Book*, by John Irving and Douglas Service. To find this in the mildewed mahogany bookshelf of your host's boat is a guarantee of pleasure, as you sink back into your bunk and turn up the oil-lamp for half an hour's random reading. It has certainly given us many happy hours, although our glass-fibre boats and the crowded waters we sail in would be barely recognizable to Irving and Service; so we gladly acknowledge our debt of gratitude to them for the idea behind this new 'Week-End' book for sailors. Although they offered some fairly useful advice — about tinned cheese, sailmaker's whipping, how to give an order aboard ship, etc — most of the information they offer goes above and beyond mere practicality. This aspect we particularly liked.

For there are a good many books published today about how to sail safely and efficiently. Yachting has grown specialised; cruising men and racing men, coastal and blue-water types, monohull and multihull fanciers, are all catered for splendidly and copiously. If you need to build your own mizzenmast, improvise a trysail, or programme your onboard computer to find English Harbour Antigua, half-a-dozen experts will have written books on it.

What seems to be lacking, though, is any book about how to *enjoy* your cruising. We have always found that our own pleasure depends only partly on the boat's smooth forward progress through the water towards a well-charted harbour. It is a more complicated enjoyment than that; it depends on eyes, and ears, and ideas, and a sense of being part of a long, island tradition. We were always turning vainly to our bookshelf in the cabin to find out why only the Royal Yacht Squadron was entitled to fly the White Ensign, or whether that black thing was a shag or a cormorant, and where it had come from; what sort of ship that distant gaffer might be, and what it felt like to sail aboard her; how they light buoys to make them flash nine times regularly and then stop, or whether it was true that the Navy always writes ship's logs in pencil. We wanted to know how other people sailed, whether round-the-world heroes and heroines ever burned the porridge; we wanted ideas on how to amuse our ten-month-old baby on a long windward passage, and how to calculate tonnage. When we were bored and becalmed, we found after a while that we did not want to practise our sun-sights or memorize the rules of ocean racing and the IALA buoyage system. We wanted, instead, to learn to play a hornpipe on the penny-whistle with minimum effort, to sing the Aldeburgh Cod-Bangers Song, or to read a bit of rousing sea writing by an author we had never encountered before. And, because our boats have never been very big, and the bookcase is always half-jammed with binoculars, flares, pilot books, and oddly shaped pieces of ex-engine, we really wanted all this in one neat volume, to dip into between the thousand small crises of shipboard life. Call us frivolous if you like; say that we should have been teaching ourselves Morse code or overhauling the sheet-winches; but that is what we wanted.

So we wrote and collected for this book. It took time; we kept on thinking of new and indispensible chapters — on lighthouses, on rum, on how to dress overall; we kept on finding out new and fascinating sea-facts that we had to share. Finally we have finished. There is nothing in this book that you cannot read while a coat of varnish dries off, or the shape of a buoy becomes a bit clearer in the haze, or the marina-master at Cowes decides whether or not to move you across to yet another berth 'to make room for the 40-footers'. You will find no useful instructions on how to anchor under sail, or tie a Blackwall Hitch in three-strand polystyrene round the handle of your digital satellite navigator and use it as an emergency sea-anchor. On the other hand, you *will* find the correct flag signal for 'I can strongly recommend my washerwoman', a perfectly accurate account of a bingo game below decks on a Trinity House lighthouse tender, and a chapter which will settle all idle arguments about whether red sky in the morning is bad news for sailors as well as shepherds.

This book, in short, may never save your life. But we hope that it will enhance it. Good sailing.

Paul Heiney
Libby Purves

1985

A cruise in our company

Where lies the land to which the ship would go?
Far, far ahead, is all her seamen know . . .
WORDSWORTH, Sonnets

If you want to know a man, sail with him. The confident, athletic chap in the pub turns into a cringing poltroon at the first hint of trouble; the shy, balding bank manager turns into a roaring Cap'n Bligh, cramming on sail recklessly against a darkening sky. The puny little weed in bifocals turns out to be a hero on the fore-deck, and the girl who looks as if her maid dressed her hair twice a day is transformed into a fierce Valkyrie, bending winch-handles and cursing fit to frighten the fish. Meanwhile, the lady champ of the tennis club, tough as a blonde bulldozer on court, turns out to need two gallons of fresh washing water a day and to have a morbid fear of raindrops; and the crisp, authoritative ex-naval officer proves unable to make a single decision while stranded at 45 degrees on the Brambles. You simply cannot go by appearances; you have to get on a boat with someone, put out to sea, and see what happens. After you have once sailed with them, everything they ever say to you, every suggestion they make, can be correctly valued. If Adlard Coles personally tells you that a harbour entrance is 'difficult' you believe him; if Fred Twitte of the Mud Lump Yacht Club tells you the same, you remember that this is the man who failed to get into Plymouth Harbour because he considered the breakwater to be 'in the way'; and you dilute his advice accordingly.

So really, before you evaluate the various pieces of advice, opinion, and information scattered through this book, you ought to know how we two cruise, and what we want from cruising. The only way to find out is to take one cruise in our company; the one we have chosen to recall, from our detailed logs and diaries, is the one we loved best, and will most want to remember when we are old. It had, as you will see, a bit of everything. And as H W Tilman wrote, of his much greater voyages:

> I cannot hope that anyone who reads of these voyages will partake of the pleasure of those who made them, or even of the pleasure that I have had in thus re-living them . . . There, sailing the sea, we play every part of life; control, direction, effort, fate; and there can we test ourselves and know our state.

CRUISE OF THE YACHT *BARNACLE GOOSE* TO WESTERN IRELAND, JULY 1980

This first *Barnacle Goose* was a Contessa 26, ideally suited for a two-person crew; she had a Hasler wind-vane self steering, and an unreliable 7hp petrol engine; no racing instruments, but a workmanlike Seafarer echo-sounder and seavoice VHF; 15 fathoms of anchor-chain spliced to 15 more of warp; and a wardrobe of four headsails and an infrequently used spinnaker. By this cruise she was perfect; we had made one long cruise in her (a satisfying 999 miles exactly by log!) and refined her over a good many week-ends. We both knew exactly the speed and direction in which to throw used tea-bags to clear the guardrails; we knew precisely how to stow every last pillow in order to keep it dry, and could change headsails virtually in our sleep. We were provisioned-up for several weeks, equipped to bake bread aboard, and carried full fuel and water tanks; we had, for once, thought of everything down to the spare bulbs for both sets of navigation lights.

Which made it all the more humiliating when, at 1230, in good visibility in the middle of Plymouth Sound, we collided with another yacht on starboard tack, and limped back to a Royal Western Yacht Club mooring-buoy with a bent bow fairlead and an imminent insurance claim. The other boat, we were relieved to find, was actually at the end of its holiday cruise; the damage to ourselves was slight enough to permit a second departure by 2000; but it did not seem a good omen!

We had determined on a straight run to the Fastnet Rock, and a landfall in Crookhaven, a quiet and wonderfully sheltered little harbour at the extreme south-western tip of Ireland. The great danger in cruising these waters is to make one's landfall too far east, and go into the pleasant port of Kinsale; the coast between there and Crookhaven is so beautiful in its own right that you may spend your month there, and never round the Mizen to see the real, wilder, west. We resolved to close our ears to the siren call of the Kinsale marina, and the gentle havens of Glandore and Castletownsend, and peg on ever westward.

The first night was quiet, with light westerlies until a calm dawn, and on Sunday a fresh southerly wind sprang up to take us west of the Lizard by lunchtime. Through the night and into Monday morning, the wind shifted perversely between NE and W, settling down to a remorseless headwind of force 6 or 7 by early afternoon. The sea had become lumpy enough to make us resort to our dignified and gentlemanly practice of heaving-to at every change of watch, so that the rising watchkeeper could get his/her trousers on without concussion. On a passage of 270 miles in a smallish boat, comfort takes precedence over speed! We grew damp, smelly, and disheartened, watch by watch; the skies stayed grey, the wind perverse; by Tuesday at 0530 Libby was taking off the No 1 jib and rolling the main deeper and deeper; we made barely 4½ knots into a choppy sea. An RDF fix at dawn yielded such a nonsensical result that we ignored it; by 1015 we were back up to the No 1 jib and steering an optimistic 270: for Fastnet. It is an anxious business, this Western Irish landfall; if you are too far north, you will at least see Ireland and find a light or a mountain that you know, but if you are too far south, you may perfectly well overshoot Mizen Head, miss the Fastnet, and plough on into the Atlantic forever. We trust our Walker trailing log entirely, but always spend an uneasy hour or so at this point in an Irish voyage.

This time, we smelt Ireland before we saw it; in the dawn, the NW wind blew us unmistakeable scents of green grass and damp earth; it was a magical moment. At 1530 Paul sighted Cape Clear Island, and as the faint line of grey rose and took its mountainous shape in the sunset, he played the *Londonderry Air* haltingly but happily on the penny-whistle. The island grew, and glowed, in the dusk; with a bit of help from the engine we rounded the Bill of Cape at 2245, and slipped across Roaringwater Bay to Crookhaven, our heart's desire. The poetry of our arrival was slightly spoiled by an unaccountable mass of lights, like a small town, at the harbour entrance. Muttering disgustedly about caravan sites and developers, we continued to ghost up the harbour entrance, until the lights took shape as — so our log records it — 'An effing great gunboat'. We never saw the Irish Navy by day; it vamoosed overnight, no doubt to stake out some other harbour and frighten a few more yachtsmen.

At 0130 the anchor was snugly down, the traditional lump of Libby's Auntie Magda's fruit-cake was cut, and the whisky poured. We had been at sea for 83 hours, and only used six hours' worth of engine. It felt good. We slept in peace.

Crookhaven is a wonderful harbour; long, deep, sheltered and rich in fine little bars. We sat in Daddy Nottage's in a warm glow of satisfaction, walked along the coast to the top of the beetling cliffs at Brow Head, and rowed back out to the boat to cook our traditional 'Arriving Curry'. One rest day, however, was voted to be enough; so rather tired still, and a little jaded, we set off to catch the fair noon tide around Mizen Head. The north-westerly, fresher again by now, brought us to the headland rapidly, in time for the fair tide northwards; but then a fearful decision loomed. Should we carry on, and risk a difficult search for an unlit anchorage in the strange waters north of Castletown Bere — or tamely sneak into Castletown, where we had been before, and spend a quiet evening in the pub? Eventually a compromise was reached — we would go into Berehaven, that fine stretch of water like a miniature Solent that lies behind Bear Island, but this time we would try the eastern entrance and get into a new anchorage, Lawrence Cove. This sounded a sporting little enterprise, with a considerable section of the pilot-book devoted to telling us to leave a submerged rock a cable and a half to port (yes, but how do you know when a submerged rock . . . ?); but rather to Paul's disappointment, the Glénans Sailing School has erected a line of magnificent perches with red and white bands, which lead you safely into Lawrence Cove without even taking the hand-compass out of its pocket. Beneath the shadow of Hungry Hill we anchored in eight feet of water, and carefully took an anchor-bearing on a rusty old tank and a grey rock. The grey rock flapped its wings and took off a few moments later, but as the wind was down, we decided the risk was little enough, and finished the whiskey bottle instead of plotting more bearings. Another O'Sullivan's bar sold us a new bottle, and we slept in peace until the morning awoke us with the sound of the returning wind.

Bere Island is a beauty. It is rich and green and rocky; the view from the summit of the island takes in Bantry Bay to the east and the whole sweep of Atlantic coast to the west; we saw wild orchids, and wandered through the sad little village of Rerrin, once crowded with the men from the wartime Atlantic Fleet, now deserted and tumbledown. The shop, however, sold us some fine sausages; and if we had not been low on bottled gas, we might have entirely avoided going to the mainland town of Castletown Bere. The wind was fresh westerly, and gave us a hard beat up the sound; but we arrived, and did our errands, and finally cleared Customs, as we had failed to do at Crookhaven.

This was the moment to head for our real westernmost goals; we meant to make our way up the coast to Valentia — one of the last safe harbours for 100 miles, and a convenient point for visiting the Blasket Islands or the Skellig Rocks — and just for a bit of bravado, we meant to get there by way of Dursey Sound. This narrow channel divides Dursey Island from the mainland, and to weave through it saves several miles of sailing out round the Bull and Cow Rocks. It also presents a challenge. 'Entering the Sound from the South', says the Irish Cruising Club Pilot 'a peculiarity about which strangers should be forewarned is that having rounded Crow Head the bay presents the appearance of a cul-de-sac as the similarity of colour of the island and the mainland shores disguises the overlap'. They also warn of a disturbed sea, and a rock in mid-channel 'with the tide setting directly onto it'.

We set out towards these amusements at 0900, and beat hard against a freshening westerly till noon. Six rolls had collected in the main by the time we came into the lee of Dursey Island; we turned gratefully up the Sound, and found to our slight disappointment that the cul-de-sac view did not apply in foggy weather: the nearer shore was too obviously the less befogged. After one shrieking false alarm ('Get back! It's the Rock!') we dodged a few lobster-pot buoys and emerged into a confused sea on the northern side.

The fog that had deprived us of the trompe-l'oeil view was still in evidence, but we assumed gaily that it would clear up — as it so often does late in the day in the west — or at least, grow no thicker. The forecast was for westerly force 5-6, and we did not associate so brisk a wind with this wet fog; also, we were so glad of a fair wind northwards that we did not consider the problem of feeling our way up this ragged coast with diminished visibility. You may judge how silly we were.

Scarriff and Deenish, two solid islands, were both just visible. Once past them, it was guesswork for half-an-hour, and the compass and log; then Bolus Head appeared. So far so good. We came abeam of Bolus at 1640, but only sighted Canduff, the end of Puffin Island and the next headland to be weathered, at 1750. It was not a comfortable hour, crossing the rocky stretch of St Finan bay, virtually blind; especially as the forecast changed to tell us — just as we hardened sheets to weather Puffin Island — that a westerly gale force 8 was 'imminent'. The sea became lumpy; we both felt suddenly tired; the wind came north-westerly, making us work hard for our four knots northwards. In turn we lay on the bunk, gathering our strength while the other steered across the increasingly wild sea.

Another nerve-wracking blind crossing, three white and choppy miles up to Bray Head; we strained to see it in the windy whiteness, dreading to see it to windward. The swell set us in a good ten degrees; we could only just make the course. The Irish Pilot book had warned:

> The wild and rocky west coast is usually a lee shore; if a yacht is overtaken by bad weather and the low visibility which often goes with it, and if an anchorage known to her skipper is not near at hand, he will probably have no choice but to get clear of the land . . .

Perhaps we should have done so. But the prospect of putting out into this lumpy Atlantic, abandoning all hope of getting back to harbour until the visibility improved greatly, was so uninviting that we kept on groping. We raised in turn the dim shapes of Bray rocks, Schala Rock, Gillaun, and the point we named 'Shangri-La . . . land of heart's desire' — Reenada, where we could turn off the harsh wind and make for Valentia lighthouse. It was a wild, rolling, downwind passage, on a difficult compass course to hold without a gybe; as often before, we blessed our ready-rigged preventer line which clips onto the boom-end in seconds without knots or fumbling! The log says:

2045 — SURFED into Valentia Hbr — vis still 1 mile — Main off — anch off pier.

The days run — only 48 miles — had left us limper and wiser than many a longer sail. The next morning rose miraculous; the fog lifted before our eyes; and we saw that this haven we had so gratefully made after such unease and discomfort was magnificent. It was mountain-girt and green, blue and grey and studded with white cottages; and what is more, in the grip of Valentia Festival Week. A rather improbable pipe band marched down the main street of Knightstown, and we followed it in our damp boots.

We needed rest. We ate at an eccentric restaurant called the Galley Kitchen (haute cuisine in the wilderness), and studied the plaque on the lifeboat-house, most remarkable for the fact that the MFV *Granat* of Dublin seemed to have been rescued eight times in eight years, at one time being towed in three times in six months. One wondered what the lifeboat crew used to say to the *Granat*'s men each time. Then we ran into a splendid couple living aboard a home-made Saga 40, with beams taken from an old banana warehouse; drank a few drams with them, and climbed over Beginish Island, trying to get through the scrub to an elusive conical lump called 'pilot's look-out hill' on the chart. We never got there, but cut our legs to ribbons on the thorns. After a perfect sunset, watching the shearwaters bathe around the boat, we slept well and sailed the next morning towards the harbour-mouth we had entered so precipitately two days before. So alarmed were we, in retrospect, that tempers frayed in the short sea off the entrance, and Paul stamped on his sunglasses.

We sailed out towards the Blaskets, inspected Inishvickillane ('home of the fairies'), but reluctantly abandoned an ambition to land at this westernmost anchorage of Europe; we had a northerly, which makes the anchorage unsafe, and so tacked north-easterly up Dingle Bay, to anchor at Ventry. We were rewarded by the sight of our first real curraghs, pulled up on the sand — prehistoric, practical, skin shapes on the lightest of frameworks. The shop in Ventry was a treat, too; it seems to sell nothing but cow-wart ointment and potatoes.

The next day the wind turned obligingly westerly again, and whistled us up Blasket Sound, northwards again to even wilder shores. We wanted to anchor in Brandon Bay or Tralee Bay, and to see more curraghs. We saw a few in the Sound, and saluted the trawler *Morning Star,* draped in seagulls; passing on round the dramatic Sybil Point we made eastwards, by the Three Sisters rocks, and after some debate decided on a quiet anchorage in Smerwick Bay. The weather was still far from settled; a westerly gale would have given us few escape routes from Tralee or Brandon Bay; but Smerwick seemed well sheltered from everything but a strong northerly. Visibility was down again; when we anchored, at 1750, we already felt unaccountably uneasy. It drizzled; we went ashore only briefly, to an uninhabited stretch of road; the late forecast promised a southerly gale. At least we were in shelter.

We were not in shelter. Along this coast, almost the worst mistake to make is to anchor under a windward sweep of mountainside; the wind shrieks down the rocks, gathering momentum, to hit you on the water with as much force as if it had come over open sea. Only the swell is missing; and Smerwick harbour managed to kick up enough swell in 200 yards to make us appallingly uncomfortable. We abandoned the idea of a second anchor, in case we got a tangle; at least if things became impossible we could run northward out of the harbour, and go God knows where — up to the Aran islands perhaps. 'Or Greenland', Paul said wildly. 'It'll have to be north'.

From Wednesday night to Friday morning we hung there in horrible Smerwick, in the rain and the gale, thinking, among the white water, about the chain-joining shackles we had put on our cable in the spring. Would they hold? We got a little neurotic. We baked some bread to cheer ourselves up. We ate it. Then we got neurotic again. Neither could sleep much.

When escape came, on Friday, we hauled up our anchor (thanking it fulsomely for saving our bacon) and sailed with a gentler westerly force 5 to Sybil Point. Our goal was Dingle. Dingle is the only town on the 30-mile peninsula; the hub of Dingle Bay life. In Dingle, we thought, there would be pubs. People. Possibly even a launderette. 'Bingo halls!', shouted Paul. 'A cinema! A Town Hall!'. We had had enough of solitude and privacy. Brighton Marina would have looked like heaven. We had not seen another yacht for nearly a week.

The only drawback was that the entrance to Dingle is difficult (says the pilot) without local knowledge. It is easier if you can follow their instructions to 'pass between Reenbeg and Beenbane points . . steer for Flaherty point . . when abreast a wall which runs down the hill between Flaherty and Foghera points keep the northern end of the lighthouse in line astern with a small but obvious notch in the skyline beyond'. Suffice to say that Reenbeg, Beenbane, Foghera, Flaherty, wall, lighthouse and notch were all entirely invisible by the time we got there. We made out a few shapes and — crying 'Launderette! Bingo! Pubs!' to steady our nerves — groped up the channel entirely by echo-sounder and instinct. Two poles installed by some benefactor were of great assistance; and we anchored on a shortish scope, in not much water, close to the pier. We were in a big, shallow lagoon; we had come to a bustling little town, and we found our haven in James Flahive's pub. This is, when you can see it, an important leading mark.

Dingle provided the balm to our slightly battered pride; in every snug we went into they would say: 'Ye came on a yacht? From England? Dat little yacht?' and make gratifyingly respectful signs of the cross. We felt like Marco Polo, having arrived there; and all the local fishermen solemnly told us that Smerwick harbour was 'wild and nasty' and that they would never go there by land, let alone sea. Like Valentia, Dingle shook off its mist for half a day to show us its beauty; then pulled the blanket round its head again.

From Dingle, south again around the evil Bolus Head, towards Scarriff and Deenish; an exciting entry through boiling rocky water into little Derrynane harbour (where once more the wind blew down off the mountain and blew us clean out to sea again) and then we ran roaringly southwards from the Bull Rock to the Mizen, eating fried sausages and singing sea-shanties, happier at sea than we had been in many a foul anchorage. We rounded the Mizen at sunset, and groped in the darkness up Roaringwater Bay for Schull, cursing the fact that no chart gives you both lights — Fastnet and Crookhaven — to enable a decent fix to be taken on this unlit coast. Luckily, the Schull authorities have now lit Copper Point Beacon, so this nice harbour is accessible at night to strangers; we also admired the new leading-lights of Schull, and anchored happily a little after midnight, feeling as if we had come home after our adventures on the west coast.

After this, we played around; Cape Clear Island's little North Harbour for a night; the inland sea of Croagh Bay; a challenging grope through Barrel Sound to Crookhaven; and a party in Schull to celebrate our wedding, which Irish friends had missed earlier in the year. When the day came to go home, we drank a last-evening pint in Tommy Newman's bar, and resolved to come back before long.

We had a third crewman for the long passage home; Libby's brother Andrew. The idea of two-on four-off watches was very attractive after our usual rigorous two-handed watch pattern; we upped anchor at 1415 in Schull, threw Paul's old bedroom slippers overboard as an offering to Neptune, and made for the Bill of Cape Clear.

It blew from the east! In defiance of all probability, it blew, what is more, from the *south*-east! To beat all the way out to Ireland in July can be considered normal ill-fortune; to beat all the way back looks very like conspiracy. Neptune must have disliked the slippers a lot. Paul and Andrew grew seasick; the wind freshened to force 6; Libby reefed gloomily alone and sat at the helm through a violent electrical storm and a monsoon shower of rain at three in the morning. By dawn the next day Paul was even sicker, Libby forcing biscuits and water on him like a Jewish momma, and Andrew was having trouble with a badly cut hand. He had to wear bandages and a foul pink rubber-glove, which was frequently seen in the companionway, gripping the coaming in its shiny moist pinkness while its owner threw up over the side. By 0100 on the second night at sea the storm jib was up, a deep reef in, and all the crew miserable. By 0400 it became clear that the wind — now SW — was reaching gale force; 12 months earlier, in just this patch of sea, the Fastnet disaster had begun with just such a gale. By 0625 the forecasters allayed our fears a little, by saying that force 8 was the most we might expect; even that was depressing enough. But the *Goose* was going like a lady, unperturbed and well-balanced under minimal sail; at first light the day proved to be sunny, and in that bright gale we saw the shapes of the Scillies ahead. We resolved on New Grimsby as our anchorage, as being a more sheltered entrance; but again charts let us down. The Scillies chart is hopeless for making a foul-weather approach to New Grimsby — by the time you are across its border into the detail, you are too close for comfort — so your fixes are always way off the chart onto a second, sodden, plotting-sheet. At last we saw Cromwell's castle, and all was well. We were, however, horribly wet. We sat numbly in the sunshine, listening to accounts of mayhem in St Mary's harbour, but not ourselves much troubled by swell, and felt too weak even to eat a curry. We all had plain toast, and took a trip to Hughtown on a local boat.

After a day's rest, we set off on a windless, sunny, holidaymaking morning for Falmouth and our cruise's end. The engine worked reasonably well for once, although the gearbox was remorselessly filling its drip-tray with oil; and for eight hours we motored. Entertainment was provided on the VHF radio channels by the plight of a Greek tanker which was nearly drifting onto the Scillies with 'a brokken pomp'. At last it started up again, and we heard the salvage tugs go home disappointed. Another diversion was a seagull, which floated for ages on a piece of driftwood, looking like an RYS member bobbing disapprovingly around in Cowes Roads, honking and settling himself on his broad white tail.

We came at last to Falmouth; shippiest of all harbours, secure and beautiful as it always is. And once again it was carnival day, as it had been all those miles westward in foggy Valentia; we came ashore and watched the frivolous procession go by, then cleaned ship, supped well, and took the train homewards. It had been a 700 mile cruise, in just over three weeks; a rough one at times, at others sublime. The little boat had done us proud.

Keep your fingers crossed

I have great comfort from this fellow;
methinks he hath no drowning-mark upon him;
his complexion is perfect gallows.
SHAKESPEARE, Tempest I, i

It is wonder that my great-grandfather ever got to sea. Like all seafarers of his time, whether they be Cape Horners or, like my great-grandfather, coastal fishermen working out of Bridlington harbour, superstition determined the pattern of their working lives as much as the weather. He firmly believed that if the first person he met in the morning was a woman he would not put to sea.

Remembering him to be a happily married man, that is why I question his ability to carry on his trade and yet keep faith with the lore handed down through centuries.

As yachtsmen, we either ignore them completely, hoping the power for good invested in our latest Satnav will outweigh the misfortune of having a single magpie fly over the marina this morning, or we decide to ignore it at our peril. For a reluctant sailor in search of a good excuse *not* to set foot afloat, our maritime history is rich in excuses. Most yachting starts on a Friday night. This provides the best excuse of all:

Friday sail; Friday fail.

If the owner then suggests an early Saturday start, ask to see his inventory. He will doubtless reassure you that he has flares, lifejackets, harnesses and so on. You counter this by asking him to show you his coal. Not any old lump of coal but coal taken from the high-tide line which brings luck, and you would be well advised not to sail without any. That's what you tell the owner anyway! Try him on the gold ear-rings. A gold ear-ring on board a ship brings good luck too.

If the ship is carrying a 'caul' then you could not be better placed. (Except perhaps by sailing to a lifeboat rally). A caul is a thin membrane which sometimes covers a baby's head at birth and ships carrying a caul were believed to be unsinkable. They are much prized objects amongst sailors who still believe that a baby born with a caul will never drown. Cauls can still be found in shops, changing hands for considerable sums of money.

Whilst on the subject of birth, it is worth remembering that babies born at the time of rising tide will be boys; girls are born on the ebb. For the birth of our son, I arrived at the hospital, less than a mile from the River Thames, complete with Almanac and proudly divined that if the baby was born before midnight (that being the time of high water at London Bridge; the nearest point of reference) it would be a boy. *Reed's* and I can report total success.

If you have a boy and he happens to be born at Christmas, then he will grow up to be a captain, and if he is baptised on the right arm with water from the flood tide, he will never drown.

If he should also be born with a caul, he is likely to be sufficiently buoyant to have to be tied down in strong winds.

If you have not found an escape route, question the owner on the launching of his boat. Was it done with wine poured from a silver goblet which was then thrown into the sea? Not if he's like most of the owners I know! It is an old custom that apprentice shipwrights were thrown into the wash of a newly launched ship. If the owner was already in receipt of the bill at the time of the launching, that is one custom he may have upheld.

It is more likely the boat was launched with champagne; if so, I hope the bottle smashed. When Edward Heath's *Morning Cloud I* was launched, the bottle twice refused to break. At the launching of *Morning Cloud III,* a lady fell from the quay and was injured. It was seen by many as a bad omen. You will remember the tragic loss of *Morning Cloud III* in a gale off the South Coast; you may not realise that *Morning Cloud I* was lost at her mooring in the same storm.

As omens go, the *Titanic* could not have had a worse one. As she steamed towards the Old Head of Kinsale, en-route for America, the lighthouse hoisted the signal 'Bon Voyage.' As the *Titanic* came abeam and was about to reply, the signal halyard snapped and the flags were taken away on the wind.

But cheer up. You can always bring yourself good luck by nailing a boot to the mast. If that doesn't get you thrown off the yacht, nothing will.

If the weather is poor, it was widely believed that it would cease if a woman showed herself to it naked (although it might be easier to weather the gale than survive the storm resulting from asking this favour of your skipper's wife). The French, typically, had their own refinement of this custom: for fair winds, Frenchmen whipped the naked bottoms of cabin boys at the mainmast on Monday mornings. Perhaps that's what they mean by the Monday morning feeling.

Ships that pass in the night,
and speak to each other in passing;
Only a signal shown and a
distant voice in the darkness;
So on the ocean of life
we pass and speak one another,
Only a look and a voice;
then darkness again and a silence.
LONGFELLOW,
Tales of a Wayside Inn

Ships that pass

1 — Sails around the coast

When the original 'Week-End Book' headed one of its most evocative chapters, *Ships that Pass,* it did not have in its mind's eye the lumbering shape of the Townsend ferry or the sombre thrash of the Red Funnel. For these may be the ships that pass us by today, but when John Irving took his readers on an imaginary tour round our coasts, his horizon was dotted with working ships under sail; ships we shall not see again. He saw no diesel engine or radar scanner when he described a Ramsgate trawler, but a black-hulled vessel with yellowish sails, ketch rigged with a gaff as long as her boom. The fishing boats of Boulogne, now no more than blips of irritation on a coastguard radar screen as he fights to keep his traffic lanes clear of 'rogues', are no longer the Boulogne luggers, square sterned, with forward-raking mizzen and long, unsupported bowsprit, scouring the Varne Bank for herring. A search for today's working ships under sail would be regrettably brief.

But we have chosen ships under sail you *might* see. Some you will have to search for, but all have been the workhorses of a previous generation. If one of these lovely craft turns out to be a 'ship that passes' you are indeed lucky.

We begin on the North East Coast where, as a child, I first went to 'sea' not knowing that the ship I was aboard, the *coble* (or cobble if you come from Yorkshire) had the richest history of any craft between the Borders and the Humber. My cruise, an hour round Bridlington Bay, was under engine, there being no longer any working cobles under sail. But in the days when the coble was fishing, piloting or even salvaging, she would have been powered by a dipping lugsail rigged from a single mast; these ships were never sailed with the mainsheet cleated. The Scandinavians have left their mark not only in the height of the bow but in the curve that leads to a flat, raked tramsom, giving the whole vessel the shape of a wave. The Viking invaders' influence is there too in the decoration: you will see no coble in Yorkshire that is not painted in the brightest of reds and blues, sometimes yellow; deep reds for Flamborough cobles, white outside with a red streak. Filey cobles; blue inside sometimes with red and blue planks alternating.

The most influential factor in their design was the method of launching: beach launching. The coble is unique in that she has two side keels at the stern to enable her to beach stern-first. No safer boat under sail has ever been devised to survive the waters of the east coast, in particular the rough and stormy seas off Flamborough Head and in the approaches to Whitby and Staithes. From Staithes, a fishing hamlet clinging to a crumbling cliff and occasionally smacked by the force of the North Sea, George Bayes, writing in 1953, remembers a conversation with a coble builder:

For an hour, while he worked, I chatted to one of the last men of his craft on the coast. His talk, like his workshed, is fascinating — full of odd things and old things, rough-grained, seasoned, like the timber his hands have wrought with these forty years and more.

'How is a coble built? Well, now, I should be able to tell you, if any man can. There's only three of us left between Whitby and Flamborough, so there's not many that can contradict me, eh?' Absently, he picks up an adze. 'That's what I call the shipwright's right hand, you use it see, like a croquet mallet,' he swings the heavy-headed steel thing illustratively. 'A slip, and that will give you a nasty gash. It shapes the timber of the posts and ribs. A coble may be either clincher-built — the planks overlapping each other — or caulker-built, that is with the planks flush and the seams caulked with a mixture of tar, oil and pitch. Lasts for ever, that does. Now, if she's clincher-built, first I make the shell, shallow as a true coble should be, for ease in hauling her up the beach. Then I fit the ribs in. With a caulker-built boat the ribs are put up first, then the shell is fitted on them, but come and see.'

He leads me through the long, littered workshop, which smells of oil and tar, of sawdust and the good smell of wood. 'There' he says, and slaps the half-section of an oak tree, a two-inch sponge-cake slice from a trunk five feet across. His hands run lovingly over the coarse grain. 'The ribs of a good boat are curved to the natural shape the tree grows. They'll never spring, never bend, never break, even when the wood's all but green. And they're best of English oak. Years ago they used to make the bottoms of oak too. Russian stuff it was, but good stuff. Nowadays the bottoms, like the sides, are of larchwood, locally grown, mine comes from Hackness.

'For smaller boats, river craft for instance, the ribs are made from one straight piece of timber, which is put in the steambox — that long, coffin-like thing there — and cramped to shape in a mould. Good enough, but it wouldn't do for a coble.'

'Plans?', Mr Hopwood chuckled and slapped his thigh as a wave might smack the bow of one of his boats. 'Just after the Armistice I built a big boat. Nine or ten-tonner. Forty-foot long, she'd be. I built her to the shape of a coble that was in Bridlington harbour at the time. I took one man with me. We had the coble beached and we took moulds off her, from stem to stern, five pairs of 'em, between a tide and a tide.'

INSHORE CRAFT OF BRITAIN
Edgar March
(David & Charles)

Under engine, the cobles still earn their living in Bridlington and Scarborough and Whitby harbours as pleasure boats or transport for day-anglers. I wonder how many of the owners know the old coble fisherman's rule for counting herring?

You pick up two herrings in each hand and that is called a warp. You give thirty two warp to the hundred making it one hundred and twenty eight herrings. The herrings were carried away by the merchants in quarter cran baskets, four baskets to the cran, which is a measure for a thousand herrings.

As the chalky cliffs of Flamborough give way to the shifting sands of Spurn Point, as the cran of herring gives way to tons of coal, the coble disappears and the working craft of the River Humber reign. Two types of craft in fact, but you will be lucky to see either of them. It is only the work of the Humber Keel and Sloop Society which has kept alive the last two surviving examples of Humber working craft; the Humber Keel, ***Comrade,*** and the Humber Sloop, ***Amy Howson,*** both a curious marriage of seagoing vessel and canal traveller.

Comrade, to be seen in Beverley in the winter and about her work on the Humber in the summer, was built, in steel, as recently as 1923, not principally as a seagoing ship but to trade within the estuary and work the canals; the largest keels worked as far inland as Sheffield. The rig is a square mainsail with topsail, making the keels close-winded for canal and sandbank navigation and being set on a single mast. The two together could be lowered for passing under bridges. Inheriting a little of the bargeman's love of paint and pattern, the mooring posts forward were often painted in bright colours, tillers

were carved and highly decorated. The restoration of *Comrade* was completed in 1976 and at the time of her relaunching she was the first Humber Keel to sail the river for 30 years.

A Government job creation scheme helped to preserve the other pride of their fleet, the Humber Sloop, *Amy Howson.* The Humber Sloops, at first glance, are similar to the Keels except the rig which was gaff. Remembering these ships were over 60 feet long, with spars and sails to match, the rigs were nevertheless considered interchangeable, the heavy mast and gaff being left ashore while the barge sailed inland setting only a jury square sail; the mast would then be re-rigged for open estuary work. *Amy Howson* served her time carrying coal from the West Riding to Beverley, oil seed from Hull to Brigg and chemicals to Howden Dyke. It was not until 1951 that the last of the Sloops ceased trading, making the Humber Keels and Sloops the last working square-riggers in Europe.

These little known craft of ancient lineage (*Keel* or *Ceol* being Anglo-Saxon for a ship rigged with square sail on a single mast) still have to earn their living either as homes for exhibitions or in the hands of the members of the Preservation Society who are encouraged to sail them.

(The Humber Keel and Sloop Preservation Society is at 'Glen Lea' Main Road, New Ellerby, Hull.)

Leaving behind the shifting sands of the Humber, we head for the bulge of East Anglia. Once past Grimsby we might have expected to see the Lowestoft sailing drifters at work or even steam drifters working their way out of Great Yarmouth. Pride of place on these craft was given to the kettle which, in view of its status, was kept in a highly polished state by the youngest aboard. The rule was that in winter it should never come off the boil and in summer was kept full of cold water which the crew drank from the spout. But the fleet of occupation in Lowestoft and Yarmouth is now made up of oil and gas rig supply vessels, fast motor launches and helicopters. No longer the Beach Yawls; 50 feet long, carrying crews of ten strong men to man ten pairs of oars, taking stores and provisions to ships at anchor in Yarmouth roads.

South, beyond Southwold, once the home of a score or more of these beach boats, we heave-to for a while at the shallow, shifting mouth of the River Ore, that leads to Aldeburgh and we sing the Aldeburgh Cod-Banger's Song:

When we come to Harwich Pier,
The folks all flock from far and near
To see us heave our cod on deck
and smack 'em on the head with a BLOODY great stick.

CHORUS
Sing shack fol the day,
ridle fol the day
Yo Ho for smacks-man's life at sea.

And when Orfordness is astern and the Sunk lightship and Harwich Harbour ahead of us, we could almost be back in the Humber, amongst the flat-bottomed barges earning their living between the big ports and the hidden quaysides at the head of a muddy trickle of water; we are now in the homeland of the Thames Barge, a name to cover a multitude of craft; the Mulie Barge, Boomie Barge, Stumpie Barge and Spritsail Barge.

The first cruise I ever made from the Crouch took me up the Wallet to anchor the night in Hamford Water; that oasis of peace within the maze of the Walton Backwaters. The wind had dropped to a gentle breeze by evening and slowly, creeping over the flood and carrying just enough canvas to give her steerage, sailed the first Thames Barge I had ever seen. She could not be mistaken for any other vessel afloat.

The untrained eye might confuse the Ramsgate Trawler with the Lowestoft Drifter but there can be no confusion over these estuary monarchs; built to work but beautifully built too. H Alker Tripp, cruising the Thames estuary at the turn of the century wrote:

The Thames barge is no modern contrivance, but she is still pre-eminent. Dependent on sail only, she is the largest sailing-vessel in the world which is regularly handled in all weathers by two men only. In and out of these channels she threads her expert course, laden with grain perhaps or cement,

and then again up some creek or inlet miles landward she searches her way to a farm-wharf among the fields. She loads. When she makes again seaward, she goes as a 'stackie,' having a haystack on deck, and the mate abaft of it at the steering-wheel steers blindly, his outlook nothing but hay. He is obedient to the shouts of the skipper, who straddles the hayrick. All among the delicate modern refinement of turbine and wireless of other vessels, the whole affair seems grotesquely primitive — occurring as it so often does upon London River itself; but it maintains a justification strictly up-to-date, for, in open competition, ***it pays.***
SHOAL WATER & FAIRWAY
H Alker Tripp
(Conway Maritime Press)

The Thames Barges are survivors. Like old soldiers, they have never really died. A regular fleet was still working under sail as late as 1956 but it was not until 1967 that the last of the line, the *Spinway C*, was sold marking the end of 300 years of barge trading in the Thames Estuary. The barges have the air of the least manoeuvrable of craft — but how often we week-end sailors are put to shame by declaring impossible a creek or quayside which was once a regular berth of a Thames Barge, complete with stackie!

In his recollection of the heyday of the Thames Barges, Hervey Benham writes:

Similarly when it comes to handiness the barge is a marvel within limits. A Royal Corinthian one-design turns up the Crouch over a spring ebb in a westerly breeze. That sort of talk the barge just doesn't understand. The yachtsman can thread his way with impunity in among craft moored thick in a tideway. The sailorman must plan his tacks ahead; it does not pay him to tempt fortune by cutting close to windward of a buoy or anchored craft with the tide setting on to them. He thinks ahead, too, in making and taking in sail, setting the mainsail while she lies head to wind, perhaps before she swings to the tide he intends to use; brailing up during a convenient moment's calm under the lee of a high building or passing steamer; dropping a flying jib when the wind is over the starboard bow; catching her on the port tack to let go the tops'l sheet.

There is nothing about this fundamentally different from the art exercised by the yachtsman handling his ship in the congested conditions of the contemporary yacht anchorage or in the tumble of a seaway, but there is a more constant call for the art, a heavier price to pay for a mistake. To imagine mistakes are never made is nonsense. Barges are not infrequently ashore or in trouble through elementary miscalculations, and if, when barges and bargemen are but a picturesque and glamorous memory, a legend circulates among yachtsmen that their seamanship was infallible, it will be the merest nonsense. But the yachtsmen will do well to equal the bargemen's imperfect standard.

Compared to a keel yacht, however, all have the characteristic of weaving about under way, always luffing and bearing away slightly round the leeboard. A yacht will find her own way to windward; a barge needs continual help at the wheel. Because she answers slowly, the amateur gives her too much helm, and leaves a wake like a serpent in pain; the experienced skipper feels and anticipates the swinging of the ship's head, checking the movement to come before the last is finished. He does not use much helm, but he is always gently using some. The coasters which sail on the chine rather than on the leeboard are of course the best to steer; craft like the *Venta* could be left to sail themselves. They will heave-to, under mainsail and backed foresail, or in a strong breeze under foresail and tops'l sheet. They will come off a lee shore manfully; they had to in the days when open beaches were used for discharging. And they do not share the dislike of so many working craft for bearing away. An amateur with a real sympathy for boats can sail them adequately, but long acquaintance is needed to sense when the mainsail may (in light airs) be trimmed almost entirely on the sheet and when the vang must take up its strain. Nor will an instinct for the right amount of leeboard be quickly acquired.

Every barge's suit of sails (save in Goldsmith's fleet) has its own varying dimensions and proportions, but most rigging is standard. I should like to know who was the first to establish almost universal practice by placing his main brails on the winch to port of the mast-case; his middles and lowers by the mast-case winch; his peaks on cleats seized to each after shroud; his tops'l halyard cleating on the port side of the mast and his tops'l sheet on a cleat on the sprit; his tops'l clewline on the middle starboard shroud cleat; his foresail halyard on the fore port shroud cleat; his staysail sheet opposite to port. Who, I wonder, ordained that first the stanliff and then the fore starboard and middle shrouds should be bent over the mast head of every correctly rigged barge? And, most fascinating of all, who was the genius among sailmakers who cut the baggy foresail which yet sets to windward without touching the sheet?
DOWN TOPS'L
Hervey Benham
(George Harrap)

If the cut of the headsail is as inspired as Hervey Benham suggests, I wonder which sailmaker would do better business today; the computer tapping whizz-kid sweating over his keyboard or the 'genius' with his needle and palm, waiting for the kettle to boil, cursing the weather, the customers, and occasionally kicking the cat?

The working of these ships always seems more akin to the techniques of procession than manoeuvring. It is not a question of a twitch on the helm and round she spins or crank at a winch and off she cracks to windward. D H Clarke and his wife lived aboard the sailing barge *John and Mary* for 11 years and in describing their maiden voyage from Brigg to Mistley, they give us an insight into the workings of those ships that no old barge hand, dismissive of his own skills through familiarity, could give us:

I peered into the dimly lit after cabin and saw that Mollie was sitting at the table knitting. 'Come on, darling,' I said quietly. 'We've got to go about.' I hated myself for having to drag her out, but there was absolutely no alternative. She put on her duffle coat and came up on deck, and whilst I waited for her night-sight to improve I explained exactly what I wanted her to do.

'Put the bowlin' *twice* around the shroud,' I said anxiously, 'and then pass the tail over the standing part and *hang on to it tightly with one hand.* It's going to kick like the devil in this wind, and if you lose it you won't be able to grab it again. With this sea running she might get into irons without the help of the bowlin', so for heaven's sake be ready for the sail flogging. And hang on to the middle shroud with your other hand — one hand for the ship, and the other for yourself. Remember?'

The oldest rule of the sea. She would remember that.

'Now, I've got to unrig the starboard rolling wang, and tie the end of the other to the rigging so that I can set it up as quickly as possible as soon as we're round,' I went on. 'Don't worry about the wheel — I'll set her on course. You just stay here for a minute.'

I made sure that *J & M* was on a steady course and then I ran forward and slacked off the rolling wang tackle, passed the wang back around the shrouds and made it fast to the foot of the spreet, unfastened the port rolling wang and passed it outside the shrouds, fastening the rope tail to the port forward shroud, nipped back to the tackle which I had left lying on the deck, overhauled it, and laid it ready for instant use on the port side deck, and then ran back to the wheel. She was still on course.

'Right-ho, darling. Now you go and rig the bowlin' and keep hanging on to it until I yell.'

Just in case — I was beginning to shiver inside myself in awful anticipation of what was to come — just in case we shipped some heavy seas, I silently closed the sliding hatch over the after cabin. I had a sudden vision of Mollie and myself being swept away, leaving only Kester and Sym and Tigger down below — it had happened before, even in large square-rigged ships! — and then I was concentrating hard, peering to windward to try to pick the most advantageous moment to go about.

Mollie had disappeared into the blackness forward. Screened by the mainsail, with any possible silhouette blanketed by the foresail, it was impossible for me to see whether she had slipped overboard, or whether she was standing by and ready for action. And there was not very much to be seen to windward; a fleeting glimpse of white crests, an occasional slash of bloody water as we rolled upright and the navigation light cast a hellish glow, but nothing else. I couldn't pick a suitable lull from seeing, only from hearing and feeling for a break in the rhythm of the sea and the wind.

I guessed — right or wrong? — and began to luff. ***J & M*** seemed to falter in her stride with surprise. I gave her no chance to halt: I wound on the wheel furiously until a heavy ***clunk*** told me that it was fully over. I dropped the fid, clawed up the deck to windward, grabbed the capstan handle, felt it into position by touch, lifted the pawl, and lowered the port leeboard as rapidly as I could. Even as I worked, ***J & M*** came into wind.

The cacophony was terrifying! First, I heard the chain fore-sail sheet clank on deck, then it lifted and clanked again . . . overhead, faintly, I heard the rustle of the topsail as it lost its curve . . . then the mainsail flicked its tack. It was like an orchestra tuning-up. And then came the frustrated power! By my right knee, the iron traveller thundered across the main-horse, paused, and crashed back to starboard; the heavy, spiked, mainsheet block slammed ferociously against the mainhatch head and did its best to snap the mousing which held its hook to the traveller. Slashing and thrashing, with unseen ropes cracking like whips and with chains rattling as if the tormented ghosts of all creation had suddenly arrived, the sails and all their adornments began to flog. ***J & M*** shook to her keelson. It was appalling!

Keeping well clear of the berserk traveller and knobkerrie mainsheet block, I ran to starboard, fitted the winch handle, and cranked and cranked the starboard leeboard slowly upwards.

The mizzen flicked once, and then began to flog — we were nearly round.

Gasping for breath, hoping that the leeboard was fully up, I flung myself across to the wheel, lifted the fid, and raised my head to sense the wind direction. The mainsail was still flogging — but now it was more on the port side of the horse than the starboard.

Suddenly, the traveller gave a final *crash,* and stopped. We were round. I spun the wheel furiously, standing facing the spokes and using both hands. And as I worked, I roared out into the night:

'LET DRAW!'

For a moment, nothing... Then I heard the clank of the foresail sheet, the slither as it passed across the horse,and the final crash as the sail blew into position. Mollie was O.K. We were round safely.

EAST COAST PASSAGE
D W Clarke

I have always thought of bargemen as good humoured men; to navigate the shallow, muddy waters of the Thames for a living must have called for some sense of humour. In the words of the old bargeman's rhyme:

We've wallowed in the Wallet,
Awash with sodden deals
And slipped from Southend jetty
The sou'easter at our heels.
Stern winter had the will of us
On black December days,
Our kedge is on the Buxey
And our jib is off the Naze.

Like the old barges, *we* can still sail the swatchways, take the 'overland' route through the fingers of rock-hard sand that spread seaward from the estuary. We can still creep up to an anchorage off Brightlingsea and, looking westwards in the dusk, see Mersea Island as it must have looked when the Colne was a nightly anchorage for scores of barges; not just a handful earning a living in the holiday trade.

Perhaps the lure of this unprepossessing maze of mud and water is in its unchanging views and ever-changing channels; but while we can still follow in the wake of the bargemen, there are few clues left as to the lives they led. Writing 50 years after first going to work the barges, Chubb Horlock speaks not of wind and weather but of warmth and sustenance:

Most of my barging before joining the *Memory* had been in the summer months and I soon learned that working a barge in winter was a different kettle of fish. Having to turn out at six or seven in the morning with a freezing northerly blowing was no fun, especially as we did not keep a fire in all night; coal was too expensive for that.

When we were about to get under way my job was to help heave up the anchor and generally help with the sails. When everything was set, I would go below and light a coal fire to make tea for breakfast. In the winter the fire would be left in all day but in the summer I had to light it every time we

SHIPS THAT PASS 1

wanted a cup of tea. No hope of bacon and eggs for breakfast; it was nearly always the previous day's cold meat, plum jam, (cheapest), and tea. We always ate aft in the skipper's cabin, but cooked in the fo'c's'le, so even when we had a hot meal it was usually cold by the time we came to eat it.

Lighting the fire was not as simple as it sounds. Very often there was no paper on board and I was not allowed to use paraffin to start a blaze; again it was a matter of expense. We used 'churls' to start a fire and cutting them was another of my jobs. To make a churl you took a piece of kindling wood and made five or six cuts on each side with a sharp knife so that the thin slivers of wood bent over to form small curls. Light one of the churls where the wood was thinnest, gently add another, and in no time you would have a good blaze going. Nearly all the bargemen of the time used to 'borrow' coal from Wm Cory & Sons and it was always reckoned that all sailormen had free access to any of Cory's coal lighters. Not so Captain Haste. He always bought our coal in port and therefore did not use it very freely.

After breakfast I would wash up the dishes, then clean out the fo'c's'le and cabin.

The food was very plain but in fair amounts except when we were windbound. Meat pudding was the favourite meal because you could not overcook it and consequently could have it at any time. Spotted Dick was part of the Sunday meal, although you could count the raisins in it on the fingers on one hand. In the Ipswich barges they always had their gravy on the Spotted Dick; I was nearly sick the first time I tasted this delight.

MISTLEYMAN'S LOG
Chubb Horlock
(Fisher Nautical Press)

Our cruise continues and with every mile we get a little closer to the ancestors of our modern yachts. Perhaps we shall see them creeping out of the Swale or hiding behind Mersea Island but when we see our first Smack, our first Oyster Dredger, we shall know that we are looking at an elderly member of a family of which our own yacht is the newest born.

Unlike the Thames Barge, working the same waters as the Oyster Dredgers, these smacks were built for speed, built to sail to windward, designed to handle swiftly in narrow channels. Constructed with vertical stems and fine bows, they are unmistakeable for their low freeboard aft to make easier the lifting of the dredge, and their flush deck to make on-board handling of the dredge an easier business. I have sailed on board one of these ships, *Kathleen.* Built in 1894 at Brightlingsea as a yacht but faithfully to the lines of an Oyster Smack, working her was an experience to be recommended to all lily-handed sailors who, like me, had never felt the drag of sisal across the palm. You glance around for winches and see none and pause to consider the size of the gaff and mainsail. You are asked to throw a Blackwall hitch round a hook on a tackle and haul tight the bobstay and wonder what was wrong with rigging screws. You can be convinced you are aground when it is only the thud of the waves as they meet the stern under the long counter.

It was only a two-day sail but this old girl managed to inspire most emotions; frustration at her reluctance to tack unless the helm was hard over, with the slightest hesitation on the part of the helmsman detected and leaving her shivering in 'stays' and then fear as the topsail stuck with the wind aft and not enough searoom to round up. But I remember also her power to calm us later at anchor when her timbers sighed and groaned a little as she wallowed to the slight swell. But we were pleasure cruising; on a working ship where a living had to be earned, navigation was only half the wet and miserable story. Edgar March remembers his day with the oyster dredgers:

Oyster-Dredging can hardly be enjoyed for its own sake, as can trawling, wildfowling, and most of the inshore fishermen's occupation; it is a great deal too much like work. But I have had some happy days at it.

It was six o'clock of a bleak, raw morning when I met two Mersea dredgermen friends on the Hard for my first taste of it. They were Charlie Hewes, one of the wisest old hands that ever chucked a dredge and sailed a smack, and that grand old Mersea character, oysterman, and wildfowler, the late 'Sooty' Mussett. I recall how that half-dark Hard seemed suddenly to become alive with merry little bearded figures all jesting and chattering as if it were they who were out for a holiday, and I (a sleepy and rather morose figure just out of my warm cot) embarking on my daily round of toil.

Nor shall I ever forget how that fleet of smacks got under way. Boat alongside, anchor windlass clinking, patent blocks clickety-clicking, peak up, jib set, anchor away, foresail set; it was going on all around me almost as quickly as I can write of it. So in the grey, early dawn that humble, exquisite little armada, perhaps fifteen of those lovely eight-to fifteen-ton-carvel-built cutter smacks, some of them seventy years old, streamed off out of Thornfleet and Besom Creeks. Most of them were going to work on the Main[1] and below Tollesbury Pier, but we were to dredge in the narrow Thornfleet Creek itself, all in among the moorings and the yachts on them.

It was all new to me. The tide was on the flood, and we sailed slowly over it down the Quarters. There Charlie put the helm down, and as she wended and 'Sooty' downed staysail he took the tiller out and laid it on the deck. 'She steers herself,' he exclaimed with a grin. 'Now chuck your dredge.' I flung it over, my splash sounding to me much like theirs. 'Now pull it in.' I hove on the bass rope, and in it came — upside down. 'Now let *me* show you,' said Charlie. The deft twist which sent the dredge so that the tide catching it, opened it out was soon acquired, and before long my dredge was as often full as empty and inverted.

'Make fast.' Neatly I slipped a clove-hitch on the thole-pin stuck in the rail. Safe there, anyway. But no. 'Do you get your dredge fast that'll jam and break that owd pin off,' came the reproving voice. So I learned that a dredgerman's hitch is only a single round turn and the end backed over. A fast dredge then jerks out the rope, which can be slipped off the pin in a moment.

Hove to in the tideway, the smack was working. The dredge ropes quivered as she hoed three paths in the creek bed. We were working only one dredge each, though in more open water with less 'soil' on the ground we might have had two or even four each. 'Ruck your peak.' She was forging ahead now under the weather mud. As the drive went out of the mainsail, she backed off obediently. 'Haul your dredge.' Again hand over hand on the bass rope. Heavier work than I expected, and how the bits of shell in the rope do cut the wet hand! Ah! At last the dredge breaks surface; its handle is across the bulwark, a couple of shakes to clear some of the weed and water, and, grasping the wooden batten that extends the wire and string-mesh bag, I shoot out on deck old shell, weed, limpets, crabs — a fine sample of the creek's bottom. Splash! Over goes the dredge again.

Charlie and 'Sooty,' fingers nimbly diving into their heaps, are tossing oysters into the wooden tub before I can find one at all; old shells and full ones look alike to me. Charlie ferrets out half a dozen. 'Nothing more there,' he says. I pick up the 'sheards' (how these chaps do love to have a fancy name for everything; these are only bits of board such as the gardener gathers up leaves with) and bundle the rubbish overboard. Charlie's boot has given the crabs their quietus; tingle, spawn, and limpets are in a heap for dumping later. I straighten my back and see we are drifting broadside across the bows of a moored yacht. But before I have a chance to see more it is time to haul again. 'Give me trawling,' I reflect. 'You do get a spell at that while the net is over.' The pronunciation 'drudge' acquires a new significance.

[1] The mainland — that is, the Bradwell shore.
INSHORE CRAFT OF BRITAIN.
Edgar March
Vol 1 (David & Charles)

The men who built these smacks were as revered as the men who draw today's Admiral's Cuppers. The men who sailed them with precision, knowing how to squeeze the last half knot out of the old girls became as recognised as any Olympic helmsman. Little wonder that the best of the smack skippers were wooed by the big yacht owners of Victorian times and, as a result, gave the East Coast a reputation as a breeding ground for fast, tenacious sailors; a reputation it might not have gained at the hands of the barge-master blindly and contentedly steering from behind his 'stackie.'

After the richness of the Thames, how poverty-stricken we feel in the Eastern Channel. No Deal Luggers beached facing the Downs, ready to carry messages to ships bound down channel or up to London River; no Rye Trawlers or Hastings Luggers. Indeed, not till we arrive at the Solent is there even a chance of sighting an Itchen Ferry, not, as might be suggested by her name, merely a river transport for the benefit of Southampton residents living either side of that river, but a craft often as short as 16 feet and designed for the sheltered waters of the Solent.

But we have to round Anvil Point, carefully work our tides past Portland Bill and make landfall off Start Point before we have another chance of seeing a chunk of maritime heritage under sail; the Brixham Trawler.

In fact, only one Brixham Trawler, *Provident.* I have yet to see her enter Salcombe Harbour home from a cruise and see the sun in the vast spread of her sails: modern terylene they may be but tan, and closely matching the colour of her original canvas which would have been preserved with a cocktail of grease, red ochre and seawater, a mixture known as 'cutch.'

The Brixham Trawlers were powerful vessels with little to match them anywhere in Europe except perhaps the Breton Tunnymen, (look out for *Biche* in Poole Harbour). The biggest of the Brixham giants was nearly 80 feet overall and drawing no less that 11 feet.

Built to work at sea as well as in the lee of Start Point, these ships would make passages to Ireland or even up the East Coast and work a season off Bridlington or Scarborough. *Provident* is now owned by the Maritime Trust but in the care of the Island Cruising Club, a club

whose membership is open to all, and those who can find the cash can sail *'Provi'* during the season with a little help from a crew of 16. John Corin writes:

An old saying amongst sailors is 'Grumble you may, but go you must'. It is often true for the amateur as well as the professional.

Anyone who chooses a holiday which involves getting out of a warm bunk after midnight and putting to sea in a sailing trawler, with wind force 6-8 forecast, may be regarded an eccentric. Most of the crew of *Provident* one September night in Alderney Harbour would have admitted the judgement. She was due back on the other side of the Channel within 24 hours. The 1755 forecast gave a possible force 9 for Wight and portland sea areas; the 0030 forecast mentioned nothing over force 8, while the reported wind at St. Helier, Jersey, was a mere force 5. The skipper decided to sail. Alderney Harbour is an uncomfortable anchorage in bad weather, but it promised to be much more uncomfortable outside.

For the other occupants of the anchorage wind and weather may have been enough to disturb their sleep, but *Provident* probably ensured their wakefulness. For any who peered grumpily out through their scuttles she would have presented a dramatic picture, preparing for sea, with all lights switched on, and the crew stumbling about the deck, in their oilskins, to the accompaniment of flapping canvas and creaking spars. To all this the rhythmic clank of the anchor cable being wound in formed a steady descant.

Leaving the harbour under sail involved a careful gybe and once outside, with a beam wind, it did not seem so bad after all, but a thunderstorm with a violent squall caused the ship to roll heavily, a reminder that the weather could be all the forecast said.

At 0600 the wind was still well on the beam and *Provident* was logging eight knots with full main and mizzen set, staysail and No 3 jib. The last sail, and the absence of topsails were the only concession to the weather. Steering seemed not too difficult, but wind and sea began to increase. Every so often, perhaps as a wave gathered under the quarter and there was a surfing action, the ship would run straight and true on course with hardly a spoke needed on the wheel. Then she would fall off into a trough, gripe to windward and demand a considerable effort to get the wheel over to starboard and maintain the course. A three quarters of an hour 'trick' at the wheel was enough for the helmsman.

Between 0700 and 0800 some rain squalls came along, heavy enough to flatten off the seas. In that hour she logged nine and a quarter miles, so it is fair to assume that *Provident* must have been touching over 10 knots on occasions. In seven and a quarter hours just over 60 miles were covered on that passage. It was extremely wet on deck, but only once, when altering course for a steamer, did anything that could be described as a heavy sea come on board.

The Brixham trawler's mainsail was made with vertical cloths, the theory being that if a heavy sea burst the mainsail there would perhaps be a useable area left. The mind of the summer yachtsman boggles at the thought of the violence of weather which could bring a sea on board to burst *Provident's* mainsail. Some years ago Mr Howard Thomas a retired smackman described to me a winter gale in the 1930s aboard the smack *Inspire BM13*. 'We had our gear down when it came on to blow a very stiff breeze of wind (sic). So we handed the gear while already under two reefs in the mainsail. The skipper said that the glass was very low and we had better haul the jib in. The staysail was already reefed, and we put two reefs in the mizzen. It then came on very stiff indeed and we stowed the mizzen altogether. By this time we had the topmast housed too. So we ran for it.'

Force 6, wind speed 22-27 knots, is defined in the Beaufort scale as a 'strong breeze'. Mr. Thomas's 'very stiff breeze of wind' was probably force 8, a full gale, with winds of 34-40 knots. When it 'came on very stiff indeed' it was probably force 10, a storm, 48-55 knots, or even worse. It certainly remained a lively memory for him 40 years later.

The kind of weather which yachtsmen meet in exceptional circumstances, like the trip back from Alderney described above, was routine in winter for the smacksman of old and he had to shoot and haul his gear in that sort of weather. Doing 10 or 11 knots in heavy weather in a vessel like *Provident,* just once in a while, can be exciting and exhilarating for amateur sailors. They know that they will not have to face it day after day in order to earn a living. The professionals endured life aboard such craft as *Provident* because they had been brought up to it; it was perhaps the only way of making a living, and a poor one at that. Whatever else it did, it made them superb seamen.

PROVIDENT — AND THE STORY OF THE BRIXHAM SMACKS
John Corin (Top's'l Books)

The modern rig, — the bermudan rig — is a yachting innovation. It is designed for speed and to go to windward; a performance rig. But the great virtue of a gaff rig aboard a working boat is that it can effectively stop a craft, not often a requirement of a cruising yachtsman. And if the business of the ship is fishing, then gaff rig gives him a controlled drift to leeward ideal for dredging and trawling. That's why, when we arrive at Falmouth where, like the Thames estuary the business is oyster dredging, we find once again the small, nippy gaff-rigged craft; the Falmouth Working Boats or Quay Punts.

'There's no finer sailors than the Falmouth Working Boat skippers.' I was once told over the bar of Fowey Yacht Club. 'If the lads from Falmouth were contesting the America's Cup, it would be ours tomorrow!'

If they ever compete for the 'Auld Mug' under gaff rig he may well be right but his pride can be appreciated when you see the Falmouth Working boats creaming through the anchorage off Falmouth, spread of white canvas, concentration on the face of every man taking part in racing which is as hotly contested as anything to be seen at Cowes. The bye-law stating that dredging for oysters in Falmouth Harbour can only be carried out under sail, has kept this fleet alive not only in competition but in the winter months working the oyster beds in the creeks off the River Fal.

November the 5th aways spells fireworks in Falmouth; it is the date of the Silver Oyster Race, a major event in the racing calendar. It marks a major victory for working boat owners many years ago and is now almost a 'holy' day on which no owner will dredge. To compete, you have to own a boat that is still dredging under sail and the solid silver, life-size oyster shells are magnificent prizes. Should your cruise take you to Falmouth, look out for *Morning Star,* built in 1812 and still working!

Once round Land's End, we are in the home waters of the Bristol Channel Pilot Cutter, the last of the pilot cutters to work under sail and one of the last of them *Cariad* is now in the care of the Maritime Trust. These ships were built to race but not for silver cups; first pilot to meet an incoming ship got the job so these cutters raced for a livelihood. They had to be many things to many men; seaworthy for the gales and steep seas of the Bristol Channel, swift to make over the fast flowing tides. They had to be quick in tacking when working close enough to ships to allow a pilot to board and still be stable when hove-to on pilot station. No wonder they emerged as a classic amongst sailing craft. Here Captain George Buck, a retired Bristol Channel pilot, remembers his days of piloting under sail:

Piloting was also a very risky job as we usually boarded with the punt. The usual method was to ask the captain to put the ship in the position you wanted, across the sea making a lee, then the skiff would sail under her lee, out punt and the pilot and man would row to the ladder. The man in the skiff would get back into the wind again and then come back under the lee to pick up the punt in the smooth water. This was not a difficult job in the daytime but in night it required a lot of skill and judgment, as with an empty ship and fresh wind she would drift to leeward, and if the skiff lost the wind she would drift down on to her.

Before the pilots amalgamated in 1918 it was a cut-throat affair and we would do anything to get to windward of another skiff, but we were all the best of pals ashore. I have known four skiffs leave Pill on a morning tide and race as far as 50 miles SW of the Land's End. At night they would show no lights and by daylight one at a time would be missing, until only one was left and then she had the first chance. But this did not always turn out for the best, as often the one which gave up first had the first ship, since the western skiff would not bother to speak to ships at night, in order to make sure she was the western boat at daybreak.

Another trick in addition to sailing without lights to get to the westward of another skiff was, in a calm, to get out a long sweep and push all night, and it was surprising how she would slip through the water when the sea was smooth with the aid of a big oar. No 17 once chased us up the English Channel as far as Start Point and at daybreak was not in sight. We spoke to a steamer bound for Bristol and he told us he did not want a pilot there.

We told him we would come for any pilotage he cared to pay but all we could get from his was 'I don't want a pilot here'. My mate told him we had come purposely for him and he replied 'I did not ask you to come' and was soon out of hailing distance. We started to work back towards the Lizard and the next day we boarded a larger steamer off the Longships. We were away three weeks that trip for one ship and when we arrived home we heard that the steamer which would not stop for us off Start Point had picked up his pilot off Lundy Island, but this only happened occasionally.

Once we were hove-to about 5 miles SW of the Wolf Rock, the wind had died away to a flat clam, the sea like a mirror, very dark without a cloud in the sky and the stars shining in the water the same as in the sky, all the lighthouses showing their lights all around the horizon and the Lizard light flashing in the sky. I was on 12 to 4 watch when a ship's masthead light came in sight. I took a bearing and saw she would pass a long way to the north of us and, having no wind, the only thing I could do was show the Bristol signal on the flashlight, though as the flashlight was usually used by fishing boats in this area ships generally gave it a wide berth. We were expecting one of Pyman's ships along, called the *Cober,* she being five days out from Gibraltar. I decided to call one of the pilots (we had two on board) and when he came on deck I suggested calling the other pilot, launching the punt and pulling as far as possible to get as close as we could, then to show the flashlight and hail her with the megaphone. We pulled until she was abreast of us, still more than a mile away, showed the flashlight and started to hail her, but eventually had to give up and had started to pull back to the skiff when we saw her port light come in sight and she came towards us, and sure enough it was the *Cober* bound for Bristol. I put the pilot on board and he towed me back to the skiff. The captain told the pilot he was lying in his bunk and heard us hailing 'We are the Bristol pilot', but they had not heard us on the bridge.

The next night we were still in about the same place and still a flat calm. In the 12 to 4 watch I heard my mate come below and tell the other pilot a ship was in sight a long way north. I turned out and suggested another pull, the pilot agreed and this time he took an oar and we made the punt fly through the water, stopping now and again to show the flashlight. We were just deciding to give up when she went hard-a-starboard and steamed towards us. She was bound for Bristol and of course I expected to be towed back to the skiff as we had pulled much farther than the night before, but when the pilot suggested this to the captain he told him he had lost a blade and a half of his propeller and wanted to make sure of his tide. The pilot looked over the bridge and told me but I did not care, being happy to think we had another ship, and started to row back. After pulling for some time I stopped to see if I could pick up the skiff's light but with so many stars in the water I could not find it but could see the Wolf light and knew if I pulled in that direction I was bound to find her, also my mate would show a light. It seemed I had been rowing for hours alone in the world and I started singing to keep myself company. Then I stopped rowing, looked around and saw a light and was close to the skiff. My mate was pleased to see me back. The two pilots were EW Born and RM Stenner, Pilot Born on the *Cober* and Pilot Stenner on the *Clara,* one of Burdock & Cook's ships. When Pilot

Stenner rejoined us he said the captain told him he had loaded grain in a Russian Black Sea port and damaged his propeller in the ice and was ten days from Gib when we boarded him. I have often wondered how many miles I pulled that night and thought it strange that it should have happened on two successive nights.

Roger Robinson, who sailed with explorer Bill Tilman who also had a penchant for these craft, is restoring *Olga* a cutter built at Barry in 1909. He tells me:

'Unlike many craft that have been converted into yachts, these were principally built to take people — not cargo. That's what makes them such wonderful boats at sea. You can leave the helm, wander forward, put the kettle on and she'll still be on course.'

Have you noticed how often the kettle appears in any discussion of ships at sea? It may have been a face that launched a thousand ships but it's a kettle that has kept 'em going.

Red sky at night

Weather to believe it?

Whatever the glass is doing, whatever the sky and the wind and the waves are up to, some wise fool will appear at your elbow and recite a poem about it. 'Ahar', he will say, knocking out his ancient pipe on his ancient wellie; 'When zhunder-clouds be in the sky, A zhunder-storm be drawin' nigh'.

And who can contradict him? He stumps off, muttering darkly about mackerel's tails and St Swithin's day, and the rest of your week-end is ruined by fears of a freak typhoon.

To counteract this mixture of folk-wisdom and superstition, and to temper the deep belief, embedded in most of us, that anything which is in dialect, and rhyme, must be true, we searched out all the seamen's weather-proverbs we could find, and offered them in turn to an expert. Michael Hunt is British TV's longest-serving weatherman, and a lifelong student of meteorology. First we drank a bottle of claret and ate some mackerel to get us in the mood; then, one by one, in tones of gloomy foreboding, Libby recited the poems and Michael delivered his verdict on them. Here we go:

Long foretold, long last;
Short notice, soon past.

'Basically very sensible. When a depression is large and deep, it becomes sluggish and moves slowly. It shows its hand a long time ahead, but stays a long time too. There are no big rapid falls, just a slow persistent leakage of pressure. That's very sound indeed: such depressions linger for days. As for 'short notice', that might be an active secondary depression, forming on the southern side of the big parent depression, in the Northern Hemisphere. And they *whistle* through with rapid falls and rapid rises.'

Sharp rise after low
Foretells a stronger blow.

'Very sound. There are two factors: this could be a secondary cold front — the wind has veered to W then veered sharply to NW with almost a line-squall effect. Or it could be that the cold front of a depression just gone through, the wind veers, and we pick up the cold Polar-Maritime north-westerlies. In winter, you see, with relatively warm seas, large cumulonimbus clouds with attendant sharp gusty squalls will form over windward coasts. Funny that we should have begun with two of the soundest proverbs — frankly, over 50 per cent of them are not worth the paper they're written on.'

Seagull, seagull stay on the sand;
It's never good weather while you're on the land!

'Nothing in it! Especially nowadays, when seagulls have adopted a different lifestyle. They don't of necessity come inshore to get away from bad weather. They usually come to scavenge on the rubbish-tip.'

The higher the gulls, the harder the gale.

'I would have said the opposite applied. Nearer the ground, there is less wind; sensible gulls stay low in bad weather. Really, you know, there is rarely anything in these animal-behaviour sayings. Look at that business about cows lying down when the rain is coming — on any normal day when rain is spreading from the west, half of them are lying down and half of them standing up'.

When the sea-hog jumps
Stand by your pumps.

'What is a sea-hog? A porpoise? they jump in good weather, don't they? What does it mean?'

If fowls roll in t'saind;
Covr yr head f'r rain be t'hand;
If t'cockerel craws as ye're going to bed
T'sun will rise with a watery head.

'Rubbish, most certainly. The cock crowing at odd times, ever since the betrayal of Christ, has been taken as a bad omen. That might be the root of it. But it isn't meteorology. Any better ones?'

If St Swithin weeps, the proverb says
The weather will be foul for forty days.

'Now this *is* interesting. It is one of a whole range of sayings where the indicated date shouldn't be taken too literally. They chose Michaelmas, or Martinmas, or St Swithin's day, just to fix it in people's minds — the actual *date* is not important at all, but it does contain a measure of meteorological truth. St Swithin's day is on 15 July and the point is this: in very general terms early and middle summer are more settled in this country than late summer. So if by St Swithin's day, or thereabouts, you've had the change to unsettled weather, this second phase has begun. Or take another common one, which you find versions of in many countries:

If Candlemas day be fair and bright
Winter will have another flight.

'In Germany, they say that shepherds would 'rather see a wolf than the sun', on Candlemas Day. This is 2 February; and here the point is that if in early February you are getting fine, clear weather — that's cold, easterly weather with clear skies — then we're still feeling the Continental anticyclonic effect. If its cloudy and unsettled that Continental effect is breaking down, and we're starting to let in the westerlies which bring wetter, milder weather. Both these proverbs are about weather types changing. Ignore the exact date, and there's more than a grain of truth in them. Next?'

March, March, as black as a ram;
Comes in like a lion, goes out like a lamb!

'These things are bedevilled by this rhyme business. Ram — lamb — how often do you see a black ram? All that this one means is that by the end of March, spring weather is usually established. So what?'

Rainbow to windward, foul fall the day;
Rainbow to leeward, damp runs away.

'Ah. A great deal depends on the time of day and the direction of the wind. It must also be remembered that a rainbow cannot be seen once the sun's elevation exceeds 42 degrees — so in summer you can't see a rainbow in the middle of the day. If we assume that the wind is westerly, the proverb has some validity. An observer must have his back to the sun to see a rainbow — so in the case of a morning rainbow he must be facing roughly westward, with the rainbow and the associated area of rain lying upwind, and the rain still to come, for the proberb to work out. If the rainbow, with the area of rain, is to the eastward (the leeward, in this case) it must be retreating from the observer. Remember that it is impossible to see a rainbow to the west in the late afternoon, because the source of light is behind it. Remember also that you can see a rainbow at night, with the moon as the light source. Nocturnal rainbows are less intense, and the colours very pale.'

Fog in the morning, sailors warning
Fog in the night, sailors delight.

'Absolutely nothing in it. Sorry.'

When the wind shifts against the sun.
Trust it not, for back it will run;
When the wind follows the Sun,
Fine weather will never be done.

'I think this is about winds backing — anticlockwise — and veering. In general terms a backing wind heralds the approach of a depression, a veering wind means it is moving away. General terms only, mind!'

Comes the rain before the wind,
Halyards, sheets and topsails mind;

Comes the wind before the rain,
Soon you may make sail again.

'This one is very general; there are endless versions of it. It probably refers to a squall line; the rain comes — there's a sudden wind-shift and squalls. Or the spatter of large rain drops you get for five minutes or so before a sudden thunderstorm. Not universally reliable, but then so few of these rhyming things are.'

If it raineth at tide's flow,
You may safely go and mow
But if it rain at the ebb
Then if you like, go off to bed!

'Oh really now. The tide ebbs and flows every six hours. All this can mean is that, other things being equal, the weather might be going to change, or then again it might not.'

No dew after sun,
Fine weather's on the run.

'That's better. It's rather interesting. The idea is that for dew to form you need clear sky and light wind — *no* dew means either that cloud is increasing, or wind increasing; both indicators of changing weather. The ground cools most, forming heavy dews, under clear skies and in light winds. There's another saying that heavy dews foretell fair weather — same thing.'

When the mist rolls o'er the land
The rain comes pouring off the sand.

'I don't know where you found that one. I don't understand it. Do you? No. Well then.'

Red sky in the morning, sailors' warning.

'Or shepherds' warning. This is the most famous of all; and it is reasonably valid, if properly interpreted. We are talking about a red atmosphere, which means that the blue light is filtered out of the setting sun's rays, which in turn means that the atmosphere particles are small; which again in turn means that the particles are dry. So red sky at night means that the atmosphere for about 500 miles to the west of you is dry . . . and no rain is on its way from the west. But red sky in the *morning* — to the east — means the upper atmosphere to the *east* of you is dry, and in changeable weather that is likely to mean the next rain is not far off to the west.'

If the sun goes pale to bed,
'T'will rain tomorrow, so 'tis said.

'Here there is no reassuring red sky at night; there may also be a layer of altostratus or cirrostratus giving that white, pale, look. Cirrostratus and altostratus at sunset, and a falling glass, and backing wind, taken together, do mean rain, probably before morning.'

When round the moon there is a brough
The weather comes in cold and rough.

'Yes, and there's another version — *'The bigger the brough the bigger the breeze.'* Or, *'the further the ring, the nearer the rain.'*

A brough, or ring, is a halo round the moon. It is caused by the presence of a sheet of cirrostratus ice-crystal cloud, which is normally associated with the approach of a warm front, and hence rain, from the west. If it is a true halo, set far from the moon, that is a sign of bad weather, especially in winter. It is caused by refraction through the ice-crystal cloud. Don't confuse it with a harmless corona, a coloured ring near to the moon, formed by diffraction through water-drop cloud. That's a settled sign. One of the best pieces of weather-proverb poetry is:

"The hollow winds begin to blow
The clouds look black and the glass is low
Last night the sun went pale to bed
The moon in haloes hid her head
Look out my lads! A wicked gale
With heavy rain will soon assail."

That contains the three essentials, the triad of weather forecasting: wind, sky, and barometer. Consult all three. Never mind all this rubbish about sea-hogs and rams.'

Enough blue in the sky to make a Dutchman's breeches and it will clear.

'True. A cold front is coming through, and the clearance shows itself as a little bit of blue on the windward horizon. If the wind is also veering and the glass checking, we have a line of frontal clearance. But the wind may well *not* decrease.'

Mackerel sky and mares' tails
Make tall ships carry small sails.

'Well, mares' tails — hooked cirrus — are certainly a sign of the warm front of an approaching depression; but it may be a long way off, and in summer it may not develop. Watch the glass, watch the wind, if you see mares' tails. Also watch the cirrus to see if it is thickening. Mare's tails don't often appear at the same time as altocumulus — mackerel sky. There's a lot about that —

"Mackerel sky, mackerel sky,
Never long wet and never long dry
Mackerel scales, furl your sails
Mackerel clouds in the sky, more wet coming than dry
A mackerel sky, not 24 hours dry . . ."

The thing about extensive bands of altocumulus cloud is that they mean the approach of an occluded front, and such fronts are generally fairly weak. They are attractive clouds, so people look up at them, and make up poems, and assume that they will mean rain, or change (which they possibly will, all other things being equal). There's even:

"A mackerel sky, let all your kites fly."

The sensible thing to say about mackerel sky is that when you see it you might as well watch your triad — sky, glass, and wind — more carefully than you usually do.'

If the clouds look as if scratched by a hen
Be sure to furl your topsails then . . .

'Hooked cirrus again: mares' tails. True enough'.

If woolly fleeces deck the heavenly way
Be sure no rain will mar a summer's day.

'Oh come now! All this can mean is that, "if it stays fine, it will stay fine — so long as it stays fine." Small fluffy white cumulus is fine as long as it doesn't develop.'

If wind be north east three days without rain.
Eight days will pass before south again.

'If it is wintertime, easterly winds mean a continental anticyclone is established. If it has been easterly weather like this for a few days, it may well be a week before southerly winds ahead of a depression can make their way up from the south-west. In general terms, this one has a grain of truth in it.'

The winds of the daytime wrestle and fight
Longer and stronger than those of the night.

'In the eastern counties "a westerly wind goes to bed with the sun"; in the west, the opposite applies — easterlies die down at dusk, generally. The reason is that the wind at the surface is markedly lighter than the wind at, say, 3000ft, because the ground slows down surface winds by friction. The turbulence which 'mixes' the winds at the two levels, and so keeps up the speed of that surface wind, is brought about when the ground is heated — in the daytime. At night, stability increases as the ground cools, so turbulence decreases and the friction effects of the earth's surface produces a progressive falling off and backing of the surface wind. This effect is most marked when cooling is most marked — that is, when there are clear skies. Offshore, of course, there is very little diurnal variation in the sea temperature and hence very little diurnal variation in wind speeds.'

Better it is to rise betimes
And make hay while the sun shines
Than to believe in tales and lies
Which idle people do devise!

'Quite right too. Especially in summer, rising betimes is good policy; there is a common pattern of days which start fine and slowly deteriorate until a teatime shower. As for the idle tales and lies, we've just heard a few of those.'

How big is she?

Tonnage, Tunnage, and downright bluff

The question is simple enough: 'How big is she . . .?', but the answer calls for a little more thought. There is a remarkable scope for confusion. Take the case of the wealthy man with his top-class ocean racer. He would proudly tell you that he raced a 'one tonner.' Then you might bump into a man who had bought his first little cruiser.

'It's a lovely little five tonner . . .' and you would glance over your shoulder at the racing man and wonder why he was being so uncharacteristically modest. Then you look at your own boat and peer at the fine print on your Certificate of Registry. It states quite clearly that you are a 'seven tonner' but how does that explain the fact that the man on the mooring next to you, with an identical boat, is a 'ten tonner' and why are you both minute alongside the 'one tonner?'

The answer is quite simple. Tonnages have nothing to do with tons in the sense of tons of coal. In that case, it is a measurement of weight but afloat, a ton is a measure of a boat's capacity.

'Ton', in the nautical sense, is a remnant of the days when ships seemed to be principally engaged in the noble business of wine shifting. A 'tun' was a cask with a capacity of about 250 gallons and the bigger the ship, the more 'tuns' it carried and hence its 'tonnage' was larger. It might be refreshing to revert to this system. It might not do much for handicap racing but it would make the measuring much more fun!

A ton these days, in shipping terms, is now taken to be a capacity of 100 cubic feet.

If we think of our yachts as being small ships (and who doesn't?) the capacity will be measured and computed in the same way as if you were the *QE2* for the purposes of registration. It takes a surveyor using a set of mathematical formulae, and a ruler, to calculate what is called your *Gross Tonnage.* This is a measurement of the volume of the boat beneath the deck level. If you have a wheelhouse, the volume of that would be calculated and added and you end up with a figure which represents the volume of the boat if she were empty. That is your gross tonnage.

However, it's not a fair figure because so much space is taken up by engines and tanks and so these are measured and subtracted from your gross tonnage to give a fair idea of the carrying capacity of your boat. This figure is your *Net Register Tonnage.*

If your yacht is less than 45 feet overall, the 1894 Act of Parliament no longer allows you any of the above but asks you to be content with a figure called your *Register Tonnage* which, without going into the mathematics of the whole thing, can be taken to be a cross between your gross and net register tonnage. This amendment came into force under the 1975 Act and more changes are due, so be warned; you could lose weight overnight and not feel a thing.

You can now forget about gross tonnage and net tonnage since the tonnage often used to compare the size of yachts is its *Thames Tonnage.* Modern yacht design has rendered this a little deceptive, but by and large it has been in use since 1855 when it was introduced by the Royal Thames Yacht Club as a rating for racing yachts against which a true allowance was allocated. It is now only used when comparing cruising yachts. The formula is:

$$\frac{(L - B) \times B \times \frac{1}{2} B}{94}$$

where L is the length 'between perpendiculars' in feet (not including the bowsprit if you have one) and B is the maximum beam measured to the outside of the hull. If you see an advertisement for a 'nice little five tonner' it is the Thames ton to which it refers.

Unless your yachting is on an extremely grand scale or consists of really weight-conscious racing, you will hardly be concerned with your *displacement.* It is a figure generally used to express the size of naval ships. Meeting a 20,000 tonner at sea is not taken to mean an encounter with some super-yacht but with a warship or, in some cases, a merchant ship. These are usually referred to by their gross or net register tonnage, but the displacement is the actual weight of the ship. It is the

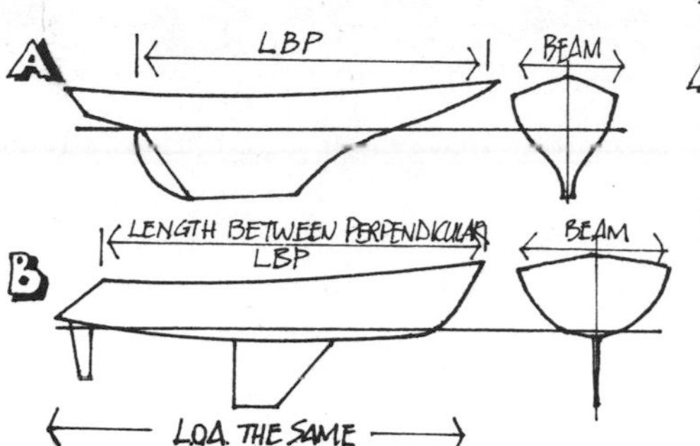

THAMES MEASUREMENT

A. MID-20TH. CENTURY YACHT WITH OVERHANGS AND MODERATE BEAM.

B. MODERN YACHT (80s) FOR SAME LOA. HAS LONGER LBP. AND MUCH MORE BEAM, GIVING BIGGER THAMES TONNAGE. WATERLINE ALSO LONGER.

figure you would get if you put the vessel on a set of scales. Archimedes holds the key to this calculation since a floating ship *displaces* its own weight of water.

That leaves us with the racing man and his shiny machine which he calls his 'one tonner.' If it were a Thames one tonner it ought to be about 12 feet long, even less if it were 1 gross ton. The French are to blame for this confusion (along with so many others in the yachting world). They introduced a cup awarded to yachts racing under their own tonnage rules, the first one presented being the 'One Ton Cup' in 1898. Since then, yacht handicapping has developed and we enjoy a headache-inducing system whereby, after several computer hours, a yacht is awarded a rating figure which is related to its theoretical potential speed. It is expressed as a length, but is in no way similar to the figure you would get if you ran a tape measure down the hull. Since a yacht's maximum speed is related to her length, the logic of the system begins to come clear.

There are five classes of 'ton cup' yachts which race level under the International Offshore Rule. The rating for each 'tonnage' is a maximum figure. (This may also be directly related to your bank overdraft figure).

ONE TON	30.5 ft rating
¾ TON	24.5 ft
½ TON	22 ft
¼ TON	18.5 ft
MINI-TON	16.5 ft

There is also an even smaller MICRO-TON to a different system of measurement.

It is worth mentioning a further system of measurement known as the *owner's apparent length.* Since yachts pay harbour dues on the basis of their length and not their register tonnage as do ships, some formula is needed when the owner is asked by the harbourmaster, 'how long is she?'

To arrive at an answer, the owner should take the overall length of his yacht and multiply it by a factor which is always less than one. The size of this factor will vary and has to be decided in each case and is based upon the owners assessment of the harbour master's power of observation!

Other people at sea

An imaginary rally

Of all the quieter delights of cruising, few are so great as to drop anchor in a safe harbour at night, *alone.* But one of the pleasures which comes close to it is to drop the anchor and, on rowing around in the dinghy, to discover one or two boat-loads of kindred spirits. Over various brews in various saloons you can exchange passage notes, compare opinions about the height of the seas you are hiding from, and note down details of each other's brilliant labour-saving ideas. We have many cherished memories of such encounters.

There was the man we met in the fog at Valentia, who had built his own ferro-concrete boat and had the curious experience of nearly drowning in the bare hull before the floors went in (it filled with rainwater and he fell in while trying to fix a pump-hose). There was a splendid old lady who had once been towed away at 15 knots in the middle of the night by Spanish fishing boats and swore that she'd 'never undressed on a boat since that night!'. There was the determined couple who were circumnavigating Ireland in an old six-metre with a mast raked like a banana and no engine. They were vegetarian, and loaded to the gunwales with exotic and windy pulses in canvas sacks. There was the man in Ramsgate who had come from Wales with only an AA road map. We are grateful to all of them for the things we learnt, and the whisky.

So here, in case tonight you find yourself alongside some deserted fishing-boat or a grumpy starlet's gin-palace, we present the ultimate in comparative sailing chat. Imagine you are storm-bound in a pretty, remote bay, surrounded by 19 other boats. None of you can leave until the gale abates; nobody else can arrive. It could be a week. There is no pub for ten miles, no road, and one farm supplying water and eggs. So you spend the week in a series of social gatherings from boat to boat, bragging and comparing and recounting and nosing around. Your companions are some of the most distinguished sailors afloat, so there is plenty to learn. Clare Francis is there, and Michael Richey in the legendary *Jester;* Hammond Innes, John Ridgway, Robin Knox-Johnston, Sir Alec Rose; Ewen Southby-Tailyour who charted the Falklands before the invasion in his yacht; and a dozen others with decades of experience between them. They answered ten questions which we fired at them, beginning with:

'WHAT IS THE GREATEST LUXURY YOU CARRY ON BOARD?'

We had our own answers ready. In Paul's case, bedroom slippers; in Libby's the paraffin heater in the saloon.

Actually, a lot of the luxuries were similarly concerned with keeping warm and snuggling down. Robin Aisher, former Admiral's Cup team captain, insists on a thick sleeping bag. Charles Stock, who sails 2000 miles a year on the East Coast swatchways, takes a pillow 'of the same quality that I use at home' and also a hotwater bottle, but denies that either is a luxury. 'Sound sleep is an obligation to self and crew'. John Ridgway, ultimate tough guy, who rowed the Atlantic with Chay Blyth, sailed non-stop around the world and teaches survival up in icy Scotland, admits to using 'a duvet bed cover'. Michael Bentine has spare dry clothes as a luxury; Clare Francis revels in 'extra fresh water for washing in', and John Foot, Vice-Commodore of the Royal Thames Yacht Club and a vastly experienced voyager, says that it has to be *hot* fresh water. Tim Severin, who crossed the Atlantic in the leather boat *Brendan* and sailed to China in the dhow *Sindbad,* finds his comfort in Cooper's Vintage Marmalade.

There were two backers for the idea of a cabin stove; Maurice Griffiths, whose yacht designs have carried many cruising people thousands of happy miles, and whose books have inspired even more, writes:

'An anthracite/coal/wood burning stove, fitted in one corner of the cabin where its cheerful glow can be seen and felt. With a polished fiddle-rail it can double up as a simmer plate for the coffee pot or soup saucepan, and it burns the rubbish'.

J D Sleightholme, ex-Editor of *Yachting Monthly* and another great cruise-inspirer, praises his old solid fuel bogey stove:

'Ten degrees frost, vest and Y-fronts in cabin' but continues:

'We now have a catalytic heater run on gas and we sit taut with apprehension waiting for it to explode. Wife sniffs constantly like retriever in bracken'. Finally, he settled for a proper pillow as well:

'Folded trousers OK, but why always Curry Lockspike knife in pocket?'

JDS also once tried to take a television 'with a picture the size of a dog-biscuit', but gave it up. Ewen Southby-Tailyour takes a portable telly, not without shame. But reception in the Falklands must have been limited, to say the least, so perhaps he is entitled to such luxury in home waters.

The other votes were for a wife (Hammond Innes), a transistor radio (Alec Rose), a tape recorder (Robin Knox-Johnston), a substance called Boatcake, made with fruit marinaded in rum (Mark Brackenbury, author of many pilot books) and 'a British flag'. This last was the luxury chosen by Tristan Jones, a redoubtable figure who holds the world vertical sailing record, having travelled from the lowest to the highest waters in the world 'to bring the Red Ensign closer to the stars'. Of the others, Colonel 'Blondie' Hasler, founder of the Observer Single-handed TransAtlantic Race, asked for Chinese rig, Bernard Hayman the ex-editor of *Yachting World* wanted an AP Navigator, and Sir Maurice Laing, the great racing man, chose his B & G Hercules as the greatest luxury. However, all of these were so practical that we refused to allow them as luxuries. They probably make better answers to the next question:

'NAME ONE THING YOU WOULD NEVER GO TO SEA WITHOUT'.

A few sensible, practical, seamanlike answers here. 'A boat', says Michael Bentine firmly. Bernard Hayman wanted a compass, so did Maurice Griffiths, although he was prepared to settle for a good anchor and chain or a leadline instead. Charles Stock says binoculars, because, 'Skilled navigation is pointless if the marks are wrongly identified in the first place. This is particularly so in the Thames Estuary'.

Blondie Hasler votes for wind-vane steering gear, naturally enough since he invented one of the best on the market; Robin Aisher and Alec Rose say they would never go to sea without a liferaft, and both Ewen Southby-Tailyour and Tim Severin want good knives. Sir Maurice Laing would not go without a Verey pistol and cartridges.

Hammond Innes claims that his one essential is his wife; Mark Brackenbury will settle for Dramamine; and Michael Richey for garlic (all very well for singlehanders). John Foot says whisky; Robin Knox-Johnston says tea; and John Ridgway wouldn't go without dry clothes. For Clare Francis the essential is Nivea cream, and for Tristan Jones — 'British flag'. So much for the first stages of packing. Now:

'NAME THREE BOOKS FOR READING ON BOARD'.

Tastes vary. Some want to revel in seafaring, others to escape it entirely. On our boat, Paul reads salty seafaring stuff until the going gets really tough, when he switches to gardening books. Libby reads H W Tilman and the Royal Cruising Club's *Roving Commissions* in calm weather, but prefers Nancy Mitford and John le Carré to shut out the rising gales. The least successful reading summer was 1983, when she was a Booker prize judge. Modern novels go remarkably badly with the atmosphere of cruising, on the whole. Anyway, here is the reading list as recommended by our panel from their own cabin shelves:

The Bible — Sir Maurice Laing, Robin Knox-Johnston
Riddle of the Sands by Erskine Childers — Maurice Griffiths, Charles Stock, Bernard Hayman, Ewen Southby-Tailyour, Michael Bentine
The Wind in the Willows by Kenneth Grahame — Tristan Jones
Oxford Book of English Verse — Tristan Jones
Decline and Fall by Gibbon — Michael Richey
Parade's End by Ford Madox Ford — Michael Richey
The Oxford Book of Death — Michael Richey
War and Peace by Tolstoi — Clare Francis
Skene's Elements of Yacht Design — Bernard Hayman
Round the World with Ridgway — John Ridgway
Down Channel by MacMullen — Maurice Griffiths
Cruise of the Nona by Hilaire Belloc — Maurice Griffiths
Heavy Weather Sailing by Adlard Coles — Maurice Griffiths
An Outline of History by HG Wells — Robin Knox-Johnston
Para Handy Tales by Munroe — Robin Knox-Johnston
Nare's Seamanship — Tim Severin
The Good Food Guide — Tim Severin

More general recommendations were for Kipling (Ewen Southby-Tailyour), Chesterton (Mark Brackenbury) and Eric Hiscock (Alec Rose). Both JD Sleightholme and Clare Francis have a weakness for huge sagas; as JDS puts it: 'huge fat paperbacks about family sagas and bad blood, orgies in the slave baracoons etc, send me to sleep off watch like being sandbagged'.

Michael Bentine claims to be 'too busy surviving' for light reading; he takes Reed's Almanac and the relevant Pilots. Hammond Innes reads cookery books by Elizabeth David, which brings us neatly to the next question.

'WHAT IS THE MOST SUCCESSFUL DISH YOU HAVE COOKED ON BOARD?'

Here a wild gastronomic adventure opens up. John Foot claims to have done grilled oysters; while Hammond Innes and Maurice Griffiths both remember bacon and eggs as the height of gustatory experience. 'For breakfast, after a dip on a summer's morning', says Griffiths, but reserves a corner of savoury memory for 'a chicken casserole with dumplings, cooked for a hungry crew after a tedious and wet passage to a quiet, almost deserted anchorage for the night'.

Michael Bentine and Bernard Hayman both speak highly of porridge ('tastes the same coming up as going down', says the ex-goon darkly); Charles Stock of well-hung rump steak, and John Ridgway of curry. Robin Knox-Johnston also remembers a curry of bully beef: 'Nobody else liked it so I had the lot and it gave me appalling indigestion, but it was worth it'.

On *Barnacle Goose* we always have a ceremonial 'Arriving Curry' to mark a significant passage. It has to have coconut chips and banana and all the trimmings, and fresh onion and apple; the remains are strapped down on deck in the centre of the lifebelt and become a mulligatawny soup for lunch the next day.

Tristan Jones' most successful feat of cuisine was Toad-in-the-Hole and chips.

There were quite a few private recipes on offer. Clare Francis likes Egg-In-Bread.

'Make hole in bread with fingers. Drop bread into frying pan full of hot butter. Drop egg into hole in bread. Turn and fry other side. Eat in fingers'. Blondie Hasler goes one further and makes the bread:

'Starting with wheat grain, ground in a hand coffee grinder and baked in the bottom half of a pressure cooker with a biscuit-tin lid over it'.

We have always found that baking bread is easy enough over a single burner, provided that, like us, you happen to enjoy really heavy, solid, lumpen wholemeal bricks which keep for days and are impossible to sick up — too heavy.

Sir Maurice Laing claims that he only ever heats up pre-cooked food on board, but another great racing man, Robin Aisher, is clearly an advanced gastronome: 'scrambled eggs, peanuts, and garlic salt'. That would, at least, sort the men from the boys fast enough in a mid-Channel lop. Ewen Southby-Tailyour 'cooks everything in garlic and red wine, so they are all successful'; Alec Rose recommends his personal stew: 'stewed steak, mushrooms, onions, carrots, suet dumplings, a pinch of mixed herbs, served with mashed potatoes and butter beans'. Tim Severin remembers bean cassoulet, made with Polish ham smoked in London, W11 but also has good memories of (hold on to your hat) 'fricassée of seagull with tinned cream'. And JD Sleightholme gladly offers his culinary secret:

'Bachelor days living alone on boat up creek, Blunt Snout Pudding. Made in pint mug and looked like greyish pig's snout when turned out. I could knock up one of those old busters from rolling dough to mug-eviction in 20 minutes by stopwatch. Used to try and beat my own best time. Cooked one every night, some had sausage and spud, other times apple and sultanas. Up they'd rise like bloody genies from some dark and steamy cavern'. Finally, let us doff our hats and remember the immensely wise words of the late H W Tilman, Polar sailor and explorer. In his years of driving ancient pilot cutters up freezing fjords, he amassed much wisdom. One of the best bits of the lot was the simplest: *'Never board a ship without an onion'.*

We shall pass rapidly over the next question:

'WHAT IS THE LEAST SUCCESSFUL DISH YOU HAVE ATTEMPTED?'

Michael Bentine and Bernard Hayman are united in a distaste for burnt porridge. Tim Severin and John Ridgway both report failure with scrambled egg made from dried egg powder; Robin Aisher would rather draw a veil over one particular toasted egg sandwich. Maurice Griffiths once made a curry with seawater by mistake. Mark Brackenbury has no doubt at all about his lowest ebb in the galley: 'tinned haggis and neeps with scotch on a passage through Cardigan Bay. It achieved a 100 per cent rejection level an hour later as the wind got up against the tide off St David's head'.

Haggis, we can confirm, causes problems. It is all right if you have an oven, and roast it on a grid so that all the fat falls out; if you boil it like the Scots do, you are asking for mutton-grease flavoured trouble and haunted, uneasy dreams off-watch.

Clare Francis finds that fish pie tends, owing to gravity, to fall on the cabin sole wrong side up; and another cook admits to trouble with a Vesta curry 'when trying to read the instructions after too much to drink'.

We ought not, perhaps, to leave the subject without a confession. Once Libby made a wholefood grain dish called Bulgar with so much salt that even the seagulls turned down the leftovers; and we have uneasy memories even today of a stew made in a saucepan which some fool had used to bleed the diesel engine into, and put back. Unwashed. Apart from that:

'WHAT HAS FRIGHTENED YOU MOST IN YOUR YACHTING CAREER?'

'Yard bills', says John Foot starkly. 'Questionnaires', says Tristan Jones, and 'The Sea', says Michael Bentine. Fog came high on the list; so did icebergs and pack ice (Clare Francis, John Ridgway), big ships (Alec Rose, Tim Severin both complain of their apparent blindness to yachts) and whales (Michael Richey, threatened by killer whales off Newfoundland). There were some horrifying experiences to recount: Maurice Griffiths ran aground 'about 1922, in the dark and a rising autumn gale. Our leaky little 22ft centreboard sloop went on the outlying Gunfleet sands off Clacton on the ebb, and our dinghy had gone adrift. The yacht lay on her side until dawn, and very nearly broke up'. Mark Brackenbury had a bad entry to Fécamp in the dark on a falling tide; JDS had such a bad time in the Adriatic once that 'I recommended my soul to Maker, like some sort of special bargain offer'. One man may have a lousy moment gybing into Newhaven harbour, and another (Robin Knox-Johnston) see great Southern Ocean rollers in a force 11 gale; the quality of private fears perhaps remains the same.

A few yachting fears are not concerned with gales and whales: Ewen Southby-Tailyour was understandably terrified by being asked to return to the Falklands to put his light-hearted yachting experience to military use. Robin Aisher, in the 1979 Fastnet race which brought disaster to so many boats, found the responsibility for other lives weighed heaviest on him. And Bernard Hayman is merely 'frightened by the attitude of many beginners'. Blondie Hasler has had, similarly, a few nasty shocks from 'some of the boats at boat shows, particularly one discovered by the late Angus Primrose which had a red sidelight to starboard and a green to port'.

See what he means. See what they all mean, really; but our own vote would go to that nastiest of all combinations; an onshore gale and thick fog. Now, a very personal question:

'WHAT MAKES AN IDEAL CREW MEMBER?'

Bernard Hayman, Charles Stock, Blondie Hasler and Ewen Southby-Tailyour all voted loyally for their wives. Short of matrimony, the favourite qualities were willingness and a sense of humour. 'A *moderate* sense of humour', warned John Foot. Quite right. Whoopee cushions and false ears can begin to pall, four days out in Biscay. Alec Rose would like someone quiet, who makes hot drinks; if you want to crew for Robin Knox-Johnston you must be fit. Tim Severin requires skill, tidiness, manners, tact, and patience; Michael Bentine would settle for 'a professional'. Hammond Innes wants a cook with an iron stomach, Clare Francis wouldn't mind 'a few brains'. Maurice Griffiths sums it all up beautifully from a lifetime's experience: 'He/she has a natural boat sense, and keeps an eye lifting whenever on deck; spots any trouble brewing (fraying sheet, shackle pin unscrewing) and puts it right; doesn't flap easily, is never late on watch, takes willing turn at galley chores; has no irritating personal habits, does not smoke, is generally calm and cheerful. But what a paragon to live up to!' We once had a crew who was so lethally incompetent (steering reciprocal courses on the grid compass, setting fire to the cabin with the stove) that Paul had to resort to spiking his cocoa with a huge whisky to stop him waking up for his next incident-filled watch at 3 am. It worked. Nothing but a pair of vast boots was seen poking from the forepeak for the rest of the night, and he woke up happy and quite unnecessarily apologetic for his lapse.

'DESCRIBE YOUR FAVOURITE YACHTING GARMENT'

'Paper knickers and a T-shirt', cries Clare Francis robustly. Both can be thrown overboard, a valuable feature in sailing underwear. Michael Richey, aboard the dry and manageable chinese-rigged *Jester,* wears his bedroom slippers as much as possible; there was a strong vote for pyjamas from Hammond Innes, Blondie Hasler (wears them as insulation under his trousers) and Sir Maurice Laing, who keeps his Viyella pyjamas on day and night on long offshore races for comfort. Javlin heavy suits are favourites with Robin Aisher and John Foot; Henri-Lloyd oilskins got honourable mentions or two.

But the real fascination lies in discovering what eccentric, much-prized private habits of dress are indulged in by really seasoned sailors. It is the novices who buy the lot off the peg from Cap'n Watts and never improvize. Far away from land, among a few trusted crew and clear of the curious eyes of marina tourists, you can wear what you want, or don't want, more freely than in any other pastime. Rosie Swale spent much of her time nude. We have known one skipper who always wears a welding mask in bad weather, because one swift wipe of the yellow vizor is quicker than a fiddly cleaning of his bifocals; also the yellow tint makes him think the weather is clearing up. A favourite like that can last for ever. Robin Knox-Johnston has sailed in the same sweater for 13 years; Charles Stock likes his pure wool duffle jacket; and Mark Brackenbury clings to 'a mildewed and collapsing blazer, which is full of useful pockets for keeping things in'. One of the sleeves is falling off, but who cares? Give me *pockets'*

Headgear reveals the wildest, most ingenious variations. Maurice Griffiths rejects the peaked hat, sou'wester and bobble cap in favour of 'a well-fitting bowler, City style. For rain, hot sunshine, and very low deck beams. In distress, it can also serve to bale out the dinghy!'

Ewen Southby-Tailyour does not own any oilskins, but one black plastic mack; on his head, over this, he always sports 'a green Arab shamagh (head-dress). There is nothing better for keeping the head and ears warm, it dries quickly and easily, prevents serious injury if hit by the boom, and when in my bunk it pulls down over my face'.

JD Sleightholme only puts on the rakish white top befitting his high yachting-editorial prestige when people are looking. His secret, seafaring headpiece is 'a motor cyclist's hat with ear-flaps. Waterproof, secure, can be worn back to front as sun visor. Flaps button under chin. Wearing it I look like the Hush Puppy dog'.

'WHAT IS THE MOST USELESS THING YOU HAVE EVER BOUGHT FOR YOUR BOAT?'

A bit below the belt, this one. But after wasting our own money on a hopeless wrist-breaking patent winch, and a pair of clever salt-cellars which clogged at a touch, we wanted moral support. We got it. Bernard Hayman and Alec Rose claim never to have bought anything useless, and good luck to them. Everyone else found bitter satisfaction in recalling money wasted on:

A wind generator ('would have been OK on sandcastle' — JDS)
A sea-anchor (Michael Richey)
Sun awning (Clare Francis)
A bubble sextant (Hammond Innes)
Chrome deck fittings ('and other useless shiny gadgets at jewellery prices' — Maurice Griffiths)
A Bloody Outboard Motor (Robin Knox-Johnston)
Anything electrical (John Foot)
The services of a Baluchi cook (Tim Severin)

and — winner, if you please, of the Golden Lemon Award for the most useless yachting purchase ever — Blondie Hasler's investment in 'about 20 gallons of semi-solid ex-US Navy antifouling paint, *without its special thinners*'.

Finally we asked:

'NAME YOUR FAVOURITE HARBOUR AND YOUR LEAST FAVOURITE.'

This question derives from a splendid annual dinner at the Royal Thames, the 'Favourite Harbours Dinner'. Six or seven members rise to their feet, clutching log-books and photograph albums, and describe their current favourite for (officially) not more than five minutes. The winner gets a bottle of champagne and the losers a good deal of applause and argument. We have in our time pleaded for Walton Backwaters, Laimpaul Ushant, and Ster Wenn on Belle-Isle. One member rather eccentrically claimed Walton-on-Thames (by road) and the Vice-Commodore announced two years ago that you hadn't lived until you had sailed your own boat into Venice. However, it is definitely the most difficult question of the ten; John Foot refused in case everyone went there, wherever it is; Blondie Hasler and Tim Severin found it hard to decide; Michael Richey said 'any port in a storm' and left it at that. But there were some enthusiastic tributes. Falmouth and Dartmouth are much loved; Dittisham and Yarmouth IOW appeared as favourites, so did Harwich. Other favourites named were Maplin, Ardmore, Carcass Island in the Falklands (guess whose), Muscat, Pulau Wei, New York, Fourni on Delos and Coll in the Hebrides. The only one which actually inspired us to plan a cruise round it was from generous-minded Des Sleightholme; a lot of people would have kept this one under their hat: 'Goes in Holland. Willow fronds sweep your crosstrees and the street organ comes on the wind as you doze in the cockpit. The tiny club has an honesty box and you help yourself to beer by lifting up a trapdoor in the floor. Showers scald you and the yachtharbourmeister beams a welcome'.

Least favourite harbours? Cowes, I fear, led with three votes — Hasler, Laing, and Aisher. No doubt the latter two see it mainly in the high racing season when it overcrowds; but we have had happy winter evenings tucked into East Cowes, watching spoons players go berserk in the pub. Other dishonourable mentions go to Newhaven, Dover (inhospitable to small boats), St-Jean-de-Luz, Barbados, Trinidad, English Harbour Antigua, Great Yarmouth in Norfolk, Brighton, Bombay, Buenos Aires, Torquay, and Villa Cisneros. Michael Bentine is the most adaptable of sailors; his favourite is whichever one he has just got into, his least favourite the one he has just missed.

We wish our 19 friends good sailing and good harbours; and thank them for staying alongside for long enough to answer the questions. We shall think of them as we use the advice, whether we are constructing Blunt Snout Pudding, baling the dinghy with a bowler hat, or avoiding Bombay harbour in favour of a run to Dittisham. Good luck to all.

Ships that pass 2

The Trinity Tender at work

Brightly beams our Father's mercy
From his Lighthouse evermore;
But he leaves within our keeping
All the lights along the shore.
Traditional hymn

Our coastline is ringed with sandbanks, spiked with rocks. Our seas flow over hidden harbour-bars, scour narrow and winding channels, and break on reefs of chalk and lime-stone; our shores are a graveyard of ships. Even in the age of radar and sonar, Decca and satellite, approaching ships are made safe primarily by seamarks: lights and beacons and the buoys that gleam, flash, ring and whistle by night and day. These are the signals that have, over the centuries, effectively belled the cat.

The lights and marks do not belong to the Navy. Nor do they owe their being to the Department of Trade and Industry, or the Customs. They are the entire responsibility of the Corporation of Trinity House, 'a guild of shipmen and master mariners', granted a charter in 1514 by Henry VIII, and a gay coat of arms in 1573 by his daughter Elizabeth. Its flag bears four Tudor ships in a St George's cross, its members are known as 'elder brethren' and 'younger brethren'; its badges are ancient and ornate. Were it not so intimately involved with barnacle-encrusted buoys, lonely lighthouses, and plunging lightships, it would be easy to describe Trinity House as quaint.

It would also be unfair. The Corporation has its roots very firmly in the practical, merchant tradition — the religious gloss of the Trinity is due as much to the medieval prudence of getting your guild some Church approval, as to the benevolent character of the work. It is tempting to think sentimentally of Southey's Abbot of Aberbrothok, who placed the bell on the Inchcape Rock:

When the Rock was hid by the surge's swell
The mariners heard the warning bell
And then they knew the perilous rock
And blessed the Abbot of Aberbrothok.

— but a solid concern for trade, rather than blessings, is what has fed the determination of the Trinity Brethren, and they support their work directly from the Light Dues paid by merchant ships to every British port.

Five ships, or tenders, do that work at sea. Standing on the upper bridge-deck of the THV *Winston Churchill*, as she loads in Swansea Docks, the tradition and the merchant practicality both lie evident beneath you. Under the Tudor ensign and the golden lion on the flagstaff, a sleek new heli-pad is loaded with prosaic stores: water, diesel, food and laundry for the keepers of the Lundy light, of South Bishop and the lonely Smalls, of Bardsey and St Gowan. On the foredeck six huge steel buoys are lashed, their new green and red and yellow paint striking an oddly festive note amid the sober marine tones of white, rust, and black. Red can shapes with caged bells and heavy lanterns are Merkur and West Usk, bound for the Bristol Channel; tall green cones are for the Copperas Rock and Baggy Leap stations off the Devon coast. Towering 20 feet above the deck in waspish black and yellow stands the pillar shape of West Culver. Out on the darkening sea, their shabbier twins await replacement and reconditioning; to take on new names and replace, in their turn, other weary cones and cans.

This was the moment of the fortnightly relief. Each ship has two complete crews of 36, and as the sun set splendidly on the Gower peninsula, it was the Starboard Watch that Commander Woodman took out through the lock gates, and down the track of a bright half-moon. Richard Woodman is 39, one of the youngest Tender captains.

He came to Trinity House from a merchant line, as many do, and is now its enthusiastic historian, with a book published on what he calls 'the Hidden Service'. Hidden, but not unrecorded. Triumphantly he quotes a memo of August 1745, ordering 'that Mr Widgeon go down in the Trinity Sloop to clean the buoys in the South Channel'. Mr Widgeon is his first recorded predecessor, and from him the line of ships and men stretches unbroken from sail, to steam, to the diesel-electric, 1451-ton *Winston Churchill*. And the shade of Mr Widgeon no doubt appreciates Mr Woodman's present command: for she is, even to the most amateur eye, unquestionably a nice little ship. A length of 220 feet and a draught of barely 13, together with the ability of the captain to drive the engines direct from the bridge with his own hands, make her a satisfyingly compact, human-scaled vessel. I was seized by the irrational conviction that I could drive her out of harbour myself, buoys and all, and slip along down the Bristol Channel in the moonlight. It was pleasant to watch Woodman too, clearly enjoying himself. To attain a similar professional status in the merchant marine, he and the other officers would probably have had to serve in VLCC's — gigantic, awkward, unstoppable tankers, plying dully on instruments from Gulf to European oil terminals.

Instead, in these little ships they slide amid reefs to mark them, creep up on wrecks, lower the ship's boats to manoeuvre tightly in the rocks and surf, load and fly tiny helicopters to the tall lighthouse. 'It is the last pure seamanship job going', they will tell you, and it breeds contentment. Several of the officers are yachtsmen in their fortnight off, and get something of the same sort of fun at times out of the work of *Winston Churchill:* using anchor, wind, and tide to position the ship to its task, sneaking over a sandbank on the last of the tide to paint a remote buoy against the clock, anchoring for the night amidst the cliffs and the calling seabirds. Even progress is a little regretted, as endangering that high-keyed seamanship. 'In the days before the helicopters, the only way to relieve a lighthouse in bad weather was to take a boat in stern-to amongst the rocks', said Woodman. 'My first time, I couldn't believe it. The coxswain didn't mind, but I thought it was suicide'. And he turned up-channel in the darkness.

A familiar, but unfamiliar, sensation. When you look out on a buoyed channel, at night, it is a pleasant sparkle. When you sail down it, navigating a small boat, the syncopated flashes cease to be decorative, and become a pattern of lights that registers and confirms your safety. But see it yet again, from the deck of a Trinity tender, and it means even more. As we steamed up the Bristol Channel that night, to anchor until dawn off our first buoy, at Barry, I stood at the bridge window next to the young third officer, Paul Dorricott. He was, I gradually realized, not so much following the buoys as *checking* them. We gazed at one in particular, West Nash, whose duty is to mark the western edge of a shoal by flashing nine times every ten seconds. Unquestionably, it had just flashed ten. And ten again. Eleven. Nine. 'Damn. Oh Damn' said Mr Dorricott, softly, trying again with the binoculars. Ten. Ten. Nine. Ten. It is the junior second officer who gets out in the boat and adjusts rogue buoys; even at night, even in a choppy swell. Ten. The Captain was called, and considered. When he ruled that there was no likely confusion, and that the ship could do the job in the morning, Paul Dorricott smiled into the dark, and huddled further into his uniform sweater. 'I wouldn't have minded really', he said, convincingly enough. West Nash flashed nine, and slid astern. John Snape, the first officer, joined us. '*My* first job was changing the lantern on East Spile buoy, in a snowstorm, force 6'. How was it? 'Horrible'. Woodman, the historian, says that climbing a pillar buoy, whipping around in a high wind 'is the modern equivalent of hanging onto the topsail-yard'. If a third mate has more than two knuckles intact, he added, he is not doing his job. We anchored, and adjourned below for a chicken sandwich.

It is a clever system of promotion. No officer can be alienated from the main dirty work of the ship for long. The most junior deck officer goes out in the boat with the men, clings to the rocking buoys, and climbs slippery rocks to lighthouses. His next step up will make him mainly Navigation Officer, living in the disciplined dry quiet of the bridge and the chartroom; but let him become First Officer, with a Captaincy in sight, and he is back in a grubby boiler-suit, sweating on the foredeck in charge of the buoy-work. John Snape was out there at 0730 the next morning, easing aboard the great clanging, dripping, slippery mass of the Merkur buoy. Lying afloat, it had looked no more impressive than any other red can buoy. Aboard the ship, it was revealed as a 12-foot giant, a fat red cage over which eight men could clamber, checking gas pipes and silencing the great bell. Its clean, refuelled twin was humped across the deck, the chain checked and reconnected, and the Merkur relaunched to clang and flash for three years more. Not undisturbed: in two months the ship will be back to check the gas; in six months back again; in a year, Merkur will be back on deck for a swift coat of paint, and a few red splashes will join the rest on John Snape's boiler-suit. 'And so round we go. Like painting the Forth Bridge', said the Captain, and darted across to the engine telegraph. 'One-five-oh, quartermaster'. We steamed on.

With Snape, I clambered around the grubby red shape that had been Merkur. Close up, a buoy is startlingly simple. I had naively assumed that in the electronic '80s, some little silicon brain the size of a pea would be telling the buoy its job, building electricity out of waves, sending reassuring messages to some nerve centre ashore. Instead, a gas flame jerks and pops inside the dioptric lantern lens, and a simple knob turned up and down adjusts the number of flashes. Later, when Mr Dorricott was dispatched to cure the rogue West Nash, I went with him in the boat, climbed the tall pillar leaning to the hard Severn tide, and understood for a moment what it must be to cling half sick to a tossing buoy at night, 15 feet above the icy January swell, and fiddle with a sharp gas flame that pops twice a second. Your hands are icy; the heavy lantern-glass, slung on your forearm, pulls every muscle coldly down. If you are really unlucky, they told me, you have to change the lantern. It weighs around a hundredweight; only now are lighter alloy versions beginning to appear. 'Well, standard and simple is the rule'. Steel and gas are reliable — and re-lightable. 'Out we go with a packet of Bryant & May, and there you are. Lit.'

The work went on: Merkur, West Usk, West Culver; the anchor laid out, the ship sheered alongside, the seaman leaping over onto the buoy and rising with it on the derrick; the muddy chain checked on deck and slowly let out again, the links marching overside like a procession of iron lemmings. At every buoy, the second officer Bob Bushnell painstakingly checked the position with old and new equipment: Decca and sextant and arcane landmarks from the Local Knowledge Book. 'St Hilary Radio Mast in line with Chimney on left-hand side of Convalescent Home . . . eastern end of the Barry Holiday Camp roller-coaster with the TV mast behind... yes, walk out chain'. Twelve long hours after *Winston Churchill* had steamed up to her first buoy of the day, Richard and Bob were scuttling from voice-pipe to compass to engine-telegraphs above the bridge, lining up a waterfall, a hillock, and a lighthouse off Ilfracombe in order to pick up the slimy green cone of the Copperas Rock buoy without hitting the Copperas Rock itself. By eight, the old mark hung streaming in the derrick, with a curt entry in the book about the need for a heavier sinker. As the new weight was hauled from the open hold, a wonderful aromatic smell of chandlery arose: tarred marline, coir and sisal, huge fenders the size of a prize sow; varnish and paint and cotton-waste. Dazed with fresh air, I leaned over the upper rail, as Ilfracombe slid away to port. The ship passed into the dusk, bound for a rendezvous at dawn off Penzance, to pick up a lightship and tow it north. 'Always a different light, on these Western coasts', said the Captain happily, pausing a moment to admire the point ahead. 'Always a new sea. Paul, take a look at the Morte Stone as we pass and see if the radar reflector has come off again. Someone is tying up to it, blast him'. The Worms Head to Watchet chart lay open by the radar's glow; quartermaster Roberts stood impassively at the wheel; 90 miles to Land's End.

After manual work and fresh air, comes beer. Below decks, in a long compartment at the stern where the lightsmen once bunked, (before the helicopters took over the job of crew-changing), the men have installed a pub. It was bingo night: the starboard watch has a bingo machine, spewing numbered pingpong balls to the lilting call of Dafydd from the engine-room. With the draught bar at one end, and the old cramped bunks at the other, we bent our heads obediently in the long room, marking hard. 'Legs . . eleven. Eighty-eight, two fat ladies, sixty-five, old age pension . . .'. Gwilym Hodge, the Chief Steward, got the machine from a club. It goes home with him at the end of the fortnight. 'If the other lot want to play bingo they can pull tickets out of a bag'. ('Seventy-six, seven and six, was she worth it?' called Dafydd). Hodge himself is a prize asset to morale: not only does he own the bingo machine, but he has a butcher's training and a cook's respect for food. This ship has freshly-butchered steaks, home-made puddings, and laver bread and salt fish to please the Swansea men. 'My cooks, any cook, are the centre of a ship. This is a good crew, because the men come from different places, Holyhead and Liverpool and the Isle of Wight; Mr Stewart the quartermaster is Irish. It is a happy enough crew'.

The beer flows slowly, for the men can be called out at any time to tend a buoy or relight a towing-light. In the warmth after the long day, we talked of the scarcity of jobs for seamen, of exciting wreck-hunts when the double bang of Concorde makes every soul on the ship jump out of his skin; of bad and good officers, of terrible tangles of freezing chain, of tomorrow's towing job. 'A long tow is a rest, now, after all the buoys'. A healthy chauvinism prevails: this crew, this ship, this service, is the best. Some 'other crews' are terrible, though all crews unite against 'the office'; the office, however, is an ally compared to 'London', and the service itself, London and all, is understood to close loyally together at any comparison with — say — the Royal Navy. 'Oh dear no', said one man, horrified at the idea. 'I could not abide all that salaaming'. And the carpenter, a fine-featured Liverpudlian, touched his forelock and mooed satirically. In the sixties, the pay on Trinity ships was far worse than most, and men joined mainly for the coastal work and the chance to see home. Now, pay has outstripped other sailors' jobs, and it is a good place to be. The West Coast tender, too, is special — with all the dirty weather, the Atlantic gales, and the deep icy waters, she also has rare joys: steaming up on a balmy day past the greys and greens of Holy Island, beaching a boat on a tiny islet to paint the West Mouse beacon white again, and sit and rest while it dries. One former second mate recalls his early task of shoving the sheep clear of the fresh paint: was this, he would wonder, the proper task of a Navigation Officer?

The fog whistle was sounding by two. In the Captain's cabin, Richard Woodman slept in his clothes; on the bridge, the watch officers stood warily close to the radar screen, and on the upper deck the hourly lookouts shivered in the damp air. Cape Cornwall appeared in a clearer dawn, and after breakfast we glided across a flat Penzance Bay to meet *Siren,* the South Coast tender, and her charge, Light-Vessel No 95. As she lay quiet above her rippling reflection. I borrowed the record book and read 95's story. A photograph of her in her days as *Varne* lightship; a laconic entry about drifting off-station in 1966; back in 1962, serving as *Kentish Knock,* she was towed back from another drift, by another tender, *Vestal.* Otherwise a quiet life since 1939, a slow drift towards the scrapheap, arrested now by the Brethren's decision to try her out as an automatic lightship. The boat wallowed across the water towards her, weighed down by two tons of towing chain; the two captains exchanged professional pleasantries on the VHF, and a formal dip of the ensign; and No 95, in her dull old red paint, rolled her meccano lantern-tower and followed obediently astern. 'Funny about these little red ships', said Bob Bushnell, watching her affectionately, 'they follow us for miles, you know. I've never found out what they want'. The chain gang returned, very dusty.

Two hundred and twenty-three miles to Holyhead. After the early-morning exertion of the tow, the ship settled to the routines of passage. Snape, up since four, cleaned off the coal dust and dozed in a flowered armchair in the mess, while the valve radio chuntered gently through *Pick of the Week.* Bo'sun and seamen washed down the boats, or painted in the sun; the captain typed another chapter of his book in his cabin. Above him, on the silent bridge, the watch officer glanced between towline and passing tanker, to the chirrup of the radar. Someone's forgotten coffee-mug balanced on a capstan; cooking smells rose seductively through ventilators. Far below, in the oily gleam of copper piping, the engineers moved deafly through their banks of dials; aloft, the towing flags lifted to a growing westerly breeze. The bo'sun came out to retrieve the coffee mug, and for a moment we stood and watched light-vessel No 95 foaming and plunging along, throwing up odd sheets of spray as the Longships lighthouse fell astern.

Distance-judging at sea

This chapter is reproduced exactly as it appeared in the original YACHTSMAN'S WEEK-END BOOK. We have never found a better summary of the subject. It was written by John Irving.

DISTANCE-JUDGING AT SEA

'Tis distance lends enchantment to the view
And robes the mountain in its azure hue.
CAMPBELL

The following standards of distance are approximate only — but may be of some use when recording the beam position of a yacht as she passes a buoy, beacon or similar aid to navigation. The observer's eye is here assumed to be about 8 feet above sea-level — the eye-level, in fact, of a man standing up in a small ship's steering well. For greater heights of eye the approximate distances given below would be slightly greater.

In general, distance-judging at sea is, to begin with, somewhat of a disillusionment when the estimates come to be compared with the correct distances as measured off the chart. Usually the estimate will be found to exceed the correct distance, for distances over water invariably seem to be greater than they really are. Then again, the light can affect an estimate unless it is taken into account. On a bright clear day, and with the sun shining down on to the distant object, this usually seems to be nearer than it is. On the other hand, on a grey and overcast day the opposite seems to hold good, particularly so if there is any mist or haze about.

For the man with his height of eye at 8 feet above sea-level the sea horizon will be distant about 3¼ miles. Had his eye been between 5 and 6 feet above sea-level this distance would have been about 2½ miles. That is to say, therefore, that our 8-feet-up man, seeing a light-vessel with her waterline resting apparently upon the horizon, or another yacht or vessel precisely hull-up, or anything with its base just touching the horizon line (e.g. a beacon), or a power vessel under way and showing her bow-wave just above the horizon — all these objects would be approximately 3¼ miles distant.

A steam-vessel, or other ship, with the bow-wave showing just below the horizon line, or a beacon base, or a ship's water-line just below the horizon, or, again, the surface of exposed rocks or a shoal just touching the horizon line — will be between 2½ and 2¾ miles away.

At 2 miles distance (from the 8-foot observer) a large navigation buoy should be visible, in smooth water, but its shape and colour will as yet be indistinguishable to the naked eye. At this distance also the shape of a flat — e.g. the ensign of a light-vessel, can just be distinguished. At a distance of 1½ miles smaller-sized navigational buoys can be made out in smooth water, but their colour and shape will be indistinguishable. At a distance of 1 mile to 1¼ miles the shape of the smaller buoy can be made out with the naked eye, as also can the colour and markings of the large type of buoy. Details of flags should be discernible at this distance as well as the portholes and main-rigging of a large vessel. A man moving to and fro on board a ship or on shore shows up detached from his background as a black mark, but his limbs and features are, of course, indistinguishable.

Between 600 and 800 yards distant a moving man ceases to be a mere dark spot and resolves himself into a featureless vertical mark. At 400 to 500 yards distant the movement of a walking man's legs are noticeable, and the rower's arms in a dinghy can be seen working. At 200 to 300 yards distant a man's face — without features — is discernible and the swirl of the tidal stream about a buoy can be made out with the naked eye.

Of equal importance at sea is the ability to assess the distance of an object on the horizon when it is first sighted. This applies especially to night work when a distant light is suddenly raised. The chart of the Light List will always give the height of the object in feet above sea-level: multiply the square root of this height in feet by 1⅒, and the result is the approximate distance in nautical miles the object can be seen by an eye at sea-level. If the observer happens to be above sea-level — which he is almost certain to be — then to this distance in miles must be added a second obtained by multiplying the square root of his height of eye in feet by 1⅒.

Just as approximate distance-judging is possible — and with considerable accuracy if practised frequently — so is it possible to measure angles with tolerable accuracy without a sextant. To this 'parlour trick' can, moreover, be added the kindred art of ascertaining compass direction without a compass.

Taking the latter 'trick' first. In the Northern Hemisphere turn a watch face upwards to the sky and so that the hour hand points exactly at the sun. Then the imaginary line drawn through the centre of the watch from a point midway between the hour hand and the XII of the dial through the axis of the hands runs true north and south.

The true bearing of the sun can then be found by noting the number of 'minute' graduations of the watch dial between this north-and-south line and the hour hand. Multiply this number by six, and the answer is the number of degrees the sun is east or west of south depending upon whether the time is a.m. or p.m. At the same time, and in the same manner, the degree-bearing from south of a prominent object should be ascertained. Then, using the watch-dial as a protractor, the relative bearing of any other objects can be found and referred to this true bearing for, as said before, each 'minute' graduation of the dial corresponds to 6° of arc.

Yet another form of extempore protractor can be made out of a sheet of newspaper. Tear the corner out and then fold it, edge to edge, three times upon itself: smooth it out again and pencil in darkly the lines of the creases. Each of the angles now made at the apex of the corner is exactly one 'point' of 11¼°. With the point of the paper held close to the eye both horizontal and vertical angles up to 90° can be measured with quite a fair degree of accuracy.

It may on occasion be convenient to know the angle subtended by different parts of the hand when held out at arm's length. For example, the nail-joint of the little finger, at arm's length from the eye, covers approximately 2° at the horizon. The wide open hand from thumb tip to the tip of the little finger — again at arm's length — covers about 20°. If the fist is tight closed at arm's length, the horizontal angle covered is some 10°; extend the thumb and the angle from thumb-tip becomes about 15°. Naturally these angles vary slightly with different people, but it is well worth while one day to see with a sextant precisely what angles one's own hand can make. With such fixed measurements carefully determined and memorised almost any angle can be measured 'by hand' with very little error.

While these rough-and-ready methods can be used satisfactorily for ascertaining horizontal angles they are not likely to be of any use for a vertical 'off-shore' angle. For this, some sort of sextant will be necessary — if only to deal with angles of less than 2°. To convert these vertical angles into distance there is no need to carry sets of 'off-shore distance tables,' however, for one or two simple rules give the 'distance' in miles. Firstly, multiply the object's known height in feet by .565 and divide the result by the sextant angle in minutes — the answer is the distance away in miles. Secondly, and more simply still, divide the object's known height (in feet) by one hundred times the sextant angle in degrees — and again the answer is in miles. For small angles and small heights the old infantryman's rule is useful — 'One minute of angle is an inch at a hundred yards.' Interpreting this, divide the height of an object in inches by its vertical sextant angle in minutes, then multiplying the answer by 100 gives the distance in yards, dividing the answer by 20 gives the distance in nautical miles.

Distance-judging in fog is a precarious thing. In the first place, no attempt should ever be made to judge distance from a fog signal — the atmosphere plays too many tricks to make this worth while. When sailing close in to a cliffy shore however, it is often possible to obtain a good estimate of one's distance off the cliffs by sounding a sharp siren or fog-horn blast and then timing the echo. The normal speed of sound through air is about 375 yards a second — although fog may affect this. If, therefore, the time in seconds between the blast and its echo is noted, this number should also be approximately the number of cable's lengths (of 200 yards each) which the vessel is off the cliffs. Incidentally, a complete failure of echo usually suggests that the cliffs have come abruptly to an end.

And having thus discussed distance-judging and the use of an improvised compass and other divices for obtaining horizontal angles, one might as well complete the tale with extempore methods of ascertaining speed. Long before the comfortable days of patent logs there was the leg-o' mutton shaped longship with its sand glasses, its marked line, and its tight-lipped, stern-faced men standing about and muttering a hoarse 'Watch, there. Watch.' But before that again men knew of means whereby the speed of a ship under way could be ascertained. Read here the views of one Marcus P. Vitruvius who, in the tenth chapter of his fourteenth volume of *De Architectura* — written somewhere about 20 B.C., talks of a 'useful invention of great ingenuity handed down to us by our ancestors which enables us ... to know how many miles we have travelled. An axle is carried through the side of the vessel, and on the projecting end a wheel, 4 feet in diameter is fixed, with paddles fastened round its circumference striking the water. The inboard end of the axle carries a drum with one cog projecting beyond its circumference. In contact with this case holding another drum having four hundred cogs at regular intervals, so placed as to engage the cog of the axle drum. The second drum also has a tooth projecting beyond its circumference. Above, in an outer case, is another drum which revolves in a horizontal plane and has teeth in it which engage the cog in the side of the vertically placed drum, so that one revolution of the latter turns the horizontal drum to the extent of one tooth until its circle is complete. Tubes must be fixed in the horizontal drum in which round pebbles will be placed. In the outer case containing the drum one opening will be cut, having a pipe affixed, through which, when the obstruction is removed (*i.e.* when a tube comes over the opening) a pebble will fall with a ringing sound into a brass receptacle. Thus, when a ship is moving, whether under oars or sail, the paddles on the wheel will strike the resisting water, and being driven forcibly backward will revolve the wheel, and the wheel as it revolves will turn the axle, and the axle will turn the drum. The tooth of the first drum in every revolution strikes and moves on one of the teeth of the second drum. And so when, by the action of the paddles, the wheel has revolved four hundred times it will, by the pressure of the cog at the side of the vertical drum, move the horizontal drum on one point. As often, therefore, as the horizontal drum in its course brings a pebble to an opening, it will let it drop through the pipe. Thus by sound and by number (of the pebbles that have dropped) the length of the voyage in miles will be shown.'

A device such as this, though undoubtedly effective, might perhaps prove cumbersome if attached to a small modern yacht. In any case if so provided her speed-judging would scarcely be extempore. It is possible, in fact, that the owner would eschew the contraption of M.P. Vitruvius and his ancestors, and prefer the device of some unknown Hollander, the Dutchman's Log. Let him mark off along his deck as long a known length as possible. Then throwing a block of wood or a bottle or some other thing that will float well ahead, he notes the exact number of seconds it takes for it to pass the marks. Multiplying the distance apart of the marks (in feet) by three and dividing this figure by five times the elapsed time (in seconds) gives the speed of the yacht in knots.

There is yet another method — a cruder one still. Surely every yacht will have a hand-lead-line, or if not, a length of string can be knotted at fathom intervals (a full arm span across a grown man's body from finger tip to finger tip is close upon a fathom). We will assume that the lead-line exists at any rate. Unbend from it the lead and replace it with a stoppered empty petrol can. Pay the can on the end of the line out over the stern until the ten-fathom marking is resting on the taffrail (that piece of leather with a hole in it). By this time the can should be well astern and clear of the ship's wake. Then allow the line to slip unchecked over the rail starting a stop watch as you do so. After three and three-fifths seconds have elapsed check the outrush of the line. The marking on the lead-line at the taffrail — less ten — will be the speed of the ship in knots. Of course, if there is no stop watch, then even timing must be improvised. Let the operator say distinctly and aloud, 'I reckon that's one; I reckon that's two; I reckon that's three; I reckon th —!' and he will have measured the passing, approximately, of three and three-fifths seconds — losing the line with his first 'I' and checking it with the outbreath of the last 'that.'

No doubt there are many other improvisations for measuring time, distance and direction, and all are at least worth a test by way of whiling away a drowsy summer afternoon's sail. After all — one day, perhaps.

Looming lights

Oh! Dream of joy! Is this indeed
The lighthouse top I see?
Is this the hill? is this the kirk?
Is this mine own countree?
S T COLERIDGE, Rime of the Ancient Mariner

To raise an expected lighthouse in the darkness of a stormy watch is one of the deepest satisfactions of a navigator's life. The loom first rises, perhaps, on the horizon; too doubtful to allow for celebration, it nonetheless provides a source of hope and interest for a quarter of an hour. Then the flashes become clear; the navigator quietly checks the almanac, watches again for a moment in lonely pleasure, then makes his grand announcement: 'I've got the Fastnet'. The wind seems to howl with less malice; the very water running down your neck feels warmer. One can feel great affection for a lighthouse at a time like this; it seems a pity that the almanac only lists its height, characteristic, and foghorn. One would like to know more; who built it there and when, what ships fell foul of its dangers, how many keepers live there and what they have for supper. It would be pleasant to know a poem about the lighthouse, or a song, so as to serenade it during that hour while it draws closer, throwing longer streamers of light across the clearing sky.

We cannot provide all that for every light. But here, to while away that reassured and lighter-hearted time of gazing at your desired light, are a few biographies of the best ones. We sail west-about, starting with the queen of all British lighthouses —

EDDYSTONE ROCKS

In the second half of the seventeenth century, a splendid eccentric called Henry Winstanley (owner of 'Winstanley's waterworks' near Hyde Park, a great popular attraction) grew tired of losing money in ships wrecked on the small and dangerous rock called Eddystone. He therefore vowed to build a light on it, and commenced work on a wooden structure. England was at war with France, and the Admiralty provided Winstanley with a warship to protect his work; in June 1697 a French privateer arrived instead, and kidnapped the lighthouse-builder. When Louis XIV heard of the incident, he ordered that Winstanley be immediately released, saying that 'France was at war with England, not with humanity'. The importance of the light was now international.

Winstanley achieved his ambition; the light was lit in November 1698. He had such confidence in his work (strengthened after some rough winter weather) that he expressed a desire to be present in the lighthouse 'during the greatest storm that ever was'. Sadly and eerily, this wish was fulfilled; five years after first lighting, he went out to do some repairs on a November night, and the worst storm ever recorded in British waters hit the Channel. The next day there was barely a trace of the structure; none of its occupants.

Another design, a wooden tower, was lit on the Rock in 1709, and stood for 47 years before catching fire one night from one of its own candles. Henry Hall, the keeper, was 94 years old, and while he threw water upwards to put the fire out, the lead roof melted and lead ran down his throat. He lived for 12 days, and a Dr Spry of Plymouth, on postmortem, found a flat oval piece of lead in his stomach weighing over 7oz. When he wrote about this case for the Royal Society, the Fellows refused to believe him; and Dr Spry tried to redeem his reputation by doing experiments on live dogs and fowls by pouring lead down their throats to prove that they could survive.

A less gruesome and more successful history followed the great John Smeaton who built his Eddystone tower, modelling it on the shape of an English oak tree in stone. His quick-drying cement formula is still used today; his immense 24-candle tower was lit in 1759. When new cracks began to appear in the rock, the top part of the tower was taken off and put in Plymouth as a monument to Smeaton; this was in the 1870's. The present tower was finished in 1882; in 1980 it got a heli-deck, and in May 1982 Trinity House finally converted it to automatic operation. There are now no keepers to wave to, unless the ghost of old Henry Hall should drop by on a dark night.

WOLF ROCK

The rock owes its name to the dreadful wolf-like wail caused by the escape of air from a hollow where it was compressed by incoming waves. Shipping used to steer by the sound as surely as by a foghorn; but eighteenth-century Cornish villagers so hated the noise that a few of them rowed out and blocked the hole with stones. After this the rock became such a danger that Trinity House proposed to mark it with a bell-buoy; the villagers objected again, this time on the grounds that the bell would frighten off the fish. In the 1790s one Lieutenant Henry Smith put up a mast, 20ft tall, with a wolf's head figure at the top with open jaws, to re-create the wolvish howl; this was soon washed away. Finally Trinity House built a concrete tower, then a granite tower modelled on the Smeaton Eddystone Lighthouse. In July 1869 the light was finally established; in 1973 Wolf Rock was the first rock Lighthouse of Trinity House to be fitted with a heli-deck above its lantern.

BISHOP ROCK

Not an easy one to build; the rock ledge is barely 52ft wide by 153ft long, and rises sheer from a depth of 150ft; it is exposed to the full force of the Atlantic. In 1847 Trinity House sank cast-iron legs into the rock, on the principle that the waves would roll freely among the piles instead of slapping against the solid mass of a masonry tower. Unfortunately all this was swept away in 1850, before it was even finished. Engineer James Walker began again, with a small granite tower; laying the lower blocks below low-water mark meant damming and pumping; the job took seven years. On 1 September 1858, the light shone out at last, 11 years after the project began. Strengthening and rebuilding was necessary by the 1880s — a new lighthouse was effectively built around the old one, encasing it; the foundation was reinforced against the sea with massive blocks of granite bolted to the rocks.

The worst disaster near Bishop Rock was before the light was built; on 22 October, 1707, a British squadron, homeward bound from the Mediterranean, missed the St Agnes light on the Scillies, and all but two frigates grounded and went to pieces. Over 1800 men died; the Admiral, Sir Cloudesley Shovell, was washed ashore alive, but murdered by wreckers for the ring he wore.

LONGSHIPS

John Ruskin described the cliffs around Land's end as 'entire disorder of the surges... the whole surface of the sea becomes one dizzy whirl of rushing, writhing tortured undirected rage . . .' Not, in other words, a congenial spot to get lost. In the late eighteenth century, there were no aids to navigation here at all; the marking of the Longships rocks began in 1795 with the lighting of a tower on the biggest one, Carn Bras. It was the property of a lessee (a common early arrangement) who collected the light-tolls from passing ships — one Lieutenant Henry Smith. In 1795, however, Trinity House took it over and remitted the profits to the Smith family. It made a lot of profit; by 1836 Trinity House was obliged to buy out the lessees, with nearly ten years still to run, for £40,676. The original tower being only 40ft above high water, it was often under water in storms; the present tower is over 117ft high, and dates from 1875. The light is traditionally one of the toughest to man; early Victorian stories allege that 'more than one untrained keeper has been driven insane from the sheer terror of the waves'; another apocryphal tale tells of one whose hair turned white overnight; and the best of all is the yarn about the Longships Keeper who was kidnapped by wreckers eager to let the light go out and bring in ships for plunder. His tiny daughter saved the day by standing nightly on the family Bible, on tiptoe, to light the lamps.

LUNDY ISLAND

There are two lights, North and South; when the first light was put at Chapel Hill (now abandoned) it included the revolutionary innovation of a white quick-flashing light. Alas, it revolved so quickly that it looked like a fixed light; and in November 1828 a ship, *La Jeune Emma,* mistook it for Ushant and ran aground in Carmarthen Bay, killing 13 people including a niece of Empress Josephine.

The present lights were installed in 1879; the North lighthouse is remarkable for standing among large colonies of guillemots, razorbills, and herring-gulls, which seem undisturbed by its 600,000 candlepower and noisy fog signal.

BULL POINT

After a quiet first 93 years (1879-1972) this lighthouse fell down the cliff; or part of it did. Local people from Mortehoe incurred the gratitude of Trinity House by mucking in to help; 24 hours after the collapse, a buoy was laid, then a lightship; for the next two years an old Trinity House light tower was borrowed back from the Nature Conservancy and fitted with an optic; the new lighthouse was finished in 1974, with some of the old equipment in use. Bull Point is now fully automatic, with a keeper and wife on station; they will, one hopes, enjoy another 93 years of peace before any further alarums.

SMALLS

Gifted amateurs played a great part in the early development of lighthouses; the first Smalls lighthouse was designed by Henry Whiteside, a musical-instrument maker of Liverpool. The dreadful job of putting up his octagonal hut on legs began in 1775; the highest peak of the rocks only stands 12ft above high tides, and workmen had to tie themselves to iron rings in the rock for safety. The winter of 1776 proved too much for the incomplete structure; in January, Whiteside and his blacksmith went out to strengthen it, and met with fierce storms. The next month, a letter in a bottle was found, tossed into the sea by the designer, begging 'immediate assistance to fetch us off the Smalls before the next Spring or we fear we shall perish, our water near all gone, our fire quite gone and our house in a most melancholy manner'. The group did survive, but John Phillips, who had commissioned the structure, ran out of money, and extingushed the light. Trinity House took over in 1778.

A bizarre episode, apparently true, is related: one of the two Smalls keepers died and the survivor feared a murder charge if he threw the body in the sea. So he lashed it in a wooden box to the lantern-rail; passing ships noticed it and thought nothing of it, and it was three weeks before the survivor and the corpse were relieved of their dreadful vigil together. After this, three keepers at a time went out. They still do.

SKERRYVORE

Here, 24 miles west of Iona, the Atlantic waves have been recorded at a pressure of over 6,000lbs per square foot. It was 1844 before the Commissioners of Northern Lights managed to light the rock; Sir Walter Scott, who went out with the surveyor, remarked that the jobs done on Eddystone and Bell Rock were a joke in comparison. The tower eventually built is very graceful, a defiance of the sea in Hynish gneiss and granite from the Ross of Mull (the Duke of Argyll let the builders quarry freely on his estates). Even in 1844 the whole operation cost nearly £87,000.

FLANNAN ISLANDS

Though three men dwell on Flannan Isle
To keep the lamp alight
As we steer'd under the lee, we caught
No glimmer through the night.

The terrible disappearance of the three keepers of the Flannan Islands lighthouse on 15 December 1900 caught the late-Victorian imagination; W W Gibson's poem has curdled the blood of schoolchildren ever since. When a vessel reported the loss of the light, the Lighthouse Tender *Hesperus* under Captain Harvey went to investigate; her crew found no trace of any of the men; the lamp was ready to be lit, the beds made and empty, the washing-up done. One keeper had taken his boots and oilskins, another his boots; the third had left his coat behind him. The Superintendent's report finally concluded that the men were washed away by waves; the effect of the disappearance on the relief keeper who first went ashore was described as leaving him 'very nervous; very much upset . . . if this nervousness does not leave Moore, he will require to be transferred'. Gibson's poem ends with the famous lines:

We seem'd to stand for an endless while,
Though still no word was said
Three men alive on Flannan Isle
Who thought on three men dead.

But I find the telegram, sent by the master of the *Hesperus* on the night of the 26 December, far more moving. It testifies both to his natural grief as a colleague and to his dutiful and efficient concern for the light itself:

A dreadful accident has happened at Flannans. The three Keepers, Ducat, Marshall and the Occasional have disappeared from the Island. On our arrival there this afternoon no sign of life was to be seen on the Island. Fired a rocket but, as no response was made, managed to land Moore, who went up to the Station but found no Keepers there. The clocks were stopped and other signs indicated that the accident must have happened about a week ago. Poor fellows they must have been blown over the cliffs or drowned trying to secure a crane or something like that . . . I have left Moore, Macdonald, Buoymaster and two seamen on the Island to keep the light burning until you make other arrangements. Will not return to Oban until I hear from you.

BELL ROCK

Aha: another poem. Remember the Inchcape Rock? Robert Southey wrote his famous verses about its belled buoy:

The worthy Abbot of Aberbrothok
Had placed that bell on the Inchcape Rock;
On a buoy in the storm it floated and swung,
And over the waves its warning rung.

A wicked seafarer, Sir Ralph the Rover, cuts the bell off to spite the Abbot; and of course gets wrecked on the rock itself:

Sir Ralph the Rover tore his hair;
He cursed himself in his despair
But the waves rush in on every side
And the vessel sinks beneath the tide.

And serve him right. The rock had long been a menace to ships approaching the Firths of Tay and Forth; a 2000ft long reef which had claimed many vessels, but lay just uncovered at low water, and under 16ft at high water. After a terrible storm and the loss of 70 vessels on the Scottish coast in December 1799, the Commissioners of Northern Lights applied for an Act of Parliament, to include authority to borrow the huge sum of £25,000 from the Exchequer to finance a light on the rock. Work began in 1807, and in February 1811 the light shone out at last, 115ft above the water; it is standing still, the oldest serving rock lighthouse in the British Isles. Sir Walter Scott, a Commissioner himself, visited this lighthouse too, and wrote in the visitor's book:

Far in the bosom of the deep
O'er these wild shelves my watch I keep
A ruddy gem of changeful light
Bound on the dusky brown of night
The seaman bids my lustre hail
And scorns to strike him tim'rous sail.

ISLE OF MAY

There was a beacon here in 1635, a coal-fire hoisted to the top of a stone structure by box and pulley; it was highly thought of at the time, but suffered from the obvious problems of any aerial coal-fire — smoke, drenching, and above all the way that an easterly wind would blow the flames away from the sea so that light could barely be seen. In 1810 two of HM ships, *Nymphe* and *Pallas,* were wrecked near Dunbar because they took a lime-kiln on the coast to be the beacon on the Isle of May. The present lighthouse was built in 1816, to much better effect.

LONGSTONE

The Farne Islands are bleak; the early keepers of this light (established in 1826) were families, who often took refuge in the upper rooms of the tower to escape the waves covering their living-quarters. One such family were the Darlings; Grace Darling, their daughter, became a legend one night in September 1838, when the steamer *Forfarshire,* bound from Hull to Dundee, went aground on the Hawkers Rocks a mile away. The survivors clung to the forepart of the vessel, and in a stormy dawn the keeper, William Darling, saw them there, as did fishermen on the shore. Keeper and fishermen hesitated to brave the high seas around the rock in a rescue attempt; but Grace Darling persuaded her father, and went with him as second hand in the little lighthouse boat. They saved nine people in two trips; a feat of extraordinary gallantry which has made Grace's name one of perpetual honour among seamen; the Trinity House boat which carries supplies to the Longstone is named after her.

FLAMBOROUGH HEAD

There was a lighthouse here in 1669, but it was never lit. The present tower dates from 1806; it is remarkable mainly for being the first lighthouse ever to have mixed red and white flashes, with an arrangement of glass on the reflectors which gave two white, then one red.

CROMER

The present lighthouse (1837) actually stands on a golf course half a mile from the edge of the cliff; and just as well. The last one, which had worked on coal and then oil since 1719, fell into the sea in 1866. It used to have two young women keepers, in its latter days; a difficult life to lead, on that slipping cliff-edge. Long before the first lighthouse-builders came to Cromer, though, there were other lights for vessels to see: the parish church tower was one of a chain of ecclesiastical lights which had been lit as a regular work of charity ever since medieval times.

NORTH FORELAND

A very important corner to light; they lit it, amazingly, in 1505, with candles. For a short period in the late seventeenth century a temporary light was shown — one single candle, in a glass lantern on a pole. A coal-fired beacon replaced it, but burned to the ground; part of the present structure was originally an octagonal coal-fired tower, and is a listed building. These towers were very difficult to manage; in calm weather the keepers had to use the bellows to keep the light bright; when the trustees tried to enclose the light in glass to protect the fire, the glass got so dirty that the shipmasters could not see any light at all; the invention of the Argand oil lamp and its reflectors must have seemed like a miracle when it burst on them in 1790.

DUNGENESS

The steeple of Lydd Church 'like the forme of the saile of some talle shippe' used to lure vessels onto the terrible shingle-bank off Dungeness in the reign of James I; the need for a light was pressing. In 1615 an open coal fire was installed; candles replaced it when it proved difficult to transport enough coal to the remote site. Another coal fire burned next; then in 1792 Samuel Wyatt built a 116ft tower, modelled on Smeaton's 'oak tree' at Eddystone, and fuelled by sperm-oil. In 1862 an electric light — the first ever — was installed; but oil was found more effective, and took over again. The sea having receded, a new tower was built (the High Light Tower) in 1904; but the nuclear power station obscured it and a new lighthouse had to be opened in 1961. Since the whole tower has been floodlit (to assist identification from seaward) the bird mortality rate has, apparently, gone down during the migration season.

ROYAL SOVEREIGN

This extraordinary mushroom-like concrete structure replaced the old lightship in 1971. It was built in two sections on Newhaven beach, much to the amazement of locals and visitors off the ferry; the base and vertical pillar were floated out, and the cabin superstructure then floated over the pillar; then the pillar — which was telescopic — was jacked up 45ft in the air, where the platform still hangs, defying the seas to telescope it down again.

BEACHY HEAD

The problem here has always been height; light a beacon on the clifftop and the sea mist will often hide it, even when the atmosphere below is crystal clear. This was the problem with the 1828 tower and when this threatened to fall down the cliff at the turn of the century, a lower light was deemed to be desirable anyway. The lower light stands on a foundation of hard chalk about 550ft from the base of the cliffs; to build it, a coffer-dam had to be built to allow the water to be pumped clear of the building operation. The workmen got out from the cliff by a cableway, to an iron staging next to the dam; five-ton stones were slid down this cable without incident. There are 3660 tons of Cornish granite in the structure; it is solid for its first 50ft, except for a water-tank space. North Foreland now controls it, automatically.

NAB TOWER

Perhaps the oddest of all English lighthouses: a leaning-tower-of-Pisa-like structure, looking more like a fortress than a sculpted beacon. Although never having played a warlike role (like the Solent forts from which a shot has never been fired in anger) the original intention of the Nab Tower was that it should be one support for an anti-submarine barrier built across the Dover Strait during the First World War.

What we now know as the Nab Tower was the first of what were to be several such structures, built at Shoreham, and floated out to sea and then tilted into position (a bit of North Sea oil technology ahead of its time). The war ended just as the first tower was completed and, having no further defensive use, it was towed out to sea to replace

the Nab lightship. As it was lowered into place, it developed a list and has remained the subject of much on-board conversation and speculation ever since. A second 'Nab Tower' half built at the end of hostilities was broken up. Photographs exist showing both 'Nab Towers' in Shoreham harbour.

ST CATHERINE'S

This point had a light very early on — in 1323 Walter de Godyton erected a chapel and added an endowment for a priest to say Masses for his family, and show a light at night to warn ships off the Island's southern coast. The Reformation brought this to an end 200 years later; and it took until 1838 for the present effective tower to be built. Again, it proved too high because of mist; and in 1975 the light was lowered by taking 43 feet out of the top section of the tower, and 23 feet out of the middle tier. This is why it is such a peculiar shape. The second tower houses the fog signal, and the locals call them 'the cow and the calf'.

PORTLAND BILL

This dreadful stretch of coast was notorious very early in shipping history; the Corporation and Shipowners of Weymouth were clamouring for a light by the eighteenth century, and eventually a private consortium built two lighthouses on the Bill. These were so badly kept that they were often not lit until two hours after sunset; Trinity House took over in 1789, and the tower had this dignified inscription:

'For the Direction and Comfort of NAVIGATORS; For the Benefit and Security of COMMERCE and for a lasting Memorial of BRITISH

HOSPITALITY to All Nations This Lighthouse was erected by the Worshipful Brethren of Trinity House of Deptford Strond, Anno 1789'

And so on down-Channel again, towards the Eddystone where we began. All thanks to the Corporation of Trinity House for their information; also to the Commissioners of Northern Lights for theirs. Come to think of it, all thanks to both bodies for the lights themselves, served so faithfully over the centuries. If we are to think of, and thank, the lighthouse-keepers too, there are no better words to remember them by than the bald description issued by the Comissioners of Northern Lighthouses:

Not every man is suitable to be a lightkeeper. The good lightkeeper has or acquires the temperament so necessary for this job which involves residence close to the sea and which has much loneliness and isolation in its composition. While his primary duty is to keep watch at night, to ensure that his light flashes correctly to character, and to keep a fog watch throughout each 24 hours, so as to be ready to operate the fog signal in the event of poor visibility, a lightkeeper must be a man of parts. He will acquire a good working knowledge of engines; at stations with Radio Beacons and Radar Beacons he will be initially responsible for their accurate operation; he will know about Radio Telephones; from his study of the sea he will respect its immense power; he will be a handyman of varying proficiency but mostly of a high standard; he will be a useful cook and a good companion. A lightkeeper will not make a fortune but the odds are he will be at peace with himself and with the world.

Fare ye well and adieu . . .

Anatomy of a sea song

'Spanish Ladies' is without doubt one of the greatest of English sea songs, or is it a shanty? Shanties are only sung to accompany heavy work, but it is easy to imagine the windlass turning and the massive anchor rising from the seabed of some Spanish harbour as the crew think, and sing, of sailing home.

The song is also an accurate record of the seamanship in the days when it was written; believed to be the late fifteenth century. It talks of 'striking soundings clear' and 'standing by your shank painter' and 'swigging off a full bowl.' Although 400 years old, much of this seamanship is still with us and so is the long debate over the exact words of the song. Some will sing of 35 leagues from Ushant to Scilly, some will tell you it is 34. Some sing of 'cat stopper' and some of 'ring stoppers.' We have taken the words as printed in 'Poor Jack' a novel set around Greenwich and written by Captain Frederik Marryat, a naval officer in the mid-nineteenth century, as this is the first time the words appear in print.

Imagine, then, the crew aboard a ship of the English Fleet setting sail for home and bidding farewell to the ladies of Spain:

Fare ye well and adieu to you, fair Spanish ladies,
Fare ye well and adieu to you, ladies of Spain,
For we have got orders for to sail back to old England
But we hope in a short time to see you again.

CHORUS

Then we'll rant and we'll roar like true British seamen,
We'll rant and we'll roar all across the salt seas,
Until we strike soundings in the Channel of Old England,
From Ushant to Scilly is thirty five leagues.

We hove our ship to with the wind at south-west my boys,
We hove our ship to for to strike soundings clear.
We had forty five fathom with a fine sandy bottom
So we filled the main topsail and up Channel we steer.

CHORUS

The first land we made 'twas the head called the Dodman,
Next Rame Head near Plymouth, Start, Portland and Wight
So we sailed by Beachy, by Fairlee and Dungeness
Where we bore right away for the South Foreland light.

CHORUS

The signal was made for the grand fleet to anchor
All in the Downs, the ships to be moored
Let go your shank painter, stand by your cat stopper,
Haul up your clew garnets, stick out tacks and sheets.

CHORUS

Let every man toss off a full bumper,
And let every man swig off a full bowl
For we'll drink and be jolly and drown melancholy
With a 'Here's to the health of each true-hearted soul'.

CHORUS

In the first chorus we start to get a flavour of their seamanship when they sing:

'Until we strike soundings in the Channel of old England.' Sailing into soundings is still a valid navigational practice which we have used to great effect on many occasions. To take soundings in the traditional manner, a lead-line is used: simply, a length of stout line with a lead weight attached to one end. The weight is shaped so as to have a cup hollowed out of the bottom which was, and still is, for 'arming the lead' with tallow.

For coastal waters, a lead would be about 25 fathoms long and the depths would be marked using a combination of knots, leather and strips of bunting. The idea was that depths could be easily read during the day and if during the night there was any doubt, a touch of the lips would tell bunting from leather.

A lead-line is marked as follows:

1 fathom — a knot
2 — a piece of leather with two tails
3 — a piece of leather with three tails
4 — unmarked (but sometimes a knot was used for safety purposes)
5 — a white rag
6 — unmarked
7 — red bunting
8 — unmarked
9 — unmarked
10 — leather with a hole in it
13 — blue serge
14 — unmarked
15 — white rag
17 — red bunting
20 — two knots

The unmarked lengths are called 'deeps' and if the lead were cast and came to just over, say the '5' or the '9', the shout would go out,'by the mark 5' or 'by the deep 9!'

The advance of the metric chart renders the fathom, sadly, little more than a confusion so there would appear to be no harm in knotting up your own lead-line. As long as you know what it means, that is all that matters. It may seem a little obsolete but an echo-sounder battery fades faster than a knot in a length of rope.

To swing a lead, you have it coiled so that it will run free. Place yourself in the bows or wherever you feel safest if there is any sea running. You will need room to swing your arm because the object of the exercise is to get the lead as far forward of the boat as possible if she has any way on her. Swing the lead until you have established a good pendulum motion and then throw. The lead will make a splash and as you sail up to the point where the lead entered the water, the line will come vertical and the depth can be measured. Clearly, the lead has to touch the seabed and so the deeper the water, the slower you must go.

Taking soundings can often help in a landfall. After a passage from Ireland to Land's End, it is often possible to tell within ten miles or so how close you are to a dead-reckoning position and many other landfalls can be made easier in this way. Whilst not a foolproof system on its own, it could serve as a useful back-up to a shaky dead reckoning or an unsure radio fix. At best it is one more position line.

To return to our homecoming crew, it was clearly a moment of great celebration when their lead-line first hit the bottom, or 'struck soundings,' one more confirmation that home was that much nearer.

This brings us to the last line of the chorus, 'From Ushant to Scilly is thirty five leagues.'

I have heard this sung as 35, 34 or any number you care to think of. The league as a measure of distance is now obsolete but it was the equivalent of four Roman miles which to be precise, would be 3.18 nautical miles. If we take it to be approximately three miles, Ushant to Scilly would be 105 nautical miles, which is roughly the case. 'We hove our ship to with the wind at south-west, my boys.'

As we have said, the deeper the water, the slower the ship would have to be moving to take accurate soundings and since she was running before a prevailing southwesterly breeze, it could well have been that she would heave to, or stop, to take soundings.

Heaving-to is a useful but little-used practice these days. We have hove to whilst on passage at change of watch to make easy the effort of putting on oilskins in a seaway and if you are a crew of two doing watch on — watch off for several days, it is only by heaving to that there is any chance to be sociable. Only *you* can discover the best way to heave to as it differs from boat to boat. In principle, the mainsheet is hauled in, the headsail is sheeted aback; which we have found to be most easily done by tacking and not letting fly the weather sheet. The helm is then lashed to leeward.

You will be surprised how quiet it becomes. Indeed, if your boat is well balanced this is the chance for you all to go below and get warm and dry as the boat will look after herself except perhaps for the regular glance to see that all is clear. Hove-to, the boat is under little strain, and that goes for her crew as well.

'We hove our ship to for to strike soundings clear,
We had forty-five fathoms and a fine sandy bottom,
So we filled our main topsail and up-Channel we steer.'

To measure depths of 45 fathoms, a deep sea lead would have

been used which had over 100 fathoms of line. Being of such a length, a special technique was needed and this may be the reason the ship was hove-to.

The line was carried forward and held at intervals by the crew. On the order, the first in the line nearest the bow of the ship let go the lead and this continued down the line until it was felt that the lead had hit bottom and the depth was measured in that way.

By arming the lead, you can discover the nature of the seabed and this is how they would have discovered their 'fine sandy bottom.' Into the cup on the bottom of the lead, you press a little tallow, or these days, pump grease. Tallow is a fat used in the making of candles and don't despair of ever finding any. We once bought some from the most modern of Hamble chandlers where we found it hiding behind a bubble-pack of split pins. On reaching the seabed, the tallow picks up a little of what it hits and you can detect mud, sand, shingle or if nothing at all, you didn't touch the bottom or you are on rock. It's a technique of most use these days when choosing a spot to anchor, especially a first time anchorage. Before we leave the lead-line, the advantage it does have over the echo-sounder is that you can use it to take soundings all around your boat. If planning to dry out, it's nice to know that you aren't perched on the edge of a gulley which will only reveal itself when it's all too late.

'The first land we made 'twas the head called the Dodman,
Next Rame head off Plymouth, Start, Portland and Wight,
We sailed by Beachy, by Fairlee and Dungeness,
And then bore away for the South Foreland light.'

A fine description of a passage up Channel although Dodman and Fairlee, presumably Fairlight off Hastings, are perhaps not the most conspicuous headlands if sailing some distance off shore.

'The signal was made for the grand fleet to anchor,
And all in the Downs the ships to be moored,
Let go your shank painter, stand by your cat stopper,
Haul up your clew garnets, stick out tacks and sheets.'

The Downs is perhaps one of the most famous of anchorages around the British coast. It lies between the North and South Foreland and is sheltered from the West by the land and from the east by the Goodwin Sands. It has served as a pilot station and was where the Fleet would anchor awaiting a fair slant of wind to take them down Channel.

'Let go your shank painter, stand by your cat stopper,' tells of making ready the anchor for dropping. The shank is that part of an anchor which connects the flukes, or arms of the anchor to the ring at the top of which the chain of cable is attached. A painter is a length of line used for making secure and so we might suppose that 'letting go the shank painter' released the anchor ready to drop.

Anchors were held in a cathead, a piece of heavy timber sticking out from each bow, usually with the face of a cat carved in the end, hence its name. Attached to the end of the cathead was a block and tackle system used to haul the anchor up to the cathead and when it was so held, it was said to be 'catheaded.' We can assume therefore that to 'stand by your cat stopper' was to be ready to release the lines which held the anchor up to the cathead. The anchor was now ready to let go.

'Haul up your clew garnets, stick out tacks and sheets.' A garnet is another word for tackle, or pulley system and a clew garnet was a tackle attached to the clew of a square sail which was used for hauling the sail up to the yard when it was necessary to furl it. So, 'hauling up the clew garnets,' is roughly the modern equivalent of rolling up headsails in a modern yacht.

'. . . stick out tacks and sheets' is sometimes sung, 'let go tacks and sheets' which simply means letting fly as you would if coming up to anchor — under sail.

'Let every man toss off a full bumper,
And let every man swig off a full bowl,
For we'll drink and be jolly and drown melancholy,
With a here's to the health of each true-hearted soul.'

There can be no doubts as to the timeless sentiments behind the last verse.

Pipe aboard!

Patrick Purves' Instant Whistle System

In the days when only gentlemen went yachting, and rich ones at that, the Royal Yacht Squadron's Book of Signals gave as its cue for the night's entertainment to begin, the hoist 3081 meaning, 'can you spare me your fiddler awhile?' and as each owner decided whether or not the services of his private band could be dispensed with for the evening, an oilskin-clad violinist would be packing his instrument in preparation for a choppy row across Cowes Roads. Beats a push-button eight-track stereo?

But if your waterline doesn't permit the stowing of a spare fiddler, bassoonist or bass drummer on the off-chance that a few nights a year, boredom will overtake you, have you thought of the tin whistle? It has many advantages in that it is cheap, takes up no space, can't go wrong and is no great loss if lost over the side; which makes it just about the perfect piece of yachting gear. It's traditional too. You will have heads popping out of hatches in silent appreciation as you whistle your way through a few shanties in a moonlit anchorage. Practice a little at home first though, or silent appreciation cannot be guaranteed.

I learnt to play by a unique method of one Patrick Purves, a gentleman not entirely unrelated to the authors. He started some eight years ago at a stage at which most of us find ourselves. As he says, 'If you are unmusical, have no previous experience, are left handed and clumsy, you have the advantage over me, for I was all of these things when I started eight years ago. Since then I have played with folk bands, and started playing solo after two months. The Spinners say I am competent but I am no prodigy. I simply learned some tunes in the dog watches for my own enjoyment, which is what I assume you are about to do.'

From that starting point, his method commences.

THE TIN WHISTLE

A tin whistle is just that. To get a penny-whistle (they are now over £1) you need a time machine and manufacturers' descriptions will have to be ignored too. They are often sold as flageolets which strictly speaking have two barrels and thumb holes. Neither are they flutes but your eventual tin whistle might be described as one of these. They are usually displayed on a card in order of key and you should choose one that fits your fingers — it's as simple as that. Key will not matter if you intend to play alone, and for the first few weeks you certainly will be. The rule is that the shorter the whistle, the shriller it is. For big-fisted boatswains, a 'C' or even a 'B-flat' whistle is right and a cabin boy will want a 'G' but if you are of average fist size, then buy a 'D' or 'E-flat'. They are all played in the same way but a sensible sized whistle will make you feel at home much more quickly.

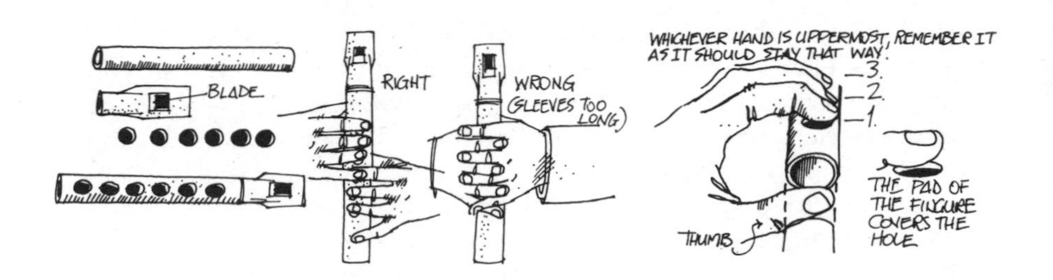

STARTING TO PLAY:

Hold your whistle in both hands. It doesn't squirm or bite. Three fingers of each hand (the three nearest the thumb) go over the holes. Remember which hand is upper-most as that is where it should stay. It is the pad of the finger that covers the hole. Strangely, you will find the little finger of the hand nearer you (which is not on a hole) is not much problem to begin with and becomes less so with a few minutes playing. You will find that it ends up slightly crooked and you can keep it out of the way by letting your hands sit on the whistle with the thumb directly opposite the middle one of the three playing fingers. You will find this easier with the elbows out and slightly forward. Then drop the elbows and relax.

THE FIRST BLOW:

Cover all the holes, keeping light pressure on the barrel with fingers and thumbs. Then put the plastic end between your lips (and teething-it helps to steady it) and *breathe*. No need to blow. If all the holes are covered you will (or should) get the lowest note on the whistle. Breathe progressively harder. The note rises a little, then there is a sort of grating noise and the note rises abruptly to a shriller note: the same note but the full length of the whistle higher, (an octave to those in the know). If you reduce the breathing pressure, it drops again to the lowest one.

On the increase of the note you should be reminded of the Snow White and Seven Dwarfs' opening cry of 'Hi — Ho!' Later, you can learn the rest of the tune.

Herein lies the secret of good, or for that matter indifferent whistle playing. A whistle has six holes and can play 15 full notes. Starting at the bottom, the eight are

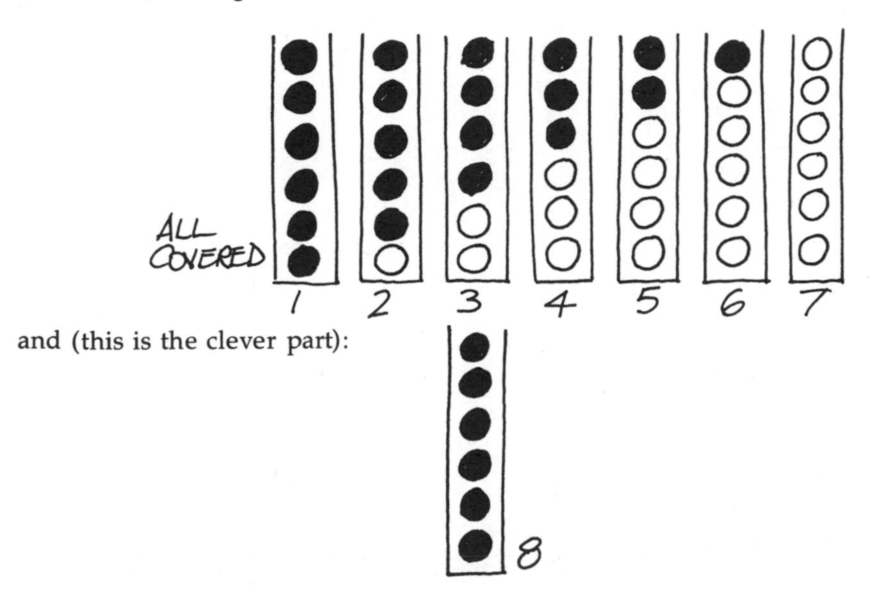

and (this is the clever part):

All covered *and* more breath pressure. Have a go at that going upwards, then downwards which is more difficult as the fingers have to find their correct holes. I suggest that when you can do this fairly fluently, you listen to it. You are playing a scale in the key of the whistle.

At this point, you may may wish to learn to read music. *You do not have to.* It is axiomatic that, say, Stevie Wonder cannot read music nor could Carolan, arguably the greatest Irish harper, who was also blind.

The scale has eight notes. The bottom one, on a 'C' whistle, is C They then go D,E,F,G,A,B, and then a higher C. There is no H. You do not need to know their names, so don't worry. As I suggested earlier, you can get more than eight notes out of the whistle. This is because when you get to the top of the scale, by stepping up the breath pressure you can slip into a higher scale. Have a go. It should be possible to collar all that in a few half hour sessions and it is then that your problems start because your eyes will start to glaze over, you will stifle a yawn, you start to toy with a shackle or a bottlescrew. You are bored . . you need some tunes to play.

PLAYING THE TUNES:

You now have all the technical knowledge you need. If you have tried to master an instrument before, you will probably have got this far and given up and for one good reason — they have tried to make you play boring tunes. Trombonists will have been given 'Three Blind Mice,' the violinists 'Etude in B' but you do not have such problems, you can play *what you like.* If you like Rachmaninov, play it. If you're a folk fan, play folk. If you enjoy waltzes and one in particular has plagued your waking hours, learn it and exorcise it. I started with 'Jesu Joy of Man's Desiring' for no better reason than I like it. The tunes don't matter. You are learning the whistle for your own pleasure, not as a stamina test.

It will help if you choose a short piece as concentration will tend to fade. Anything traditional, like most shanties, will be easier than say 'Abide with Me.' This is because every tune has a basic structure, like a hull, on which the clever stuff is pinned bolted or glued. The clever stuff is all very good and will come in time. You are learning to float. Try 'Blow the Man Down.' following the symbols for 'hole covered' and hole 'not covered'. It's easy! There really is no more to it than that.

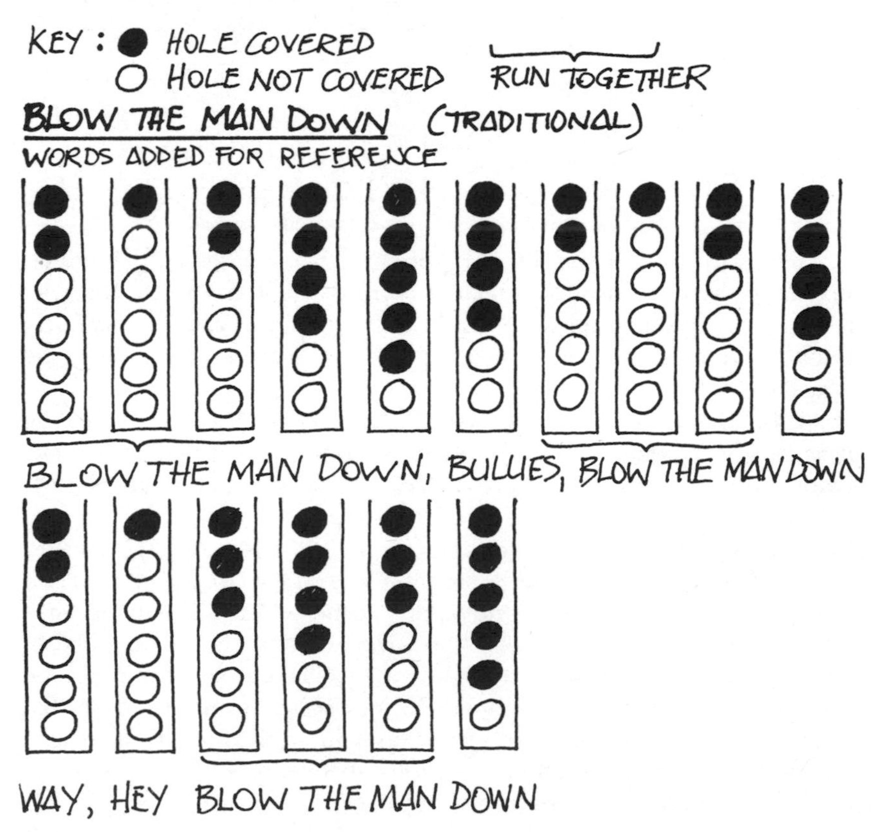

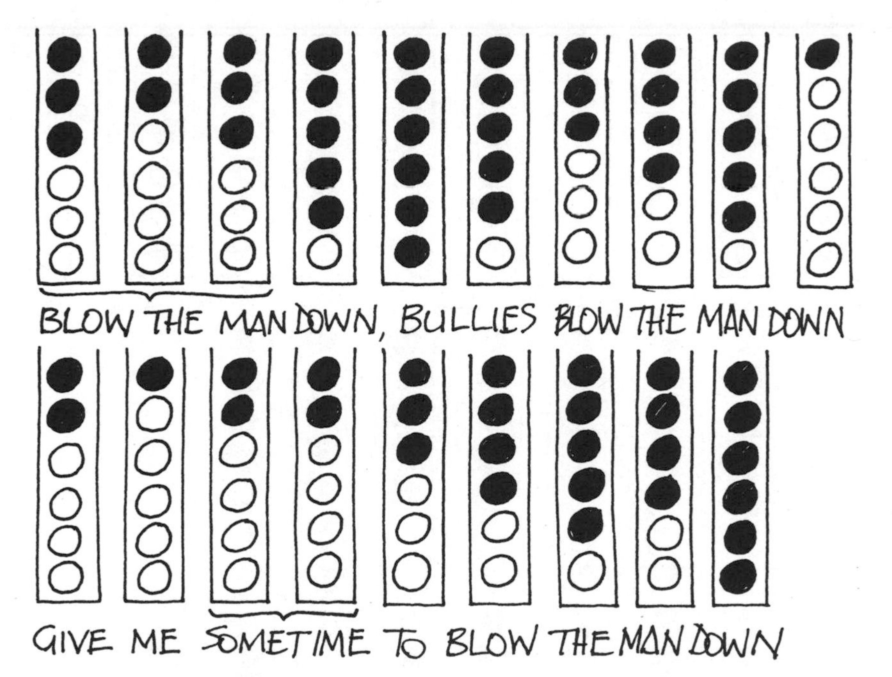

'Blow the Man Down' is all played 'downstairs' and nothing could be more appropriate. Shiver your timbers!

The next tune using the same system, is another well known one but we shall venture 'upstairs' for it.

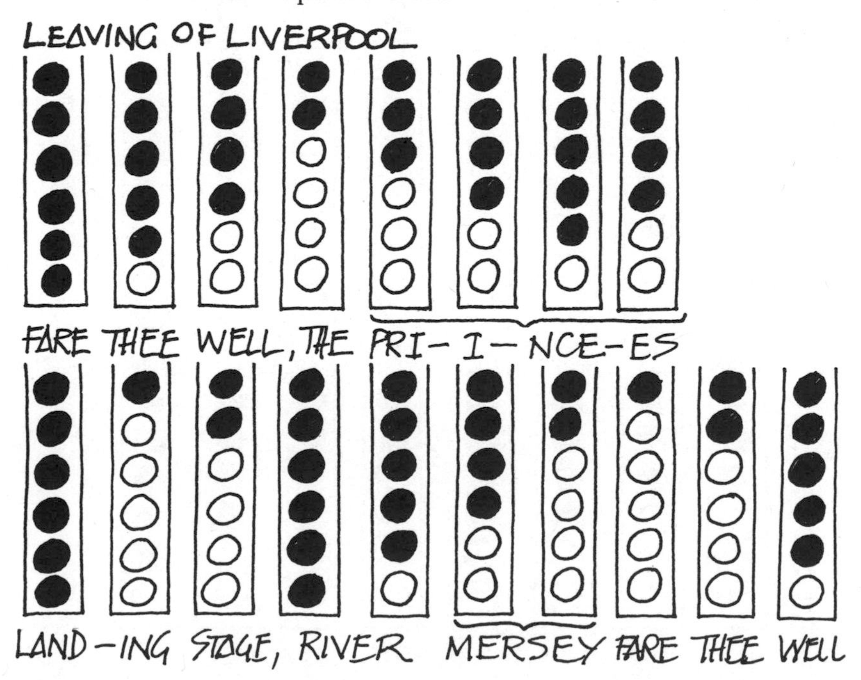

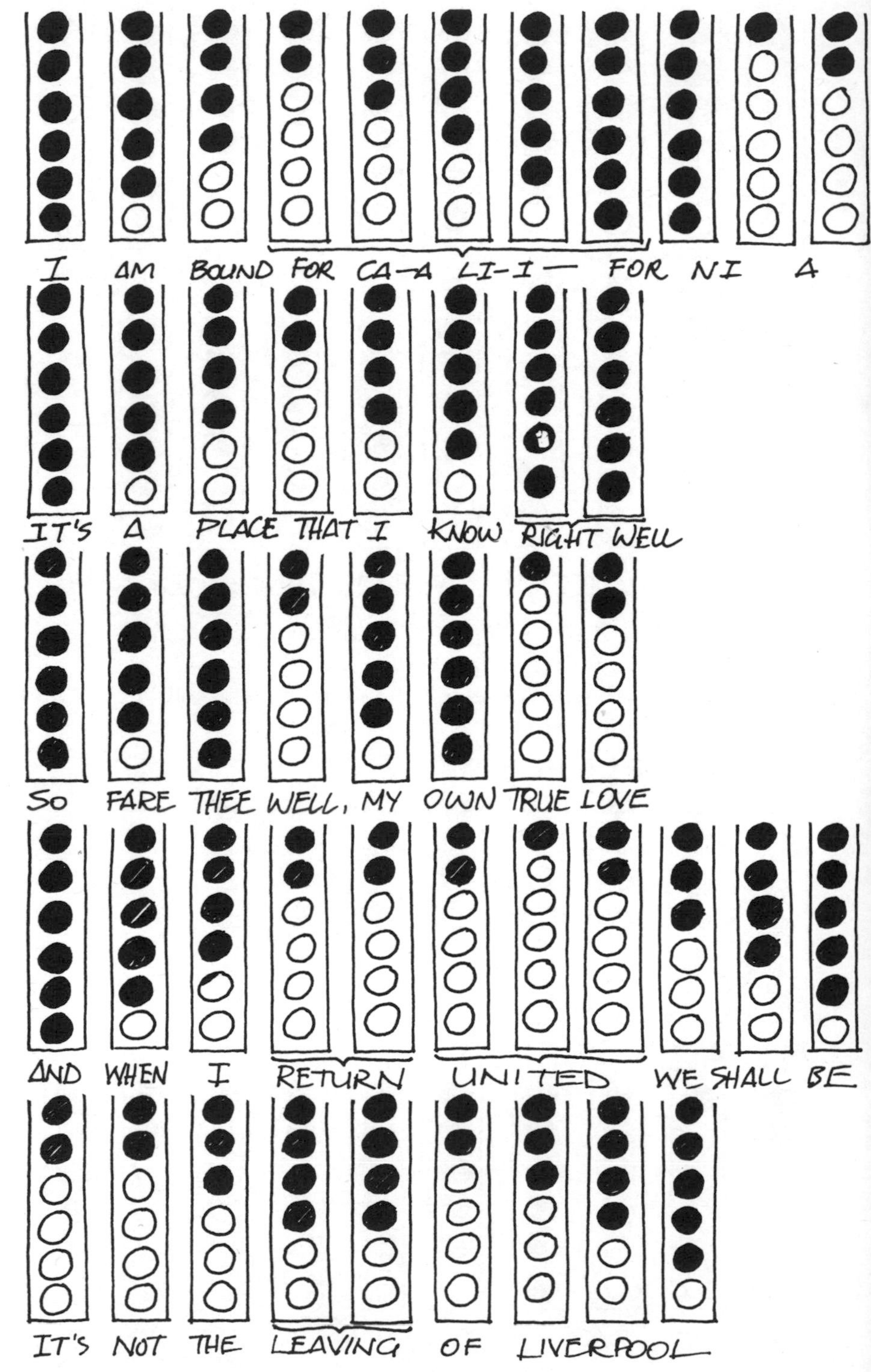
I AM BOUND FOR CA–A LI–I— FOR NI A
IT'S A PLACE THAT I KNOW RIGHT WELL
SO FARE THEE WELL, MY OWN TRUE LOVE
AND WHEN I RETURN UNITED WE SHALL BE
IT'S NOT THE LEAVING OF LIVERPOOL

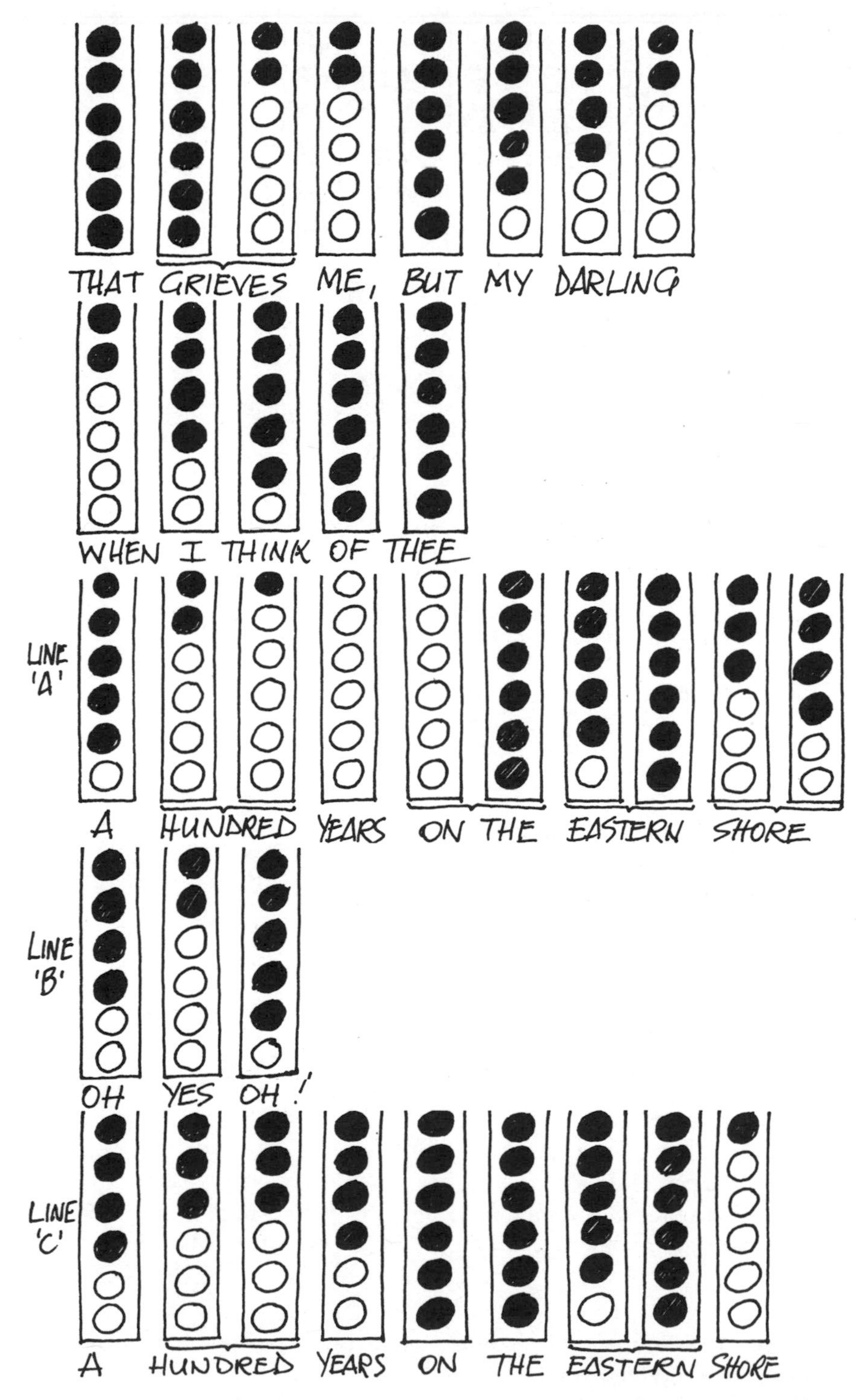
THAT GRIEVES ME, BUT MY DARLING
WHEN I THINK OF THEE
LINE 'A'
A HUNDRED YEARS ON THE EASTERN SHORE
LINE 'B'
OH YES OH!
LINE 'C'
A HUNDRED YEARS ON THE EASTERN SHORE

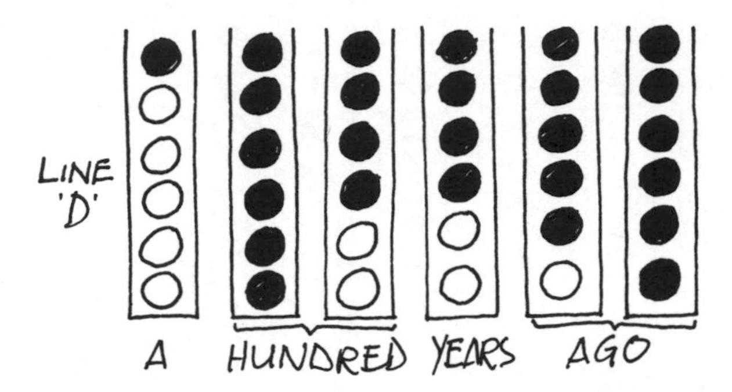

VERSE 2:
WHEN I SAILED AWAY TO SEA (LINE 'B')
MY TRUE LOVE SAID SHE'D BE TRUE TO ME (LINE 'D')

VERSE 3:
I PROMISED HER A GOLDEN RING (LINE 'B')
AND SHE PROMISED ME THAT LITTLE THING (LINE 'D')

VERSE 4:
BULLY JACK'S THE MAN FOR ME (LINE 'B')
HE'S A BUCKO ON LAND AND A BULLY AT SEA (LINE 'D')

VERSE 5:
UP TO THE TOP THIS YARD MUST GO (LINE 'B')
FOR THE MISTER MATE HAS TOLD US SO (LINE 'D')

VERSE 6:
I THOUGHT I HEARD OUR SKIPPER/
[SHOP STEWARD / BISHOP] SAY (LINE 'B')
JUST ONE MORE HEAVE AND THEN BELAY
(LINE 'D')

If you can pick your way through those, you are ready to set off on your own way. It will not all be plain sailing. To help you, there are a few tricks of the trade:

Sharps and Flats

These are notes you cannot play by just lifting a finger off a hole. try half covering the hole by rolling the finger off it towards you.

Trills

Finger up and down on the hole fast as if in the grip of some dreaded palsy or a sudden gybe.

That the log should be written
in seamanlike prose
Is a rule that every
seafaring man knows

H W TILMAN, quoted in
High Mountains and Cold Seas
by J R L Anderson (Gollancz)

The Captain's log

A ship's log is a compulsory document; in both the Royal and Merchant Navies, it is a serious offence not to keep it correctly. Naval ships send their logs monthly to the Ministry of Defence; merchant vessels send theirs to the Superintendent of their Mercantile Marine office, who sends it on to the Registrar-General of Shipping and Seamen. Page upon page of regulations insist that they enter 'date and hour of departure and arrival from any dock, wharf, port or harbour'; every muster, drill, and inspection (or reason why none happened); every distress signal seen or heard, every seaman discharged, died, or deserted (and whether he took all his kit with him); every complaint made to the master about food, water, conditions, or fellow-seamen. Punishments, births, deaths, and illnesses must be logged and signed, usually by the master of the ship.

Meanwhile, of course, the ordinary navigational details are filled in, column by column, watch by watch. The instructions to the officer of the watch in the Royal Navy specify very closely what goes in: log readings once an hour, distance run, engine revolutions per minute; every six hours the weather must be recorded, although 'during threatening and stormy weather' the wind, sea state, and visibility must be recorded every hour, and so must the barometric pressure. Distance run through the water must be calculated from midnight to midnight; and under 'Remarks', all exercises, meetings with other ships, hoisting or half-masting of colours, Divine Services, and just about everything else has to be correctly filled in, in pencil. Not a lot is left to personal taste.

Aboard a yacht, on the other hand, just about everything is left to the whim of the skipper. Techniques range from the chap who logs every hour of a passage from Hamble to Bembridge, marking down 'Sea state — calm' three times in an afternoon, to those who scribble the date, the word 'Cowes', and the telephone number of the girl who climbed so provocatively across the foredeck at Groves & Guttridge's pontoons last night. Somewhere in between are the crews like my brother's, who write copious notes in a dog-eared Korky the Kat exercise book, accusing one another of stowing wet oars in sleeping-bags, and listing their preferences for breakfast on passage ('Andrew: 2 Stugeron and Nuttella butty. Rose: 2 Stugeron and cucumber sandwich. Mike: 2 Stugeron and Snack Pot'). Their most characteristic entry of the 1980 cruise ran:

1445 Made attempt to leave for Helford River. Andrew, rising smartly to start supervising in command role, smashed lamp-glass with head and set off miserably to chandlers in heavy drizzle. Owing to confusion as to which sail was in which bag, the same sail was bent on and removed no less than three times by truculent foredeckhand. Departure postponed due to poor visibility. Have burned our boats by deflating the dinghy.

1530 Command decision made to postpone departure until after cup of tea.

1630 Beating under storm jib and reefed to 1st batten. Rose on helm. First packet of Jaffa cakes consumed. In fit of belated conscience, skipper has mounted compass. Horror! Fix has put us on the wrong side of Manacles. Decide to ignore fix. Pray God we shall prevail.

1800 Entering Helford River. Just missed forecast again. All Penguins eaten.

It may be flippant, but at least it is thorough. It is impossible to overestimate the benefits of keeping a good cruising log, particularly what the Navy would call the 'Remarks' column. Looking back at it in a dull winter, you can delightedly piece it together with your photographs — sea state, wind, view of headland, racing pigeon that landed on the deck, speed, engine problems, threatening cloud — and the jumble of facts noted down at the time will provide the basis for a splendid illustrated log that lasts for decades and will impress your most sceptical grandchildren.

Great log-writers have a few things in common. One is honesty: it is not necessary to go as far as Paul did once, after three days foggy and uncertain approach to L'Aber'vach, and simply write '0700 — LOST' — but doubts and uncertainties have a place in the narrative of a voyage. David Blagden, brave skipper of the smallest boat ever to take part in the Observer Singlehanded TransAtlantic Race, *Willing Griffin,* wrote in his log on day 33:

I've been in a bad way, these last few days. My mind has been quite out of control and my powers of judgement impaired. I have also developed a phobia of spray. I can't stand it. I have been totally soaked for days, the cabin is a disaster area — everything is saturated — my body and my clothes are encrusted with salt, yet at the least little splash of spray I cringe away in horror . . . Think of the fine figure of a fellow I was when I set out. Now I'm just a whining, whimpering weakling, all pink and crinkly and covered in splotches! Get some sleep Blagden, and snap out of it! And get out of this goddam bit of ocean!
VERY WILLING GRIFFIN, David Blagden (Heinemann/Peter Davies)

How else would he have remembered, later and on dry land, that curious detail of his spray-phobia? How would we remember, if we had not logged it, the invention (in mid-Irish Sea) of a one-pan dish named Mackereloni? How would you remember the terrible despairs of a long, wet, hopeless beat to windward for three days, unless you saw that telltale, splotched, 'Remark' against your 0500 log-reading:

'Decided to take up golf again'?

Another thing great log-writers have in common is a spare and economical style, well-suited to hurried notes where every word must count. Here is Captain William Bligh, of the *Bounty,* recording his landfall after an epic voyage in the open boat the mutineers had hoped he would die in:

My longitude, made by dead reckoning, from the island Tofoa to our passage through the reef, is 40° 10′ W. Providential Channel, I imagine, must lie very nearly under the same meridian with our passage; by which it appears we had out-run our reckoning 1° 9′. We now returned God thanks for his gracious protection, and with much content took our miserable allowance of a 25th of a pound of bread, and a quarter of a pint of water, for dinner.

No florid exultation, no self-congratulation; merely the note about the false reckoning, and the massive understatement 'with much content'.

Incidentally, Bligh's log also tells us the correct seamanlike way of sharing our dwindling provisions without argument. They had just caught a gull:

> This bird was about the size of a small pigeon. I divided it, with its entrails, into 18 portions, and by a well-known method at sea of *'Who shall have this?'* it was distributed, and eat up bones and all with salt water for sauce.

He explains, in a footnote, how the game works:

> One person turns his back on the object that is to be divided; another then points separately to the portions, at each of them asking aloud 'who shall have this?' to which the first answers by naming somebody. This impartial method of division gives every man an equal chance of the best share.

Sometimes, even though a skipper later writes a book about a voyage, it is the log written on deck, at the time, which gives the clearer impression of triumph or of tragedy. H W Tilman, the great mountaineer and sailor, made many remarkable voyages to Greenland and to the Southern Ocean; only once did he lose a crewman overboard. He described the incident of David Shaw's loss in his book about the voyage, *'Mischief Goes South'*; but it is his deck log, quoted in J R L Anderson's biography, which strikes home:

> Saturday, 27. Day of disaster. Went on deck at 0740 to find helm lashed, ship on course, and no sign of David. Called hands and gybed 0750 2 hrs on ENE course with all hands up rigging. Having found log had stopped and rotator was missing we acted on the assumption that D had grabbed at it and broken it. The log had stopped at 31¼ which indicated that he had gone overboard at 0615 as the last reading of the log at 0600 was 30. The binnacle light was still on and Tom had not been called at 0700. Having run the distance we handed sail and started motoring N and S across course, working back to the west. Roughish sea and white horses made it unlikely to spot a man, even if we were in the right area. All hands stuck in the rigging throughout altho' this was hard work as without any sails she rolled and pitched a lot. Small school of porpoises playing all day round ship, this day of all days, leaping and turning somersaults. Happy as possible, contrast with us. At 1830 I thought no more could be done so we hoisted main and stays'l and hove to for the night.

It is worth noticing how the strict hourly entering of the log, insisted on by Tilman, was the detail which gave the nearest clue to how far back the watchkeeper had gone overboard. If anything could have saved him, it would have been that; if by a miracle Shaw *had* been seen by the boat's crew searching in the right patch of water, it would have been due to his faithful entry, dead on time, of the 0600 log reading.

It was on another voyage that Tilman laid down the ruling against verse logs quoted at the head of this chapter. He was commanding the schooner *Patanela* to Heard Island in the Southern Ocean, with a young and lighthearted crew. One night in March the watchkeeper broke into doggerel, delighted to be under engine for a change:

We traverse the seas with effortless ease
No sheets to harden, no sheets to ease
No halyards to haul, no sails to hoist,
God bless Rolls, God bless Royce!

Tilman — finding this and lesser imitations in the logbook in the morning — wrote:

Attention is drawn to the entries for 4 March.
That the log should be written in seamanlike prose
Is a rule that every seafaring man knows
Only a crew of jerks or worse
Will mar this book with any more verse. HWT

Ships that pass 3

Dirty British coaster with a salt-caked smoke stack
Butting through the Channel in the mad March days
With a cargo of Tyne coal
Road-rail, pig-lead
Firewood, iron-ware and cheap tin trays.
JOHN MASEFIELD, Cargoes.

COASTER *COMMODITY* . . . of the F T Everard & Sons Line

I found the MV *Commodity* just down river from Lancaster, sitting on the mud at Glasson Dock in a cloud of tapioca. A whitened figure on deck, coughing on the sour powdery stuff, ran to steady the dusty gangway for me. 'Cattle food. Tapioca', he said. 'Sure you want to come aboard?'

I was sure. I had been trying for weeks to organize a trip on one of the F T Everard & Sons' small coasters, but their ways are unpredictable and energetic. From the office at Greenhithe wharf, they run them like radio taxis. Captain Garrett, the Marine Superintendent, had rung me up in triumph two days before. 'Two possibles. One at

Lancaster, unloading pellets, one up the Bristol Channel loading for Rotterdam. Could you be at Sharpness by five? Pity. Now the Lancaster one . . .'

The trouble with the Lancaster one, *Commodity*, was that she had no cargo to load. As she discharged her last but one, in Rotterdam, Everards had been offered a load of Thailand Tapioca pellets, *en route* for Lancaster. Calulating rapidly, Garrett had offset the desirability of getting her back to sea, out of an expensive berth, against the extreme unlikeliness of picking up anything useful in the wilds of Morecambe Bay. He took the cargo; and now she was unloading the last of the powder onto Glasson Dock wharf, with no orders to proceed. 'She might get something at Arklow in Ireland, or china clay in Cornwall for the Continent. Or we might have to send her out to steam down the Irish Sea listening to the radio. Then we *would* be on our mettle'. It is financially disastrous to have ships moving about in ballast, burning up 300 pounds worth of fuel a day with no cargo. Captain Garrett gave me my marching orders for Glasson, and prepared to plunge back into negotiation. 'Only take your passport. Could be France or Ireland. Or Holland? Lancaster to Holland in ballast, God help us no'.

So I approached the cloud of flying tapioca and the long yellow ship on the mudflats of Lune, with the beginnings of an understanding of her life. The Everard line runs 4000-ton giants and sails the world, but I was interested in the lower end of the fleet, the Home Waters Coasters of which *Commodity*, at 950-odd tons, is a middle sized example. The first ships of all must have been coasters, carrying food and stone and spice and wood; the line stretches clear from oars to sail to steam to oil. And Everards should know the trade; Frederick Thomas Everard bought his first barges a century ago.

Jerry, the dusty white deckhand, led me to the tiny mess-room and pulled six plates of spaghetti out of the oven. The three officers were in a state of ironic hilarity over theirs. 'Aye, we've got a cargo', said the Captain, a gentle, brown-moustached Edinburgh man. 'Loading Arklow for the Thames', announced one whose draped boiler-suit proclaimed him engineer. The punch line was left to the mate, a handsome battered Scotsman with a satirical eye. 'It's *pyrites residue'*. 'Pyrites! Py-ri-tes!' cried the three, and explained that compared to the horrors of the red grit to come, our present coating of cattle food was nothing. It had, I noticed, crept below through the portholes, to continue the tapioca theme even this far below decks. 'But the red stuff' said the Captain 'gets right into the paint'.

There are only five crew on *Commodity*, to handle 189 foot of ship and 900 tons of cargo. Captain Arthur Hawick, the mate, Alan McBoyle; engineer Mike Connolly, and two deckhands, Jerry Fielden and Ted Monaghan. The ship is 'non-federated' — not a union shop; the pay is on the oldest of all systems, the shareout, although the basic fall-back rate is high enough for this rarely to make a difference. The five work hard: the majority of a cargo vessel's work is in harbour, loading and unloading and cleaning. A short-hop coaster spends a lot of time in harbour. 'But we have the Library', cried Alan, hurling open a locker and snatching out a Monica Dickens, a C P Snow, two thrillers and a hymn-book. 'And the television, if you can stand it'. Hit an unfortunate trading pattern, they explained, and you can pick up the same film on four different ITV regions in a week. They were not in uniform. 'Not worth it. Tapioca. Pyrites. Chalk. Sulphur. There *is* a hat somewhere. That customs officer left it behind, could put that on for you. Anyway, uniform', said Alan with scorn. 'We're only a maritime lorry, you know'. And he went up, with the deckhands to see about the washing of the hold.

Waiting for the tide the next morning, I watched Ted and Jerry sweep carefully in and out of the iron ribs, dislodge great clouds of whiteness from the bulkheads about them, while Alan collected and threw it over the side with a bucket. Then all three hosed and sponged, while a merciful breeze blew the musty stuff offshore. 'Can be very frustrating', said Mike the engineer, watching. 'We cleaned out once, to load some grain, painted, the lot — it looked like a little picture palace down there. We get the stuff to Antwerp, and they put it straight into barges with lumps of bloody coal in them'. The cleaning team moved to the decks. Slowly the paintwork reappeared, the ship's boats, ventilators, coiled ropes, hoses and hatches lost their snowy appearance: *Commodity* regained some dignity as the tide swished in around the mudbanks.

She is smartly kept, considering the odds. Maybe she is luckier than some in her regular run from Great Yarmouth to Islay, with grain for the distillery; but the small crews spend notable energy on keeping her in order. Despite the fact that 24 hours would see every accessible surface powdered with red iron grit, all were cleaned off before sailing. 'You have to live aboard for four months', said Alan. 'You'd go mad'. Morale rose as the pilot sprang aboard from the bow of his fishing-boat, and began to guide the ship out through the winding, shifting, sandy channels of the river Lune. 'Moved more than three miles since three years ago. I write it all down in my salmon book'. There is a lesson here somewhere: the trick river Lune has been a haven for 1000 years, Glasson Dock itself has traded for 200; and it still wins a modest trade of cattle food and fertilizer, and cat litter from Spain; meanwhile down the road, those centuries have seen the great Port of Liverpool wax and sadly wane. The little ships, the modest cargoes, still thrive. 'But even now', said the ex-Harbourmaster of Glasgow, 'we get masters who haven't heard of us, going to *Gladstone* Dock in Liverpool, waiting around there'. 'Can't blame them', said Captain Hawick. 'I've been sent places I wouldn't have believed you could get a ship into. How many sugars, pilot?'

Commodity slid past the Abbey Hole lighthouse, edged over the sands. 'Feel her sucking', said the pilot, 'the wash changes'. The flat land faded quickly. The deckhands began to haul the great folding McGregor hatches shut over the dry, clean hold; the ship rolled high and vulnerable with only her ballast tanks full. The pilot finished his coffee, refused a ladder, and vaulted over to his fishing boat.

There is an oddly lonely feeling about a cargo ship at sea. So much of her has nothing to do with the business of navigating and driving along: the layout of a modern carrier, with the bridge and cabins right at the after end, and a long hold in front, is like a cottage pushing a playing-field. The bridge though, is defiantly cosy: next to the Decca navigator, radios, and charts, live boxes of houseplants and a couple of towelling coasters advertising lager. The present crew firmly disowned the scented geranium: it belongs to the regular mate, who is a woman. The indefatigable Jerry came up to hoover the carpet tiles in the wheelhouse, and I kept a rash promise to cook the ship's steak and onion tea. 'I hate cooking', said Jerry. He may not have to for long: he is taking his Class V examinations on the way to officership. Everard's founded the Small Ships Training Group, to encourage ratings to progress. There are plenty of ready-made officrs on the market, but small ships, Captain Garrett pointed out 'are not everyone's cup of tea. Some officers from larger ships are too interested in uniforms and saloons. Our guys are seamen'.

Indeed Everard's are not given to standing for any nonsense. They have had a somewhat raffish image: seamen in other lines or services will refer to 'yellow perils', or 'Flying Freds' — after Fred Everard — or worse. One Everard man told me that when he first considered trying for a job at Greenhithe, an old coasting captain said, shocked: 'Boy! have you no f---ing *pride?*' Even the compliments to the firm, from within it, have a certain iron robustness. 'They're straight. If they owe you one penny, you'll get it if it costs them a fiver to get it to you. If you owe *them* one penny, by God they'll have it'. The family, over four generations, have won approbation by working. 'They're not golf-course shipowners. Our working boss now, Ethel Everard, she's grown up with shipping. No fooling her. I wouldn't say its autocratic, no . . but if I got in here one morning and they said, get all the ships painted pink by tonight, I'd have to do it. It's their ships, their paint, their time, their money. Anyway, you have to get decisions quick and hard, in shipping. You can't have a ship off the Eddystone waiting for orders, and put it to a committee that meets on Monday'. The old dictionary from which the Founder's daughter Ethel chose the run of names ending — ITY — *Commodity, Celebrity, Serenity, Futurity, Security,* etc — still lies around the Greenhithe office. But the mixture of tradition and determined unsentimentality, oddly compelling in an era of public relations hype, is summed up best in the fact that the boardroom is lined from floor to ceiling with silver trophies won by the Everard sailing barges, in match after match through their years of glory; but that not one single barge is kept as a souvenir or company mascot. They sold the last one in 1966, and got on with building tankers.

The forecast for Irish Sea was for a south-westerly, a headwind, of force 5 or 6, perhaps gale 8. Bad news for a ship in ballast, light on the water. 'We'll bang. Bang like a brick wall', promised Arthur Hawick, staring at the scented geranium with hostility. He set course for Anglesey on the autopilot and looked around. White horses flowered around the long shape of the hold and bow; the Irish Sea began to crumple and foam. At an economical ten knots, *Commodity* ploughed on. 'Get 900 tons of pyrites in her and she'll feel deep, and steady, and grand'. The ship reared buoyantly and crashed to a wave. 'No. That wasn't a real bang'.

Woken later by a crash, I slipped on deck in the darkness. We were close enough to Ireland now for the promised gale to be blanketed by unseen land; but the wind was stiff, and the long dark finger of the ship before us rose and fell, driving through the fine rain. Every ship becomes impressive at night; self-contained, mysterious, more than a maritime lorry. In the shelter of the bridge Alan peered restlessly into the mist. The serrated edge of Ireland glowed dimly on the radar screen; the ship banged and shook, and drove on past the flashing light of Wicklow.

When the sun rose, we were at anchor, off the distant Vale of Avoca and the forbidding Arklow Rock. Beneath it jutted the skeletal form of the roadstone jetty; no harbour, only a jetty open to the swell and armed with a conveyor belt. Another ship heaved gently, loading stone. The Captain kept lookout, and talked. He did his time deep-sea, but welcomes the coasting job. Unlike the deckhand Ted, who served on the *Queen Mary* and the Eastern routes, and used to go ashore in Mao's Shanghai 'with me little seaman's pass saying PEOPLES OF THE WORLD UNITE AGAINST THE AMERICAN AGGRESSOR', Arthur does not dismiss this ship as 'a little old rock-dodger', and wish for the deeps again. 'No, my father was on Antarctic whalers off two years at a time. I don't want to leave my family like that. You see old seamen come aboard, one brown parcel, that's all they've got in the world. They live in seaman's missions. I didn't want that'. He paused to consider whether the hatches should be opened now, before berthing, to save ten minutes. 'No. Wind gets in the hold. We've pumped most of the ballast out, she'd be everywhere'.

When the time came, it took the pilot two goes to berth at the jetty; a single-screw ship with barely any ballast, in a stiff wind, manoeuvres like a cork. 'Ah, she's handy enough', said the pilot, admired the plants, and hopped ashore with a handshake. The machine on the jetty slid out to overhang the ship, and began to pour redness. It fell heaped at an angle which mate and master watched with catlike concentration for a minute. About 40 degrees. This is the 'Angle of Repose': a book in the wheelhouse of every dry cargo carrier lists substances from Alfalfa and Barley to Kaolin and Zinc; salt and silica and sulphur ('makes you cry all the time', said Ted) and quartz and coal slurry and urea ('stinks when its wet, well, it would', said Alan) — all with their desirable Angles of Repose. Arthur studied a sheet brought aboard by the agent: it gave Flow Moisture Point 25.89, safe transportable limit 23.29, this cargo moisture 19.40. The figures mean nothing less than survival: too wet a cargo will start to flow like a liquid, and overturn a rolling ship. The disaster of the *Lovat*, which went over after loading wet coal slurry at Swansea, brought in even stricter controls in the mid-seventies; there is no way that a ship like *Commodity* could get rid of a lethal cargo for her own survival at sea. I began to see why such religious care was taken in pulling and dogging-down the hatches.

The bow sloped up as the stern filled; the crew moved the ship progressively astern to make new heaps of red grit at the forward end of the hold. 'Biggest heap in the middle, see', said Alan. 'Better a bowed ship than a hogged-backed one'. The keel bit deeper in the water, the ship rose less to the swell and wind. With the cargo in reassuring 40 degree heaps, she sank towards her marks: in business again. The nine hundredth ton of pyrites fell into place, and Ted and Jerry moved to fasten the hatches against disaster. As the empty conveyor slid back, the dockers stood a moment and watched.

'Where 'you bound?'

'London River'.

An old question, an old answer.

Yo ho ho

There's nought, no doubt,
so much the spirit alms
As rum and true religion.
BYRON, Don Juan CII XXIV

The best food I ever tasted was a slice of toasted cheese: the bread was fresh, the cheese, probably Irish Cheddar, flowed like a golden liquid into every pore of the slice. It had, of course, an ingredient which no chef could dispense: we were at sea.

Nor is drink ever sweeter than when toasting the dropping of the anchor or securing to the quayside. I remember the stormy passages and the doubtful landfalls, the anchor being dropped long after dusk and under the light of the oil lamp, two glasses being poured; each with a tot of whisky, a drop of ginger wine and a splash of boiling water destined to join forces and wash away anxious memories of the previous hours.

Most yachts carry some form of drink but I suspect few carry 'grog' to dispense to wretched crews in the finest traditions of the Navy. The 'nose' of this evil potion, part rum and part water, can be guaranteed to evoke memories of aromatic fitting-out liquids usually associated with the removal of particularly noxious antifoulings; but it's role as a pacifier of men, a reward for service, seems to have died on the day the Royal Navy ceased to issue its 'tot' to seamen in 1970.

On 31 July in that year, a signal was sent from the First Sea Lord:

'Most farewell messages try, to jerk a tear from the eye
But I say to you lot, very sad about tot,
But thank you, good luck and good-bye.'

Its passing did not go unmourned. A full funeral service was held with the words 'lips to lips... splashes to splashes,' being read as the final gulp of grog was taken. Nearly 250 years of Naval history was downed for the last time:

'For grog is our starboard, our larboard,
Our mainsheet, our mizzen, our log.
At sea, or ashore, or where harbour'd,
The mariner's compass is grog!'

And so it has been since the sixteenth century. The ration was then of brandy rather than rum and it wasn't till 1655 that rum made its enduring marriage with the sea. Our naval victories in the West Indies brought rum in plentiful supply and in 1731, the daily issue to seamen was made official.

The tot, if so modest a word can do it justice, was no less than half a pint taken in two doses, morning and evening. It took only nine years for the Navy to appreciate the pitfalls of its generosity and in 1740, Vice Admiral Vernon gave the order that the half pint of rum was to be mixed with a quarter of water. Vernon bore a nickname derived from the name of a silken fabric of which his uniform was made: the cloth was called *grogram*, he was called 'Old Grog.' That was how grog got its name but it has also been known as 'Nelson's Blood,' the story being that Nelson's body was embalmed in a casket of rum before being brought home after the Battle of Trafalgar. It is not thought to be true.

For the officer class, drinking was a much more ordered affair. I don't know who or what you toast of an evening; perhaps a health to the harbourmaster and may we be away before he calls for the dues, but Nelson's own toast takes some beating:

'The wind that blows, The ship that goes, And the lass that loves a sailor.'

If you are drinking the Loyal Toast you will be pleased to hear (especially if following a substantial repast) that you do not have to stand up. You can thank several people for this privilege; or in the case of most of our yachts: necessity. It may have been Charles II returning from Holland in 1660 who rose and bumped his head on a deck-beam, or it may have been William IV trying to do something similar. Some will say it was George IV who told his officers: 'Gentlemen, pray be seated: your loyalty is above suspicion.' Or it may have been the Navy of the Restoration where officers were gentlemen volunteers and didn't have the sea-legs to stand anyway.

After the loyal toast came yet another toast depending on the day of the week.

'Monday: Our ships at sea
Tuesday: Our native land
Wednesday: Ourselves and none like us
Thursday: A bloody war
Friday: A Willing foe and searoom
Saturday: Sweethearts and wives
Sunday: Absent friends.'

If you find a few of them a little blood-thirsty, we suggest you fit them into an ocean racing context: the nearest most yachtsmen will get to naval warefare!

If you drink out of real glasses, remember never to let them ring: an empty ringing glass 'sounds the knell of an unfortunate sailor.' Even if you hate going sailing and only survive it for the drink at the end of the day, then that is sufficient reason for it has often been said that:

'A man who goes to sea without a reason,
Would go to hell for a holiday.'

We have always carried rum whenever we have sailed but not to dilute it Admiral Vernon-style. To say we only use it for medicinal purposes sounds pompous but on our boat, its role is more of a reviver than intoxicator. We never travel without our sealed, plastic 'emergency' box containing a drum of ground cinnamon, a touch of nutmeg, small pots of honey acquired from the breakfast tables of hotels, and small packets of brown sugar removed from the saucer at cafes *en route* to the coast. Our emergency store has been rarely used at sea but has become as much a part of relaxing in a new anchorage as dropping the anchor.

You need boiling water and a pottery mug; plastic will not do. There is something about a pot mug that speaks of security. Pour an unbridled tot of rum and add to it a spoonful of the honey (and a little sugar if you like it *very* sweet) and a pinch of the cinnamon or nutmeg. If you are well provisioned, a slice of lemon will complete the elixir. Allow to stand and make use of the time to silence halyards and re-check the anchor and then sit, either in the cockpit if it is a clear night or beneath the glow of an oil lamp below, and sip slowly. I have tried this under fluorescent lighting; it will not work. Do nothing for half an hour allowing the infusion to take place and only then begin to think about a little supper. By the time you have absorbed the mugful, you will thank the day you decided to go to sea, whatever the previous 12 hours have been like.

So that is our favourite warmer, a rum toddy, although it works just as well with whisky. It does have a sedative effect so I have never taken it whilst underway although I once had to silence a crew who through willingness to help and to please was more of a nuisance than an asset at three o'clock on a frosty morning in the middle of the Thames estuary. I thoughtfully made him a mug of rum toddy and did not hold back on the rum. I pointed him in the direction of the forepeak and there he slept soundly till the demanding navigation was over and he could be left to steer us in a straight line.

There are many recipes for 'warmers' so you must choose one that fits the contents of your liquor locker. If you have a large crew to satisfy and not the pocket to match it, try Mulled Ale.

MULLED ALE

Pour into a saucepan one quart of good brown ale, a tablespoon of castor sugar, a pinch of nutmeg and ginger. Bring almost to the boil and then add a wineglass of rum. Serve piping hot.

For the more generous, another punch:

PUNCH

Pour two pints of good beer into a pan, one pint of boiling water and a quarter pint each of rum, whisky, gin and add a tablespoonful of soft brown sugar, a thinly sliced lemon and a pinch of cinnamon and nutmeg. Bring nearly to the boil, strain and serve. Watch for the smiles on the faces.

The cheapest of the lot is probably Orange Mull.

ORANGE MULL.

Cut up two or three ripe oranges or tangerines, add a dessertspoonful of powdered ginger and a pinch of powdered clove. Add a pint of good strong beer and 'mull' gently.

One of the secrets of good mulling is to never let the mull come to the boil. The alcohol will quickly evaporate and you will end up with a rather odd fruit juice.

If you are cruising say in France where there is a plentiful supply of good cheap wine, try Burgundy Punch.

BURGUNDY PUNCH

To a couple of bottles of red wine, add four ripe tangerines, a wineglassful of rum, a pinch of nutmeg. Heat till nearly boiling.

Cruising in Brittany brings with it the delights of Breton Cider. It is such a delicacy that it seems a waste to try and add to it but for a little variation you might care to try a cider punch. It goes best with a little ice but fridges on board yachts are thankfully scarce and ice-machines at marinas are always under repair so the only way of cooling a bottle is to sink it. You could try wrapping it in soaked newspaper and harness the cooling effect of the evaporation of the water but sinking bottles to the depths of the oceans has the element of gamble it would be a shame to miss: a gamble that is, if you're not good at knots. A string bag has to be the best bet but if, by any chance, the bottle gets forgotten, the £2 bottle of plonk can quickly turn into the £200 bend in the prop-shaft.

CIDER PUNCH

To two pints of cider, add a thinly sliced lemon, a glass of brandy, a bottle of soda water and two spoonfuls of sugar. Mix well and serve.

CIDER CUP

To a pint of cider, add a glassful of whisky, a slice of tinned pineapple and half a glassful of the pineapple syrup out of the tin.

I have met yachtsmen in Ireland who swear by milk and whisky, presumably Irish whiskey. The only word of warning is that the milk must be fresh or it will curdle. I was told of a crew that mixed itself such a cocktail only to find the milk was 'off' and they each ended up with a beaker of solids rather than liquids; so they scooped it out and chewed it!

A more refined version of that is Atholbrose.

ATHOLBROSE

Mix a tablespoonful of best honey, a spoonful of *fresh* cream and a double tot of finest malt whisky.

But this is heady stuff. Let us not forget tea. It has done more to preserve my composure and good spirits when at sea than all the grog Vice Admiral Vernon could have dished up. To borrow the words of Colley Cibber:

> 'Tea; thou soft, thou sober, sage and venerable liquid; smile-smoothing, heart-opening, wink-toppling cordial to whose glorious insipidity I owe the happiest moments of my life, let me fall prostrate!'

Geese, Gulls, and Gannets

A guide to the birds of the shore by Juliet Bailey (by courtesy of The Wildfowl Trust)

When sailing round the British coasts it is difficult not to notice the bird life. This chapter might help anyone who is not an expert, but has more interest in the subject than to dismiss every bird as 'a seagull'.

All birds will at one time or another be seen over the sea, but a smaller number are closely associated with it. Many birds, wildfowl and waders especially, winter on the British coasts, but breed in the high north; they are unlikely to be seen in the summer, even though some are very numerous in the winter. Concentrating on the birds most likely to be seen while sailing reduces the number of birds to be considered to 29.

Unfortunately, seabirds are not colourful; they tend to be black, white, grey or brown. Sometimes the best way of recognising a species is by its behaviour. Birds plunging beak-first into the sea are most likely Terns or Gannets. Birds standing on rocks with wings outstretched are Cormorants or Shags. Colonial, cliff-nesting birds with an upright stance are Auks.

The gull is probably most people's yardstick of a seabird. There are six species commonly to be found around Britain and Ireland. Gulls are pale grey to black across the back and have white bodies. One British species, the Black-headed Gull, has a dark head, the rest have white. Their near relatives, the terns, share these features but have a black cap on a white head. Five kinds of terns occur around the British Isles in any numbers.

By far the most common and widespread in this group of terns and gulls are Black-headed and Herring Gulls. The adult Black-headed in summer is unmistakeable with its chocolate hood — no other common British bird looks remotely like it. The adult Herring Gull is larger and has a pearly grey back with a yellow bill and flesh-pink legs. Flocks of large white-ish birds standing on a beach, perched on buildings in seaside towns, or engaged in noisy aerial squabbling in harbour are almost certainly gulls.

Another common (particularly delightful) gull is the Kittiwake. It nests colonially, usually on cliffs, and has an almost human 'kitty-wau-eek' call when near the nest. The easiest way to tell it from the other gulls is by the lack of white flecks in the black wing-tips.

Though terns do not frequent towns, they can often be seen fishing along popular holiday beaches. They hover briefly then plunge head-first into the water after fish.

Another bird that looks superficially rather gull-like, with the same sort of colouration and proportions is the Fulmar. It has a stiff-winged mode of flying using air-currents and up-draughts near cliffs. A Fulmar tips and angles itself along the axis of the body, and when it beats its wings, it does so stiffly and rapidly — most unlike the lazy flapping of a gull, with the 'm' conformation of the wings so familiar in seascape painting.

Whereas gulls and terns have longish bills, the Fulmar's is stubby and has external nostrils lying in tubes along the top. It has a thick bull neck. It is an ocean-going bird, only coming to land to breed where it nests colonially on cliffs.

The Manx Shearwater also has the stiff-winged tipping mode of flight. It has almost black upperparts and white underparts. It breeds in dense colonies on marine islands in burrows, where it is nocturnal. Vast crowds of Shearwaters collect on the water towards evening before flying in to the nest. Neither the Manx Shearwater nor the Fulmar are at all at home on land, and they will not be seen walking around or standing about on a beach.

The smallest European seabird is the Storm Petrel which breeds in British waters along the western coasts of Scotland and Ireland. At only six inches long, and black with a white patch just about the tail it could almost be taken for a House Martin. It will follow along behind ships far out at sea, and has a fluttery flight, sometimes pattering along the surface with its feet dangling. Like the Shearwater it comes ashore only to breed and is nocturnal at the nest site.

A very large seabird is the Gannet which has distinctive plumage, all white except for the wingtips which look like they have been dipped 'up to the elbow' in black paint. It is further distinguished by its habit of diving for fish, sometimes from a considerable height, with half closed wings. This is seen in young birds too that still have patchy dark plumage.

Razorbills and Guillemots (both members of the auk family) nest on cliffs. They waddle when on land and have a noticeably upright stance. They are short necked and short tailed; their bellies are white and their backs are dark. This adds up to a superficially penguin-like appearance. They are not very accomplished fliers, having rather short narrow wings, and fly with a direct whirring flight, which distinguishes them from Shearwaters. But they are excellently adapted for a life of swimming and diving, with feet well to the back of the body. The Puffin, renowned for its disproportionately large and multi-coloured bill is another auk, and it nests in burrows.

The Shag and the Cormorant are also denizens of the rocky shore — the former more than the latter which also frequents estuaries. They are both large dark seabirds with long necks, and one of the ways of distinguishing them in the field is by their habit of perching on rocks and spreading their wings — almost as if they were hanging themselves out to dry. They are fish eaters and catch prey by swimming along, sitting rather low in the water, then diving. They fly low along the water with their long necks outstretched. A flock of Cormorants will sometimes fly higher, and in V-formation, and can look rather like a skein of geese.

Wildfowl — ducks, geese and swans — flock in large numbers to the coasts in winter. In summer Mute Swans, Canada and Greylag Geese and Mallard can sometimes be seen, and swans and Mallard especially can make a good living from tourists' offerings. A limited number of ducks are properly associated with the sea. The Shelduck, a large bird with a dark green head whose white ground colour is broken by black bars and a chestnut collar is most often seen in estuaries. The Eider frequents northern rocky coasts. A drake Eider in full breeding dress is largely white but for a black belly and black half-moons over the eyes. In summer it may be in more sombre moult plumage. The Eider female maintains barred brown plumage throughout the year.

Waders are, generally speaking, those birds that live on the shore and make a living feeding on the water-line, sometimes wading through the waters. They are known as shorebirds in America. There is a great deal of food to be found here, and waders are appropriately adapted to best exploit one resource or another. Some have long legs, some long beaks; some step slowly and purposefully, probing deep, and some hurry along with little steps pecking morsels off the surface; some are large, some are small. Waders tend to be brown; their plumage blending well with the rocks and sands where they feed. However, one very noticeable wader of the British coasts, the Oystercatcher, is boldly pied black and white and has red legs and a long red bill.

The seaside is the natural habitat of a few birds, some familiar inland, which do not exploit seawater. Cliff nesters such as the Rock Dove and Jackdaw are notable examples. The Rock Pipit, a small streaky brown bird, is confined to the coast.

On the following pages, 29 of the most common seabirds are described in greater detail. The list below divides them into three groups to give an idea of relative breeding abundance, though this does not necessarily represent the frequency with which they will be seen.

Indeed, as the Storm Petrel and Manx Shearwater are active only at night at their nest sites, spending the daylight hours way out at sea, landlubbers (and probably most yachtsmen too) are not likely to see them at all.

Very numerous	**Numerous**	**More unusual**
Storm Petrel	Shag	Cormorant
Manx Shearwater	Shelduck	Eider
Fulmar	Oystercatcher	Ringed Plover
Gannet	Curlew	Dunlin
Kittiwake	Greater Black-headed Gull	Arctic Skua
Black-headed Gull	Lesser Black-headed Gull	Great Skua
Herring Gull	Arctic Tern	Common Gull
Razorbill	Common Tern	Roseate Tern
Guillemot	Sandwich Tern	Little Tern
	Puffin	Black Guillemot

There is no quick route to expertise, and there is no better way to learn than to have an expert beside you. It will be useful to have binoculars and a field guide. The best of these books are arranged according to a scientific classification where the birds are grouped in families. This makes the guides accessible to experts, but they can be confusing for beginners: though seabirds will be found grouped at the front.

STORM PETRELS (Hydrobatidae)

Small black birds with white rump and weak fluttery flight. One species described, the Storm Petrel.

STORM PETREL
Hydrobates pelagicus

Identification

Size: 6 in (the smallest seabird of the area).

Plumage: Nearly all black but for white rump and variable white patch on underwing. Looks something like a House Martin.

Other features: Habitually follows ships and feeds pattering along the water with

its feet dangling. Flight is fluttery. Nocturnal on land.
Habitat and Location: Seen chiefly in the offshore and pelagic region to the west of the British Isles. Breeds on rocky undisturbed west coast islands from Scilly to Shetland.

PETRELS AND SHEARWATERS (Procellariidae)

Ocean birds that come ashore only to breed. Notable for stiff-winged mode of flying. External nostrils lie along upper bill. Two species described, the Manx Shearwater and the Fulmar.

MANX SHEARWATER Puffinus puffinus

Identification
Size: 14 in.
Plumage: Black above and white beneath, with white underwing.
Other features: Has long stiff wings and flies characteristically along the contours of the waves, with a few beats then long glides, banking to follow the contours, thus flashing black/white. Congregates in flocks on the water in the evening before heading for the nest burrows.
Habitat and Location: Breeds along the western and northern coasts of Britain and Ireland. Spends most of time in offshore waters all round coasts except at nesting time. Breeds on marine islands where it is nocturnal.

FULMAR Fulmarus glacialis

Identification
Size: 18½ in.
Plumage: Grey upperparts including rump and tail, and white head and underparts. Rather gull-like in appearance but has grey tail and lacks black on wing-tips.

Other features: Silhouette is bullnecked and the tube nostrils lying along the top of the bill can be clearly seen. It is a master glider, often flying with few wing beats and wings held out stiffly. Does not stand or walk readily, shuffles around at nest site. The voice, a harsh growling and chocking, can be heard at nest site and from flocks.
Habitat and Location: Seen all round coasts of Britain and Ireland. Nests colonially on cliffs, but is pelagic outside breeding season. Not as common in east and south of England as breeding sites are limited. Can be seen over open ocean, but readily exploits waste from fishing industry, following trawlers.

GANNETS (Sulidae)

Large birds with cigar-shaped bodies and pointed tails. Long narrow wings. Heavy dagger bill. Plunge-dive for fish. One species described, the Gannet.

GANNET Sula Bassana

Identification
Size: 36 in (very large)
Plumage: Adults white all over except for black wing tips. Juveniles and immatures dark, or patchy dark/white plumage. White plumage attained when four years old.
Other features: Great, dagger-like bill. Plunges headlong into the sea with half-closed wings when fishing, sometimes from 100 feet.
Habitat and Location: Seen all round coasts of Britain and Ireland. Can be seen about 100 miles from land, but not often in inshore waters. Breeds colonially on cliffs, usually on marine islands.

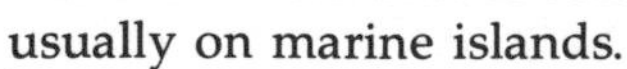

CORMORANTS (Phalacrocoracidae)

Large dark birds with cigar-shaped bodies, longish pointed tails and long necks and bills. Often perch with wings outstretched. Two species described, the Cormorant and the Shag.

CORMORANT
Phalacrocorax carbo

Identification

Size: 36 in (very large).

Plumage: Plumage of the adult is bronze-black all over except for white chin and cheek patches and white patch on thighs. Juveniles are brown with pale underparts.

Other features: Has long neck and long bill, hooked at the end. Cormorants (and Shags) perch on prominent rocks, posts etc with wings outstretched apparently to dry. When flying with the long necks extended they tend to look rather goose-like, particularly as flocks of cormorants fly in V-formation.

Habitat and Location: Seen all round coasts but only breeds locally along the east coast of Britain and is absent as a breeding bird from the south-east of England. Breeds colonially on rocky ledges. Seen in coastal waters, especially along estuaries and in quiet bays.

SHAG Phalacrocorax aristotelis

Identification

Size: 30 in.

Plumage: Adult black with a green gloss all over. No white patches on cheeks and thighs. Has a forward-pointing crest in spring. Juvenile is brown all over.

Other features: Very like Cormorant, but smaller, lacks white patches and has crest. Flies low and purposefully across water with neck outstretched.

Habitat and Location: Seen round all coasts

of British Isles though like the Cormorant only breeds in a few localities on the east coast and does not breed on the south-east coast of England.

SWANS, GEESE AND DUCKS (Anatidae)

A diverse group with fairly long necks and (usually) horizontally flattened bills. Two species described, the Eider and the Shelduck.

EIDER Somateria Mollissima

Identification

Size: 23 in.

Plumage: Males and females have totally different plumage. The female is warm brown, darkly barred. The male in breeding plumage is white but for a black crown and black belly, but by summer is likely to be in eclipse plumage then turns very dark. There is a bewildering array of intermediate male plumages. Juveniles resemble females.

Habitat and Location: Breeds colonially in sheltered localities around northern coasts. Sometimes seen further south. A purely maritime duck.

SHELDUCK Tadorna tadorna

Identification

Size: 24 in.

Plumage: Sexes similar, unlike most ducks. Appears pied black and white from a distance. Dark green head; broad chestnut band around forebody; black stripe down centre of underparts, black shoulder patches, flight feathers and tip of tail; rest of the body white. Immature has white below and grey-brown above.

Other features: It is a large, goose-like bird, and its bold plumage and preferred habitat of estuaries make identification simple. Adults congregate in huge moulting flocks in late summer at the mouth of the river Elbe and a smaller number congregate in Bridgewater Bay, Somerset.
Habitat and Location: It is found all round the British and Irish shores, chiefly on sandy and muddy coasts, especially estuaries and sea marshes. The Shelduck is a hole nester, often using old rabbit burrows, and prefers light soils or sand dunes.

WADERS

Birds of the water's edge, generally long-legged and long necked, often with long bill for probing into mud. Their feet are generally not webbed. Five species described, the Oystercatcher *(Haematopodidae)*, the Ringed Plover *(Charadriidae)*, and the Curlew, Redshank and Dunlin *(Scolopacidae)*.

OYSTERCATCHER
Haematopus ostralegus

Identification
Size: 17 in.
Plumage: Black upperparts, head, neck, chest and tail band. White belly and broad white flash across flight feathers.
Other features: Long red bill and legs. This boldly pied wader with its brightly coloured bare parts is easy to recognise. It is very noisy, with a 'Klee-eep' piping call.
Habitat and Location: Found round entire coastline on all types of coastal habitat.

RINGED PLOVER
Charadrius hiaticula

Identification
Size: 7½ in.
Plumage: Sandy-coloured upperparts, with

white underparts; a broad black band goes around the chest and over the neck. Black band (like a highwayman's mask) through the eyes. Shows a white wing bar in flight, and the tail is dark down the centre with a white border.
Other features: The black-tipped orange bill is short. A small bird of open shores, it blends in well with its background and is often difficult to see.
Location and Habitat: Found round the entire coastline on open and shingly shores.

CURLEW Numenius arquata

Identification
Size: 22 in.
Plumage: Mottled brown and rather featureless but for white triangle on rump which can be seen in flight.
Other features: A very large wader with the unusual feature of a long down-curved bill. Other birds with this are rare. The voice is a liquid 'Curr-lew'.
Habitat and Location: Found all round the coasts. It breeds mainly on uplands, but moves to the coast immediately after breeding.

REDSHANK Tringa totanus

Identification
Size: 11 in.
Plumage: Grey-brown with mottlings. Distinctive flight markings on broad white band on hind edge of wings and white rump.
Other features: Has long red legs, from which it gets its name, and long red bill.

Has a triple liquid call-note, 'Tyew-yew-yew' uttered particularly in flight.
Habitat and Location: All round Britain, but less frequent in the south of Ireland and south-west England. It is a bird of open flat land; seen especially on estuaries and mud-flats.

DUNLIN Calidris alpina

Identification
Size: 7 in.
Plumage: Grey-brown upperparts, white underparts. Summer adults have large black patch on the belly. The white rump is divided by a dark central line.
Other features: Probably the commonest coastal wader. Gathers in large flocks after breeding where, from a distance the well co-ordinated twisting flight is reminiscent of smoke. The black belly-patch is very distinctive.
Habitat and Location: Breeds mainly on peat bogs in the north of the British Isles, but flocks congregate all round the coasts, on broad beaches, mudflats especially.

SKUAS (Stercoriidae)

Their dark plumage and overall shape give them the look of immature gulls, but they have wedge-shaped tails with the two centre feathers projecting as streamers to a greater or lesser degree. Skuas chase other seabirds to make them disgorge their prey. Two species described, the Arctic Skua and the Great Skua.

ARCTIC SKUA
Stercorarius parasiticus

Identification

Size: 18 in.

Plumage: There is a pale type, a dark type and a range of intermediates. A dark phase bird, uniform blackish brown, could be taken from an immature gull. The pale phase has creamy white cheeks neck and underparts. The dark phase is more common in the south. Skuas can be told from gulls most easily by the shape of the tail. In the Arctic Skua the tail streamers, the central two feathers, extends about 3in beyond the rest.

Other features: Skuas are piratical, and the Arctic Skua's main food, small fish, is got by aerial pursuit of other seabirds, auks, small gulls, or terns, and grabbing fish from the bill, or catching it if it is dropped. The aerobatics in pursuit-flight and the tail streamers are distinctive.

Habitat and Location: Breeds on coastal moorlands of western and northern Scottish coasts and islands, but is largely pelagic, and can be seen all round British Isles in all waters.

GREAT SKUA Stercorarius skua

Identification

Size: 23 in.

Plumage: Dark brown except for a white flash on the wings across the base of the primary feathers seen on the upper and lower wing surfaces. The tail prong feathers hardly extend beyond the rest at all.

Other features: Like the Arctic Skua, it chases other seabirds to steal their fish, but it also fishes, scavenges and predates seabirds for food. It looks rather like an immature herring gull but can be distinguished by its heavier bill and the white on the primaries.

Habitat and Location: Breeds on moorland in the north of Scotland, especially Shetland; but outside the breeding season can be seen in pelagic and offshore waters in the area.

GULLS AND TERNS (Laridae)

Usually white-bodied seabirds with white heads and tails; grey across the back and upper wings (mantle). Terns are less robust than gulls and generally more graceful. They have black caps on their white heads, and have tails forked to a greater or lesser extent. Gulls have fan-shaped or square-ended tails and are generally heavier looking. Terns, sometimes known as sea swallows, are buoyant in flight, and catch fish by hovering and plunge-diving.

Eleven species are described; the Great Black-backed Gull, the Lesser Black-headed Gull, the Herring Gull, the Common Gull, the Black-headed Gull, the Kittiwake, the Common Tern, the Arctic Tern, the Roseate Tern, the Little Tern and the Sandwich Tern.

GREAT BLACK-BACKED GULL

Larus marinus

Identification

Size: 27 in.

Plumage: Head, underparts and tail of adult pure white; upper wings and across back (mantle) very very dark grey — almost black. The Great Black-backed Gull takes three years to assume full adult plumage, gradually losing the brown

chequered juvenile plumage.
Other features: Legs flesh pink. Yellow bill has red spot on lower part (a feature of the large gulls — the Greater and Lesser Black-backed and the Herring). Voice a deep bark. Could be confused with the Lesser Black-back, but the latter has yellow legs and is usually dark grey across the back, not almost black, and the size too is distinctive.
Habitat and Location: Breeds widely round coasts (except for east coast of England) especially on off-shore islands. Seen in off-shore waters, around coasts and in estuaries.

LESSER BLACK-BACKED GULL Larus fuscus

Identification
Size: 21 in.
Plumage: Adult white head, underparts and tail, upperwings and across back (mantle) dark grey. Tips of wings are black, and the contrast can be seen, where it cannot with the Greater Black-backed. The juvenile is dark brown and takes three years to attain full adult plumage.
Other features: Bill yellow with red spot. Feet yellow about the same size as a Herring Gull.
Habitat and Location: Nests on moors and cliff-tops and seen in offshore and inshore waters including estuaries and in towns. Breeds all round British Isles but there are only a few colonies on the east and south coasts of England.

HERRING GULL Larus argentatus

Identification
Size: 22 in.
Plumage: Mantle (upper wings and across back) pale grey in adult, with black wing-tips, the rest of the body white. Juveniles are grey-brown and assume full adult plumage over two to three years.

Other features: Red spot on yellow bill. British race has flesh-pink legs. This is the most common of the three large British gulls and its wailing cry is a familiar seaside sound.
Habitat and Location: Seen all round British and Irish coasts and common in seaside towns, often perching on buildings. Follows ships, but does not usually go out of sight of land. Preferentially cliff-nesting but not restricted to this habitat.

COMMON GULL Larus canus

Identification
Size: 16 in.
Plumage: Grey mantle (upper wings and across back) with black wing-tips, rest of body white in adult. Juvenile plumage grey-brown, appearing similar to adult by first summer.
Other features: Greenish yellow bill lacks red spot. Greenish yellow legs. Voice like shrill Herring Gull. Rather like a small Herring Gull, but the leg colour and lack of red spot on bill is distinctive. Another similar small gull, the kittiwake, lacks the white flecks (known as mirrors) in the black wing-tips, and has blackish legs.
Habitat and Location: Has a northerly breeding distribution and uses a wide variety of coastal habitats. Feeds mainly inland, but often flies some distance to estuarine roosts.

BLACK-HEADED GULL Larus ridibundus

Identification
Size: 15 in.
Plumage: Adult has white neck, underparts and tail, pale grey mantle and black wing-tips with white mirrors. In flight, the broad white wedge along the leading edge of the wing is most noticeable and distinctive. The name is derived from the dark brown hood over the head assumed in summer.

Other features: Bill and legs are red. This is the commonest small gull.
Habitat and Location: Breeds in a great variety of coastal and inland habitats, but requires calm shallow water nearby and avoids rocky shores. Frequents muddy and sandy estuaries and inlets all round British Isles.

KITTIWAKE Rissa tridactyla

Identification
Size: 16 in.
Plumage: Adult has mid-grey mantle and the black wing tips lack mirrors (white flecks) seen in the Common Gull. White head, underparts and tail. The juvenile has a black band across the back of the neck and a dark zig-zag strike across the upper wing surface and a black band on the tail.
Other features: Greenish yellow bill (lacking red spot) and blackish legs. Named after 'Ki-tee-wauik' call.
Habitat and Location: Breeds all round British and Irish coasts on sheer cliffs. After breeding tends to be pelagic.

COMMON TERN Sterna hirundo

Identification
Size: 14 in.
Plumage: Black cap to head, white body and white forked tail. Upper wings and back grey. When overhead, the translucent inner primaries show as a pale bar in the 'crook of the elbow' of wing.
Other features: The Common, Arctic and Roseate Tern are not easy to differentiate, even to experts. The pale elbow of the Common Tern is a distinguishing feature, as is its orange red bill. The Arctic Tern has a blood-red bill and the Roseate's is almost black. The Common usually has a black tip to the bill (lacked by the Arctic).
Location and Habitat: Breeds all round British and Irish coasts and sometimes

inland on reservoirs. A colonial breeder on beaches and dunes.

ARCTIC TERN Sterna paradisea

Identification
Size: 15 in.
Plumage: Black cap to head, white body and white forked tail; more grey on body than Common. All the flight feathers are translucent, thus it lacks the pale bar 'in the elbow' of the Common Tern.
Other features: Bill in breeding season is blood red and normally lacks black tip. Characteristically short legs.
Habitat and Location: Breeds colonially frequently on offshore islands, but much more rarely inland than Common. In Britain largely confined to the north of England and Scotland; colonies all round Ireland.

ROSEATE TERN Sterna dougallii

Identification
Size: 15 in.
Plumage: Black cap to head, white underparts and very long forked tail; pale grey mantle. Rosy tinge to breast in spring. Much whiter appearance than Common and Arctic. Long tail streamers help distinguish from other terns, projecting far beyond wing-tips when perched. (Common's do not project at all, and Arctic's only a little.)
Other features: Red legs. Largely black bill. Rarer than the Common and Arctic Terns.
Habitat and Location: Breeds chiefly on eastern Irish coasts, also colonies in Firth of Forth, Northumberland, Isles of Scilly and English shores of Irish Sea. Breeds colonially on coastal beaches.

LITTLE TERN Sterna albifrons

Identification
Size: 9½ in.
Plumage: As other sea terns, but black cap

with white 'forehead' even in the breeding season. White underparts and small-forked tail. Grey mantle. Juveniles mottled grey but distinguished from young gulls by forked tails.
Other features: Black-tipped yellow bill. Yellow legs. It is a small tern, quicker and jerkier in flight than the others.
Habitat and Location: All round British and Irish coasts except for south Wales and south-west peninsula of England, breeding on undisturbed beaches.

SANDWICH TERN
Sterna sandvicensis

Identification
Size: 16 in.
Plumage: Black cap on head is shaggy at the back, giving a crested appearance. Underparts and small-forked tail white. Very pale mantle.
Other features: Black bill with yellow tip. Black legs.
Habitat and Location: Colonies scattered around British and Irish coasts, main colonies East Anglia, Firth of Forth and Farne Islands. Breeds on sand and shingle beaches and low lying islands.

AUKS (Alcidae)

Short-necked, short-tailed, black and white diving birds with upright stance when on land. Wings rather short and narrow; fly low over the sea. Four species described, the Razorbill, the Guillemot, the Black Guillemot, and the Puffin.

RAZORBILL Alca torda

Identification
Size: 16 in.
Plumage: Black above with black head and white below.
Other features: The large black bill is later-

ally compressed and is crossed by a vertical stripe. Black feet. An upright stance when perching.
Habitat and Location: Breeds on rocky sea-cliffs, often with Guillemots, around British and Irish shores, but absent from eastern and south-eastern England. Found in coastal and offshore waters.

GUILLEMOT Uria aalge

Identification
Size: 16½ in.
Plumage: Dark brown/black above with dark brown head and white below.
Other features: Pointed long black unmarked bill distinguishes it from Razorbill. Wings are short and narrow and flies with rapid wing-beats. Feet are black.
Habitat and Location: Breeds on rocky sea-cliffs around British and Irish coasts but absent from eastern and south eastern England. Found in coastal and offshore waters.

BLACK GUILLEMOT Cepphus grylle

Identification
Size: 13½ in.
Plumage: All black but for large white wing patches (a very distinctive pattern).
Other features: Red feet, black bill is long and pointed. Juvenile has white underparts and barred white and dark upperparts.

Habitat and Location: A north-westerly distribution in Britain, but all round Irish coasts, especially Irish Sea. Less sociable than the other auks, breeding in holes and crevices. Remains close to shore.

PUFFIN Fratercula arctica

Identification

Size: 12 in.

Plumage: Black above and white below; large white cheek patches.

Other features: Breeding bird has extraordinary large triangular red yellow and blue bill. Red feet. Especially dumpy appearance.

Habitat and Location: Colonies all round British and Irish coasts except for eastern and south-eastern England. Breeds in burrows usually on islands. Frequents coastal and off-shore waters.

Flag-upmanship

Ye mariners of England
That guard our native seas
Whose flag has braved, a thousand years
The battle and the breeze . . .
THOMAS CAMPBELL,
Ye Mariners of England

Flags

It is difficult to talk enthusiastically about flags without appearing pompous. Nor is it easy when staggering onto a rainswept deck as the chill headwind of the morning tugs at the oilskins, to spend valuable minutes searching the forecastle for the ensign you were sure was there. Nor is it easy to gaze upon the crumpled, faded flag remembering:

'Old England is our home, and Englishmen are we,
Our tongue is known in every clime, our flag on every sea.'

Nor can we all expect to find the inspiration in our flags that that most individual of twentieth century sailors, Tristan Jones, found in his. When asked why he chose to attempt the world 'vertical' sailing record by taking his craft from the Dead Sea (1250 feet below sea level) and to Lake Titicaca (12,580 feet above sea level) he replied, 'What greater achievement is there than to fly the Red Ensign on the highest and lowest places on God's earth?'

Given that such sentiments beat in the hearts of precious few who go to sea, it comes as a surprise that hardly a yacht is seen without some kind of flag. It may be in the wrong place, at the wrong time, but at least it is a flag even if nicknamed the 'red duster.' Perhaps it is for purely decorative reasons that people choose to fly flags. I have heard conversations in chandlers along the lines, 'Let's have the nice blue one darling, it's much prettier . . . no, not that one, the one with the nice crown in the middle . . .'

We can spare a little sympathy for the River Thames lock keeper who, during the Silver Jubilee of 1977, warned the owner of a motor boat that if he didn't remove the dozen Union Flags he was flying, he would personally have them cut down! The public outcry against this apparently unpatriotic behaviour by this perfectly correct lock keeper was front page news and nothing the poor lock keeper could say would persuade anybody that if Admiral Lord Nelson himself had been confronted by such an offender, his reaction would have been exactly the same. (For those not convinced, the Admiralty Manual of Seamanship states; 'Afloat, the wearing of the Union Flag on a jackstaff denotes a ship of the Royal Navy, and it is not allowed to be worn by any other ship's'). But most people fly their flags (or to be correct they fly their flags but wear their colours) because everybody else seems to, so it is understandable that most of our knowledge would be derived from imitation rather than a close study of the Merchant Shipping Act which lays down the rules.

This is a pity because the history of our flags is a rich one and although their correct usage is laid down by law, to most of us the law does not apply and so the flying of flags cannot be considered to be little more than games. But it is a game to be played correctly or not at all, if only out of respect for the generations of sailors who have gone before to whom 'their flag' seemed to mean so much more.

FLAG MANNERS

There are three principal British ensigns, red, white and blue. The red and blue can sometimes carry an emblem in the lower canton, or quarter, and then they are known as 'defaced' although I suspect the people who fly them might well consider them to be 'enhanced.' The first record of ships wearing flags of three different colours was in 1617. The Navy was then divided into three squadrons each with an Admiral known as the Admiral of the White, Admiral of the Blue etc. Those of us who fly the red ensign feeling in some way we are not part of the elite who have the privilege of flying the white or the blue, might care to know that the red squadron was always the senior and the Admiral of the Red took precedence over those of the Blue and the White. The three flag system however had its irritations since each ship had to have three sets of colours but it was at the Battle of Trafalgar that Nelson, Vice Admiral of the White, gave orders for all the Fleet to hoist the white ensign for the simple reason that the red and blue could be easily confused with the French flag, and anyway, the red and blue were not easily distinguished through the gunsmoke.

Given that the concentration of gunpowder in the air is not a significant factor in modern yachting, which flag do you fly? To take the simplest case first: you are not a member of any yacht club, your yacht is not registered; what flag must you fly? The answer is quite simple, you are not obliged to fly anything. If you wish to, no-one will stop you and in that case, the correct flag is the red ensign. Should you be about to buy your first, the Admiralty system of defining flag size is to express the length of the hoist as so many breadths of nine inches. A flag of three breadths would have a hoist length of 27 inches and since the fly and hoist lengths should be in the proportion 2:1, it would have a fly length of 54 inches. The Union, in the upper canton should take up exactly one quarter of the flag (except in the case of the white ensign where the Union is reduced to accommodate the St George's cross should be 2/15ths of the width of the flag).

Chandlers seem to have adopted the standards set by television retailers whereby a 22 incher could turn out to be any size. I have yet to see anyone buying an ensign with reference to widths but clearly some good sport is to be had!

As soon as you join a yacht club and wish to hoist its flag, that is where the complications start. Assuming you joined in the first place out of respect for its members as much as for its taste in barrelled beers, then it is just as important to show respect for its flag. Yacht clubs are identified by their burgee which is usually flown at the principal masthead of your yacht. The burgee also serves to define the craft that is wearing it as being a 'yacht' as no other craft is entitled to fly one. So, in the simplest case of a yacht whose owner is a member of the Mud Lump Sailing Club and owns a single-masted yacht, he simply hoists his burgee to the masthead and his red ensign is flown from a staff on the stern. He may then put on the stern, the name he has chosen, *Mudcrawler,* and if he wished to do so, M.L.S.C. It is a good idea to fly a burgee of the correct size for no other reason than smartness and as a guide, the following figures are often used:

THAMES TONNAGE	**2**	**5**	**10**	**20**	**30**	**40**
Burgee fly length	12in	18in	24in	30in	36in	42in

If, however, you have joined the Royal Mud Lump Yacht Club which happens to be a club privileged to wear a special ensign, usually a blue, this is where the fun starts. Remember a couple of things. Because a club does not have a 'Royal' attached to it, it does not mean it cannot have a special ensign: the Cruising Association has a blue ensign. Secondly, membership of a 'Royal' club does not entitle you to wear a blue ensign without applying for a warrant, usually to the Ministry of Defence through the Club Secretary. Assuming it is granted, it is still not *your* warrant, it is your *ship's* warrant and is only effective on that yacht when you are on board. Strictly speaking, if you go ashore, you should remove your ensign but the Act uses the expression in 'effective control' and this is taken to mean that popping ashore for half an hour in search of a launderette need not cause you to remove your bunting.

Your special ensign will vary according to the burgee you are flying. If you are flying the flag of, say, The Royal Thames Yacht Club or the Royal Cruising Club, your blue ensign will carry no emblem but the Ministry of Defence have decided to give no more warrants to clubs allowing them use of the undefaced blue ensign hence the Cruising Association ensign is defaced with their 'anchor' emblem.

FLAG-UPMANSHIP (The basic rules of the Flag Game)

1 In harbour: hoist your ensign at 0800 local time (0900 in winter, summer being defined as lasting from 25 March to 30 September in the northern hemisphere). Lower your ensign (or preferably order it to be lowered) at 2100 or at sunset, whichever is the earlier.

2 Finding yourself in the company of a flag officer of your club, hoist your colours at the same time as he does — unless of course he hasn't got round to it by lunchtime in which case I would spare him the embarrassment. Flag officers are usually gentlemen of such repute that I am sure there is not one who would consider going ashore for refreshment before lowering his colours at sunset.

3 A special ensign must not be worn without its club burgee. When the ensign goes up, the burgee must go up with it.

4 Never fly a Union Flag, anytime, anywhere, anyhow.

5 Salute the flag officers of your club. Since salutes have to be returned I add this rule in the belief that flag officers have privilege heaped upon them, usually in the form of car parking space at the clubhouse and so it is not unreasonable to expect them to have to sweat for it.

Make sure he can see your ensign, or you will have a long time to wait for him to return your salute, then lower it but not so far that it ceases to fly. The flag officer you are saluting should then lower his flag and you should not hoist yours till he has started to rehoist his. To be correct, you should salute the Royal Yacht and warships as well as officers of your club. However, in the case of warships, discretion must overtake tradition and there will be many occasions when returning your salute will be something more than a mild inconvenience. I would never salute a warship in the Solent. If he had to return the salute of every yacht as he passed between the Needles and the Nab, the poor chap often seen rushing aft so as not to cause offence would soon be reduced to a wreck. It is for this reason that the sailor stationed at the stern of *Britannia* during Cowes Week must surely deserve some medal.

Incidentally, you may also salute your yacht club as you leave harbour. Your club should respond by dipping its ensign — best of luck!

Although the white ensign is now only flown on yachts belonging to members of the Royal Yacht Squadron, in the early nineteenth century its use was more widespread. There were then two white ensigns one of which did not carry the red St George's Cross. In 1835, a warrant was granted to the Royal Thames Yacht Club, the oldest of all English yacht clubs, to fly the white ensign. Some years earlier, in 1829, a warrant had been granted to the Royal Yacht Squadron for the use of the white ensign but there was nothing to say that other clubs could not apply. Many did. The Royal Southern, the Royal Western of England, the Royal Eastern and others all flew the white ensign. However, in 1842, Lord Yarborough, seeking to preserve the exclusivity of the white ensign to the Squadron, persuaded the Admiralty to restrict the privilege and so Lord Yarborough wrote to all other clubs flying the white ensign and told them to stop it. He made one error. It escaped his attention that there were two clubs with the name Royal Western. One '. . .of England' the other '. . . of Ireland.' The Irish never got the letter and continued to fly their white ensign. They might still be doing so (were the club still in existence) had it not been for the Royal St George Yacht Club who could see no reason why they should not fly the white if the Royal Western did. In search of the golden egg, the Royal St George killed the goose and by bringing the anomaly to the attention of the Admiralty, the order to strike the white ensign was issued leaving the Royal Yacht Squadron in its supreme position.

It is, of course, a matter of taste, but it must indeed be a proud man who flies the ensign of Trinity House first given them by the College of Heralds in 1573. It is distinguished by its four Elizabethan galleons sailing from fly to staff and since it predates the red ensign, to describe it as a 'defaced' red ensign is to incur the wrath of the Brethren.

Finally, on the subject of flag-upmanship, as you make your dawn scramble to the flagstaff cursing the burgee halyard that has been tapping all night, remember the warning of the Merchant Shipping Act:

'Any commisioned officer on full pay in the military or Naval service of Her Majesty or any officer of Customs in Her Majesty's Dominions, or any British Consular Officer, may board any ship or boat on which any colours or pendant are hoisted contrary to this act, and seize and take away the colours or pendant, and the colours or pendant shall be forfeited to Her Majesty.'

It could come as a shock to find a rear admiral in full dress uniform hacking away at your rigging with a view to stealing your Royal Mud Lump burgee away to the Palace!

It didn't take long for centuries of expertise in the passing of signals by flags to be eclipsed by the instant push-button VHF radio. Indeed, the only advantage the poor flag has these days is that bunting seems to do better than the transistor when wet.

It would be a shame if we were to abandon flags completely. There is some satisfaction to be had in the succinct nature of communicating, '. . . stop carrying out your intentions and watch for my signals . . .' by simply hoisting code flag 'X'. It has a power similar to that of a scornful glance from Royalty. Most yachts carry a few signals flags, the most common being the 'Q' flag to signify the end of a cross-Channel sortie. I was once recommended to carry code flag 'P', the Blue Peter to hoist above the 'Q' flag whilst waiting for the Customs officer to pay his call. 'P' signifies that 'this vessel is about to proceed to sea,' and by hoisting it over the 'Q' flag your Customs officer might detect the implied haste in your signal. I have no evidence that this works.

Code flags 'E' and 'W' are worth knowing, especially by Solent yachtsmen as they are used by large ships leaving Southampton Water bound for the Channel. Ships leaving via the Nab Tower fly flag 'E' as they round the Thorn Channel to signify they are going east, ships leaving via the Needles fly 'W' to mean west. A great help to anyone finding himself becalmed near the West Bramble and wondering which way the wall of steel is going to turn. There is a slight problem in this for an expert of the code of flag signals who does not happen to be familiar with the Southampton Water bye-laws since he might expect a ship flying 'E' to 'alter course to starboard' when in fact, she would be turning to port. He would be even more confused to see the *QE2* heading for the Needles flying 'W' and might wonder why she was in need of medical assistance.

The International Code of Signals, although created as recently as 1934, is really a distillation of ingenious systems which have their roots in the early fifteenth century. A code of 1653 required only five flags. An ensign, a pendant and one each of red, white and blue. It was this code that gave birth to the 'blood-red flag of war' when it gave as the signal for 'engage the enemy' as being, '. . . by shooting off two guns and putting a red flag over the foretopmast head.'

The code of 1746 had 16 flags which gave a range of 144 signals which soon proved to be too few and the only way to expand the code was to move the flag to different parts of the ship and thereby give them different meanings. This soon got out of hand and by 1806, a numerical system came into use which simply used ten flags and each signal was assigned a number.

Admiral Sir Home Popham took up the numerical system with such zeal that he invented his own code and set up his own press to print it. He would then pass his book round the officers of his ships. This was done at great personal expense to Popham but in those days to have one's own code of signals had something of the attraction of the personalised number plate. Flag signals were Popham's passion. He was a man with a mission and his numerical codes were his gospel. (His father was also a man of mission as Popham was the 21st member of the family!)

There was an element of guesswork involved in the use of Popham's code. Number 170, for example, could mean 'expedite, expedited or expediting,' and it was up to the man at the receiving end to make the best interpretation. If you had a word that Popham hadn't thought of, it could always be spelt out by using numbers 1 to 26.

It was Popham's lack of words that frustrated Nelson at Trafalgar. He had intended to signal: 'ENGLAND CONFIDES THAT EVERY MAN WILL DO HIS DUTY'. However, Popham did not quite run to the word 'confides'. The problem was solved by Nelson's Flag lieutenant, John Pasco who wrote some years later:

'His lordship came up to me on the poop, and after ordering certain signals to be made, about a quarter to noon, he said: "Mr. Pasco, I wish to say to the Fleet, *England confides that every man will do his duty"*, and he added, "you must be quick for I have one more to make for *close action."* I replied, "If your Lordship will permit me to substitute expects for confides, the signal will soon be completed because the word expects is in the vocabulary and confides must be spelt." His Lordship replied in haste and with seeming satisfaction:"That will do Pasco, make it directly." When it had been answered by a few ships in the van, he ordered me to make the signal for *close action* and to keep it up. Accordingly I hoisted number 16 at the top of the gallant masthead and there it remained until shot away.'

The next code came soon after Trafalgar when Captain Frederick Marryat invented his code of signals using ten numeral flags, the Union Flag, two substitutes, a numerical pendant and two distinguishing flags. Although his efforts were significant in the development of flag signalling systems, it will probably be for his books *Midshipman Easy* and *Captain Simple* that he will be best remembered. His code required four flags to be shown which gave a vocabulary of over 30,000 signals and it was his code that was adopted by George Holland Ackers in his book *Universal Yacht Signals* which, for the first time, gave yachtsmen a code of their own. Remember when reading it that those were the days when it was unusual to find a cruising yacht without a bath! Here are a few of the most useful signals:

48 Observe the Commodore carefully during the night, as he may alter course without making signals.
539 Where did you leave the Admiral?
1704 Can a vapour bath be ready at the hour shown?
4831 What time does the ball commence?
9852 Marmalade (orange unless specified).
4796 Can you spare any brown sugar?
5761 Can I have — quarts of turtle soup?
6419 I can strongly recommend my washerwoman.

The only flag which seemed doomed to extinction but has recently made its reappearance largely due to the enthusiasm of racing crews, is the house flag or 'battle' flag. They are usually to be seen flying from the forestay and embellished with some motif, usually the war cry of the crew, and being made of spinnaker cloth they crackle loudly in a stiff breeze, and often late into the night. The house flag is one of the few flags on which there seems to be little restriction. On a yacht they should be flown from the 'owner's yardarm' which is generally reckoned to be the starboard spreader or in the case of a ketch (or yawl) from the mizzen masthead. Just as a burgee tells you to which club the owner belongs, so the house flag tells you who the owner is. More commonly these days, it is used as a gin pendant and the flying of house flags generally means that corks have been drawn.

In fact, the Cruising Association has gone further. Should you find a yacht flying the CA burgee at the masthead and the CA membership flag from the spreaders, it is a positive indication that other CA members are invited on board. Never let it be said that flag signalling had no further use!

Dressing up and dressing-down

It is often the most pointless of arguments which take the longest time to settle, and this is never more true than in the columns of yachting magazines. Acres of print are devoted to the poor man with his Hong Kong-registered yacht living in Germany with an ensign warrant through a Gibraltar Yacht Club — which ensign should he fly when his wife is in charge of the boat? After an apparently logical response by an unsuspecting editor, a cascade of naval case law will surely spread itself over the next dozen issues. Never was this more true than in the case of dressing ship. The question is quite simple — which order do the flags go up?

In principle, the idea of dressing ship is a simple one. On days of national (or in the case of regattas, local) celebration, the flags of the international code are strung together from bow to stern via the masthead. No one disputes that only code flags should be used and certainly no house flags, ensigns or burgees. It was originally called 'rainbow fashion' when referred to by A D Fordyce in his *Outlines of Naval Routine* written in 1837. If you imagine a fully rigged ship of that time and imagine a string of flags from the end of the flying boom to the fore topgallant, across to the main and mizzen topgallant via the gaff to the mainboom end, it is easy to see how this name came about.

To answer the question as to which order the flags should fly, the answer is, to be strictly correct, suit yourself since no firm and fast rules have been laid down in the case of yachts. Clearly, rude words are to be avoided and after that the only principle which seems to apply is that the flags should be equally spaced and arranged to be contrasting in shape and colour. To save family feuds when it is suddenly realised that it is the Queen's birthday and the chap next door has been up all night artistically arranging his flags, the following is often used:

E Q p3 G p8 Z p4 W p6 P p1 I Code T
Y B X 1st H 3rd D F 2nd U A O
M R p2 J p0 N p9 K p7 V p5 L C S

If you have a yawl, you will have to decide whether or not you consider your mizzenmast to be of sufficient height to be included in the dressing overall since in some cases a yawl will dress as if she were a single-masted yacht. There should also be a flag flying from each of the mastheads and which flag to use will depend on the occasion whether it be local or national.

On national occasions:
British ensigns from all mastheads. At the main masthead, ensign and club burgee to be flown side by side.

Local festivals:
Club burgee at mainmasthead with no ensign. Any spare masts — put an ensign on top.

This only varies in the case of flag officers of yacht clubs who should fly their own flag from the mainmast head without any ensign.

If you are in doubt which of your ensigns to fly, should you have several, it is always in order to fly the red ensign but if you have a special ensign warrant, this may be worn but the same ensign must be worn on a staff at the stern. Dressing ship is not cheap!

Remember:
Never dress ship while underway. As the anchor goes down the flags go up and vice versa. Flags go up, and come down, at the same time as colours, and as a final piece of flag-upmanship if you have enough flag, you should continue them over the bow and down to the waterline where they should be held by a weighted lead-line.

Dates for Dressing Ship:
Accession Day, Coronation Day, HM The Queen's Birthday Commonwealth Day, HM The Queen's Official Birthday, HRH The Duke of Edinburgh's Birthday, HM The Queen Mother's Birthday.

Other occasions do occur such as the birth of royal babies and if you see a Naval ship dressed over all, I can only suggest that there is nothing to stop you doing the same.

Making up and breaking out:
This is really little more than an exercise in smartness and only requires the mastering of a simple knot. Used on small flags, it would seem to be of little use, rather like a fanfare to herald the arrival of a bus but in a fresh breeze when a flag might fly in that purposeful manner which only a large acreage of bunting (and never nylon) can, it can be done with some satisfaction.

House flags, courtesy flags and code flags can all be broken out but ensigns should always be hoisted. The exception to this is in the case of dressing ship when the ensign is flown from the mainmasthead and this is the only occasion on which it can be 'made up' hoisted and then 'broken out.'

And so farewell:
Given the love and attention we pour over our yachts, it is a little surprising that we say farewell to them with so little grace. The keys are pressed into the hands of the broker and she may, if lucky, warrant a backward glance as we stagger ashore with more gear than we thought possible to squeeze into the old girl. And then she is gone save for a few old snaps. It is a Naval custom to say farewell to their ships at the end of a commision with due ceremony and whilst it would not be appropriate in the case of every yacht to have a paying off ceremony, then your old friend might rest happier on her mooring knowing that it has crossed your mind.

The old custom was for a ship to knot together her brightwork cleaning rags and hoist them. This was replaced by a long white pennant with a St George's cross and it was a rule that the pennant had to be made on board ship and every member of the crew should have added a few stiches.

The pennant can be very long indeed since it should equal the length of the ship and to that should be added one twelfth of the ships length for every two months she has been in service since the date of her official paying off. This applies of course only in cases where ships have been doing what might be called 'overtime.' Clearly such a pennant was often of a size which meant it would require a gale of wind to keep it aloft and so it was the original custom to keep the fly aloft by attaching to it a gilded pig's bladder. Having been aboard HMS *Ark Royal* as she payed off in Gibralter before returning home to the scrapyard, I can only report that the Navy have replaced the pig's bladder with a meteorological balloon! It is also the custom that the paying off pennant can only be hauled down by the cook. Perhaps the only time on board ship when the cook gets the last word.

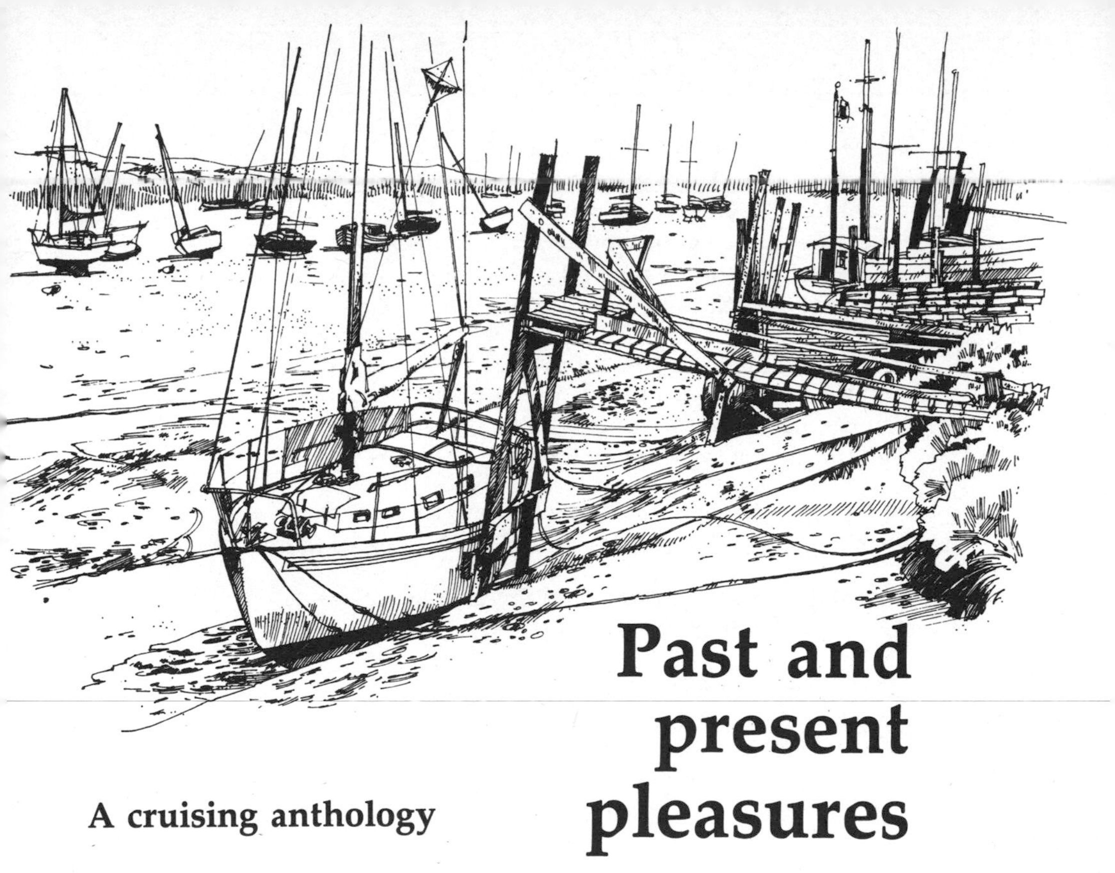

Past and present pleasures

A cruising anthology

ALONG THE COAST

Any ship, from the lowest to proudest, has due place in that architecture of the sea; beautiful not so much in this or that piece of it, as in the unity of all, from cottage to cathedral, into their great buoyant dynasty. Yet among them, the fisherboat, corresponding to the cottage on land (only far more sublime than a cottage ever can be) is on the whole a thing most venerable. I doubt if ever academic grove were half so fit for profitable meditation, as the little strip of shingle between two black, steep, overhanging sides of stranded fishing boats.
John Ruskin

FIDDLER'S GREEN

As I roved by the dock-side one evening so rare,
To view the still waters and take the salt air,
I heard an old fisherman singin' this song,
Oh — take me away boys, me time is not long.

Chorus

Dress me up in me oil-skin and jumper,
— No more on the docks I'll be seen,
Just tell me old ship-mates I'm takin' a trip, mates,
And I'll see you some day in Fiddler's Green.

Now Fiddler's Green is a place I've heard tell
Where fishermen go if they don't go to hell
Where the weather is fair and the dolphins do play
And the cold coast of Greenland is far far away.

The sky's always clear and there's never a gale
And the fish jump on board with the flip of their tail
You can lie at your leisure, there's no work to do
And the skipper's below makin' tea for the crew.

And when you're in dock and the long trip is through
There's pubs and there's clubs and there's lassies there

Now the girls are all pretty and the beer is all free
And there's bottles of rum hangin' from every tree.

I don't want a harp nor a halo, not me
Just give me a breeze and a good rolling sea
And I'll play me old squeeze-box as we sail along
When the wind's in the riggin' to sing me this song.
John Conolly

AT THE TOP OF THE CREEK

Beyond the harbour, the marina and the upper reaches of the deep water anchorage the creek winds on, shallowing until it dries completely. The offshore crowd never push further up because 'there is nothing there'.

There is an increasingly wide gulf between high tech and low tech, separating the world of the marine and plastics, alloys, micro-chips and precision engineering from the mud-and-gumboot scene at the top of the creek — the Third World of boating.

These are the people who are happy just to be afloat and being afloat is their reward for the hammering and banging, the improvisation and ingenuity, that puts a tired old boat back on the water for yet another season. The tide comes in and there is frenetic activity; it goes out and all is still, save for the shoving, squelching, cursing man who returned too late . . .

It is a lovely little world at the top of the creek, but to appreciate it you have to begin your boating there without much to lose. Then when you leave it you remember how the fat brown bubbles of the returning flood brought an excitement with them and how it felt when your boat finally floated. No other yachtsman knows the creative satisfaction of burying the garden roller to make a mooring or rigging a boat with fencing wire. Up at the top of the creek you learn the very essence of boats.
J D Sleightholme, in *YACHTING MONTHLY, 1984* (IPC)

SAILED — H M SHIP *VICTORY*

Anne sank into a reverie. Then she heard a slight noise on her left hand, and turning beheld an old sailor, who had approached with a glass. He was levelling it over the sea in a direction to the south-east and somewhat removed from that in which her own eyes had been wandering. Anne moved a few steps thitherward, so as to unclose to her view a deeper sweep on that side, and by this discovered a ship of far larger size than any which had yet dotted the main before her. Its sails were for the most part new and clean, and in comparison with its rapid progress before the wind the small brigs and ketches seemed standing still. Upon this striking object the old man's glass was bent.

'What do you see, sailor?' she asked.

'Almost nothing,' he answered. 'My sight is so gone off lately that things, one and all, be but a November mist to me. And yet I fain would see to-day. I am looking for the *VICTORY*.'

'Why?' she said quickly.

'I have a son aboard her. He's one of three from these parts. There's the captain, there's my son Jim, and there's young Loveday of Overcombe — he that lately joined.'

'Shall I look for you?' said Anne, after a pause.

'Certainly, miss'ess, if so be you please.'

Anne took the glass, and he supported it by his arm.

'It is a large ship,' she said, 'with three masts, three rows of guns along the side, and all her sails set.'

'I guessed as much.'

'There is a little flag in front — over her bowsprit.'

'The jack.'

'And there's a large one flying at her stern.'

'The ensign.'

'And a white one on her fore-topmast.'

'That's the admiral's flag, the flag of my Lord Nelson. What is her figurehead, my dear?'

'A coat of arms, supported on this side by a sailor.'

Her companion nodded with satisfaction. 'On the other side of that figurehead is a marine.'

'She is twisting round in a curious way, and her sails sink in like old cheeks, and she shivers like a leaf upon a tree.'

'She's in stays, for the larboard tack. I can see what she's been doing. She's been re'ching close in to avoid the flood tide, as the wind is to the sou'west, and she's bound down; but as soon as the ebb made, d'ye see, they made sail to the westward. Captain Hardy may be depended upon for that; he knows every current about here, being a native.'

'And now I can see the other side; it *is* a soldier where a sailor was before. You are *sure* it is the *VICTORY*?'

'I am sure.'

After this something seemed to twinkle, and Anne, who had previously withdrawn from the old sailor, went back to him, and looked again through the glass. The twinkling was the light falling upon the cabin windows of the ship's stern. She explained it to the old man.

'Then we see now what the enemy have seen but once. That was in seventy-nine, when she sighted the French and Spanish fleet off Scilly, and she retreated because she feared a landing. Well, 'tis a brave ship, and she carries brave men! . . .'

The courses of the *VICTORY* were absorbed into the main, then her topsails went, and then her top-gallants. She was now no more than a dead fly's wing on a sheet of spider's web; and even this fragment diminished. Anne could hardly bear to see the end, and yet she resolved not to flinch. The admiral's flag sank behind the watery line, and in a minute the very truck of the last topmast stole away. The *VICTORY* was gone.

Thomas Hardy, THE TRUMPET MAJOR

A shipwright's fingers are different. They are blunt and crooked, the nails are battered, and their muscular development gives them a clumsy appearance: they look infinitely less prehensile than the fingers of a clerk. But watch them when they are in action — when they operate, separately or conjointly, to effect the hundreds of tasks to which they may be set, with the precision of strength. When one looks at an animal one is prone to regard it from an anthropocentric point of view; you look at a snake, and pity it for having to creep on its belly, for you would be sorry to have to do so yourself. But when you see it pour itself over the ground you see at once that it is moving in its appropriate mode. It must enjoy moving in this manner, which for it is the most efficient manner. So it is with the shipwright's fingers. They look too heavy and big for neat and accurate work; but watch them at their job, and you will see them touch and probe and grasp and wrench, subtly and accurately and with the necessary strength as well, cunning as serpents.

W H Johnston, BUILDING A LITTLE SHIP (Allen & Unwin)

God by land and sea defend you,
Sailors all, who pass my grave;
Safe from wreck his mercy send you —
I am one he did not save.

Translated from the Greek by T F Higham

HOW TO INTRODUCE YOUR WIFE TO SAILING: ADVICE FROM THE 1940s

When we men take to a new interest like small boat cruising we want our wives, our girl friends, to come and enjoy it with us. That is natural enough. Man, a simple, kindly creature on the whole, wants his mate to share all his pleasures. And whatever happens even the pessimist must admit that most of us do at times derive great pleasure from possessing and messing about with boats; even dreadful little boats that are neither beautiful nor fast and that leak like baskets . . .

If you are an experienced sailing man and, having recently married, want to introduce your wife to all the joys, the triumphs and trials of small boat cruising which you enjoy so much, you should go as carefully as a fox stalking a duck. There may be more in the simile than you think.

Your inclination will naturally be to hustle the dear little woman aboard, tell her to stow her things as quickly as possible as you can't possibly waste this breeze and are getting underway at once, and then proceed to initiate her into the joy of a slashing breeze, a hard turn to wind'ard with the fine spray a-flying, and all the excitements which are just part of the game to you. And if the adorable creature doesn't appear to share your enthusiasm, and later confesses that she simply *loathes* boats and salt water and keen wet winds, you will probably share the disappointment of other unhappy yachtsmen with anti-yachting wives. And yet, my friend, you may well have been more than 50 per cent to blame . . .

Try to put yourself in her place. The little pal wants to come with you when you go sailing, and you want her to share this wonderful way of life at week-ends with you. But it is all very strange to her and rather unnerving the way the water looks — even the way *you* look now you've got your old slacks and jersey on and swear at having to drag the dinghy down the hard! — and the way the wind blows her hair about and makes her feel a sight. In the wobbly dinghy, then aboard the restless little yacht that you call 'the hooker,' it is all a bit upsetting, although she is putting on as brave a face as she can. She feels her world is very uncertain beneath her feet, and looks to you for moral support. She needs your consideration now more than ever.

Now is your cue. Do you take it? Do you show her over your ship painstakingly, avoiding technical jargon as much as possible, just letting her get the 'feel' of it all, the atmosphere, just getting herself *used* to the tinyness of this floating home? Do you make tea before talking of sailing — a nice tea with thin bread and butter and cake — so she will feel at peace with the world, and with you, and far, far less apprehensive, less 'strange'? If you don't you are asking for trouble, or at least a very great deal from this mate woman of yours.

It may be difficult, this business of introducing Her to it all gently. As a keen cruising man it may try your patience more than once when a grand sailing breeze or a fair tide goes to waste while you lie still alongside a towpath or at your moorings just letting Her find her feet. But if you do put yourself in Her place, and see your ship, even yourself as a tousled, bright-eyed creature, and look at the discomforts, the inconveniences, the imagined dangers of small boat life, through Her eyes, your patience will be rewarded. Let your ship lie a week-end or two in a calm spot such as on Oulton Broad or Heybridge Basin, in Birdham Lock or Torquay, or some other quiet, pleasantly situated mooring; just let your wife become used to the life aboard, to the movements of the dinghy, to the *proportions* of the new life that she has come to share with you. It will not be long before she is ready and keen to try it all outside where the sea wind blows and the white caps are hurrying. And it will have been worth it.

. . . AND HOW TO LIVE ABOARD

Do you mind if I make up my berth in my own way? If the night is cold it's a mistake, I find, to use the blankets folded; the chill comes in from underneath and down the sides. It is best if they are used singly and the spare part of the blankets is laid on the berth folded and the berth is made over that. The worst cold is that which strikes up from below and grips the small of your back through a thin mattress.

I have slept aboard a pretty large variety of small craft one way and another, in winter as well as summer over a period of some twenty-five years now, and have picked up a few ideas on comfort in little ships. One is that aboard quite small craft — like this little 5-tonner of yours — the most satisfactory bedding is a well-filled kapok sleeping-bag. You have plenty of warm material beneath you as well as over you, and if you have reasonably soft berth cushions and perhaps one blanket in addition it would have to be a frosty winter's night for you to wake up feeling cold.

The cabin lamps give their own warmth, don't they as well as the softest and most attractive light. I have never cared for electric lighting aboard very small craft, even when you have a separate generating set. There is always the recurrent need to charge the batteries and that means possibly the peace of a calm anchorage shattered for an hour or two by a popping engine. And if the dynamo is run off the ship's auxiliary engine you find you have to run the engine more than you need or want to simply to keep the batteries charged.

If you keep your oil lamps clean and regularly filled (an inkwell filler is a good thing to use because of its spout) they are very little trouble. There is nothing like their soft light. But it is a mistake to place them too low, for it tires the eyes. Where you have yours, as high up under the cabin top as you can get the lamp with a brass heat guard and a square of asbestos screwed to the underside of the deck just above it, is excellent.

Gimbals are very necessary for the cabin lamps of a sailing yacht, for you often need them when underway at night, and fixed lamps either won't burn when a vessel is heeling and pitching or they are dangerous and liable to catch fire.

I always feel a little reluctant to put out the light once I have turned in, for the cabin looks such a cheerful, cosy place, and it seems so snug and warm here, especially when you lie and listen to the wind in the rigging and the rain pelting on deck just over your head. But to-night it's peaceful, and there's only the ghost of a swell running in from the sea, making the little ship rise and fall gently as though she were breathing in her sleep. The wind is gentle too, coming across miles of marshland and meadows, scent-laden and soft with summer mellowness.

Those little sounds? Yes, they will go on all night. The gentle *frou frou,* as the French have it, is the dinghy astern on its painter, whispering to the ripples as they chase each other past; that sudden *plop* up for'd is an occasional wavelet hitting the round of our port bows, for the wind is rather across the river on our port side. That tapping? Ah, my owner friend, that sound has driven some yachtsmen crazy; others it has lulled to sleep. If the breeze dies, it dies too; but if the wind pipes up in the night your gentle tap, tap, will become a savage hammering, a positive death-rattle. And it may cause you to leave your warm bunk to brave the wind and the rain on deck to subdue the devilish clatter, only to find on returning, chilled and soaked, to your berth, a fresh tattoo will start beating about your head; and tins and jars and other round things will set to rolling and clinking and knocking in the lockers in jubilant applause. And you will groan and wish all this din would only stop for a while and let you sleep. In short, that tapping is nothing but one of the halyards swinging in the wind against the mast, and it means that you forgot to frap it to the shrouds with a piece of line. And the mysterious rattles and clinks and knocks and bumps? Your lockers are not stowed as they should be; things should not be left to roll or knock together aboard a small yacht — unless you are a fearsome heavy sleeper.

That old sea saying 'A place for everything, and everything in its place,' is an essential if life is to be worth living aboard a small boat. Everything just *has* to be put away in its place so that it won't shift and can be found the moment it is required. Nothing aboard a small cruising yacht should be left sculling around; there's no room for junk aboard a 5-tonner. And there's nothing better than a small boat to teach you orderliness and tidy habits, though to go aboard some fellows' boats it might not strike you that way.

So you are pleased with your little ship and very glad that you bought her? If you hadn't got her what would you be doing now?

Running down to the coast somewhere to stay the week-ends with friends perhaps? Imagine how crowded the roads must be and the criminally incompetent drivers that the war has produced, the traffic jams and the strain on your nerves. The roads are no place for peace of mind or even safety at week-ends, these days. It just couldn't be more peaceful and far removed from those seething crowds than here, aboard your own little ship, could it?

I've talked enough to-night, heaven knows, and it's time we doused the light and turned in. We've got to catch the ebb to-morrow morning.

Maurice Griffiths, POST-WAR YACHTING (Hutchinson 1945)

MAXIM

Six days shalt thou labour
And do all that thou art able;
The seventh, holystone the deck
and scrape the cable!

Traditional

PORT

Everyone — well *almost* everyone — knows the origin of the word starboard — a corruption of the term steerboard derived from the ancient seagoing practice of always hanging the steering oar from the right-hand quarter of a ship. (Always, did I say? Well nearly always. Some of the bigger Roman merchant ships carried a steering oar on both quarters.) But what about port? I was asked this the other day, and had the familiar experience of finding one more ragged hole in the garment of knowledge, useful and useless, with which I hide the innocence of my mind from the world.

One glossary of sea terms suggested that the origin was due to the loading port of seventeenth-century ships being on the lefthand side. This seemed an unsatisfactory explanation, and at its best only brought the derivation one remove closer; for why is a port in a ship's side called a port? Though the term 'port' was not officially adopted in place of larboard by the Admiralty until 1844, it had been in general use long before this. Falconer said in his dictionary of 1789 that the term 'larboard' should never be used when conning the helm owing to its liability to be mistaken for starboard. But as early as 1580 we find the left-hand side of a ship described as port, and it appeared that its origin might be found earlier than the sixteenth century. Even in antiquity.

And this, I think, is the case. The word comes, not surprisingly, from the Mediterranean and from the Latin word *portus,* or port. When approaching a harbour in a ship controlled by a steering oar, it was desirable to hold the land on the left side to ensure the quarter rudder's freedom. Equally, it was more comfortable to lie alongside with the steering oar clear of the quay, and hence to secure left side to. That this should be called the port side of the ship for passing out cargo should be called a cargo port equally so.

So we find that not only the term starboard but equally port have their origin in that most ancient feature of naval architecture, the steering oar, the first means of steering a ship, and in use at least five thousand years ago; perhaps before the pyramids had been raised or the Sphinx had begun its earnest, unblinking vigil over the desert. We speak history unconsciously, and in a single word may lie much of the story of man.

Douglas Phillips-Birt, REFLECTIONS IN THE SEA
(Nautical 1968)

That girl who fain would choose a mate
Should ne'er in fondness fail her
May thank her lucky stars if fate
Should splice her to a sailor.
Traditional

NIGHT IN THE RAYS'N

It is a strange fact that the moon — pleasant and companionable creature though she be — seldom makes night-sailing appreciably simpler, here among the shoals. If one desires to locate an unlighted buoy, for instance, it is practically as hopeless a task to find it by moonlight as in night unmitigated. No buoy was at the moment wanted but the shape and position of the land, if declared, would have helped. Clear though the moonlight became, the land remained invisible; it was lost in the long grey blur, indifferently the same along every horizon, save the one silvered slip of sea-line eastwards, directly under the moon.

'It's a nice little breeze,' I meditated appreciatively, as the living little flaw reached out from the greyness and fanned one's cheek, 'but its direction isn't kind. It simply is not. For a well-behaved little draught like this, it is just about as "contrairy" as a wind can be.'

Gentle though it was, the wind had been quite capable — so long as the tide had favoured and had given us gradual progress, by the beam. But the flood-tide was now running up between the shoals out of the dark sea into the Crouch, flooding through, lapping round the grey islanded shoals still uncovered, and streaming into the channels. The whole grey face of the water was moving against us. The same process would have been a perfectly attractive happening, could we have but weathered the long line of the Knoll Sand before the tide had turned southward again, for in that event it would have taken us with it up the Blackwater. As it was, the tide was busily trying to slide us back, with its insidious smooth current, back to Burnham and the Crouch.

'This ain't no good,' I added colloquially, but with settled conviction; 'we'll cut the tail of the Knoll and take the risk. The water's smooth and the tide rising. Those boards out towards the Swire Hole carry us into the full run of the tide. If the tide once really got us and took command, we shouldn't escape at all till the next ebb. We'd have to anchor.'

'I wish the North-West Knoll were still lighted,' he rejoined.

It would have been a minor blessing to-night, if need for economy had not recently occasioned its untimely dowsing. Instead of a flashing beacon of light, it was now a painted tub only, that rocked invisibly somewhere away in the darkness. Close-hauled, the yacht approached the hidden shoal-line through the grey moonlit sea. The lead had been splashing into the water, but was now hastily discarded in favour of the more primitive 'boat hook' method, and the long boat-hook was 'jabbed' downward at rapid intervals to test the depth.

'Less than a fathom, shoaling, shoaling, shoaling — no good — lee ho!'

She swung into the wind, catching the moonlight brightly on the other side of her white sails aloft as they shivered doubtfully a moment, and then filled confidently to their smooth rounded contour as she bore away on the new tack.

'A near one that,' one of us laughed. 'I felt the keel touch as she came about — not that it matters. One board further down and we'll sneak across, if the tide hasn't stopped us too much.'

The moonlight flickered, living silver, on the water; the breeze hummed for the moment alertly. It was a perfect night. About once more, the yacht was again putting the matter to the touch.

'Shoaling still, shoaling — but carry on, shoaling a little, yes, yes, all right, the same, the same, barely enough, the same, deeper, deeper, more than a fathom now.' She was over.

'Oh, the little more and how much it is,' sings the poet, and we echoed his wise word to-night, for we were now in the Blackwater tide. Sorrowfully, however, we realized that the tide had no great margin of life for our help; it had played the hindering game all too effectively. The hour was approaching two o'clock, and we decided to anchor off East Mersea and sleep while the ebb tide was running down.

'The glass is still falling. The wind backed to get into the north, and this dropping glass means it's backing further. West wind to-morrow.'

'Just so as to head us up the Blackwater,' he laughed.

H Alker Tripp, SHOAL WATER & FAIRWAY
(Conway Maritime Press)

A CHANNEL RHYME

Start Point and Beachy Head
Tell their tale of quick and dead.

Forelands both and Dungeness
See many a ship in dire distress.

The Lizard and the Longships know
Oft the end of friend and foe.

And many and many a seaman's knell
Has been rung by Manacles bell.

Gull and Dodman ask aright
A wide berth on a dirty night.

Bolt Head and Bolt Tail
Are ill spots in a Channel gale.

Over night to Portland Bill
In Channel fog it's just as ill.

And Wolf Rock and Seven Stones
Rest their feet on sailors' bones.

But from Nore Light to Cape Cornwall
Goodwin Sands are worst of all!

C Fox Smith

A WAVE

Somewhere a wave is born. It may be in the Southern Ocean, far down in the albatross latitudes where man has never been more than a brief visitor — usually now from the height of an aircraft — and great areas of sea have never been cut by a keel, or know only once in a few hundred years the passage of a single whaler. In those latitudes, between say 50 and 60 degrees south, the world is almost 100 per cent water, girdled by a wide ring of ocean where the greatest waves are born. It is these that travel farthest. In furious youth they may be 30ft high and rushing at 60 knots from the lonely wastes where they were formed, to expire some time later in small breakers at the feet of a child on Perranporth beach.
Douglas Phillips-Birt, REFLECTIONS IN THE SEA
(Nautical 1968)

THE WAY OF A SHIP IN THE MIDST OF THE SEA

When I saw her first there was a smoke of mist about her as high as her foreyard. Her topsails and flying kites had a glow upon them where the dawn caught them. Then the mist rolled away from her, so that we could see her hull and the glimmer of the red sidelight as it was hoisted inboard. She was rolling slightly, tracing an arc against the heavens, and as I

watched her the glow upon her deepened, till every sail she wore burned rosily like an opal turned to the sun, like a fiery jewel. She was radiant, she was of immortal beauty, that swaying delicate clipper. Coming as she came, out of the mist into the dawn, she was like a spirit, like an intellectual presence. Her hull glowed, her rails glowed; there was colour upon the boats and tackling. She was a lofty ship (with skysails and royal staysails), and it was wonderful to watch her, blushing in the sun, swaying and curveting. She was alive with a more than mortal life. One thought that she would speak in some strange language or break out into a music that would express the sea and that great flower in the sky. She came trembling down to us, rising up high and plunging; showing the red lead below her waterline; then diving down till the smother bubbled over her hawseholes. She bowed and curveted; the light caught the skylights on the poop; she gleamed and sparkled; she shook the sea from her as she rose. There was no man aboard of us but was filled with the beauty of that ship. I think they would have cheered her had she been a little nearer to us; but, as it was, we ran up our flags in answer to her, adding our position and comparing our chronometers, then dipping our ensigns and standing away. For some minutes I watched her, as I made up the flags before putting them back in their cupboard. The old mate limped up to me, and spat, and swore. 'That's one of the beautiful sights of the world,' he said. 'That, and a cornfield, and a woman with her child . . .'
John Masefield, A TARPAULIN MUSTER

THE GREAT DAYS OF OCEAN RACING

The majority of the yachts of the Royal Yacht Club in those days carried brass guns and an armoury of rifles and cutlasses. The cannon were used for the firing of salutes, but no doubt they also provided their owners with a feeling of security when sailing the high seas. As for the cutlasses, they came in handy to cut away rigging when two yachts of these keen sportsmen ran foul of each other in those desperately contested matches when several thousands guineas were at stake.

Some of these races literally were fought to a finish. One of the most exciting of the was that sailed by Mr. Assheton-Smith's *Menai,* Lord Belfast's *Louisa* and Mr. Weld's *Lulworth* in the summer of 1829. The three yachts had raced against each other before, and the rivalry spread to their crews, who, we are told, 'were not always under perfect control, and were apt to assert their feelings whenever opportunity, such as the fouling of two vessels, presented itself.'

Lord Belfast, with *Louisa,* had already defeated his rivals racing in the regatta at Southampton, and was determined to beat them again in the race for the King's Cup at Cowes, during the following August. In this match the three started in a light breeze and sailed down the Solent in close company to the Nab. But, returning to the westward, *Menai* ran aground so that the race resolved itself into a match between *Lulworth* and

Louisa. They sailed back through the Solent neck-and-neck, and were only separated by a few seconds as they rounded the mark boat off Yarmouth. As they neared Cowes, the two yachts came into collision. *Lulworth,* on the port tack, was about to cross the finishing line, when she ran into *Louisa,* which was on the starboard tack. *Louisa's* crew drew their cutlasses and knives and cut away 'the earing of Lulworth's boom as well as her reef pendant . . . leaving her disabled.' As the race had been sailed in the lightest of winds, the collision took place late at night, just as the roads were ablaze with light from the fireworks let off in honour of the King's birthday. In the midst of this display and while the yachts anchored in the roads were firing their cannons, the crews of *Louisa* and *Lulworth* were fighting like wild-cats and slashing at each other's rigging with their cutlasses that flashed and glinted in the light of the fireworks.

Eventually, both their owners came ashore violently angry not only about the collision, but also because they had missed the dinner at the yacht club. Mr. Weld lodged a protest against Lord Belfast with the stewards of the club. The latter gave their decision in Lord Belfast's favour but stated that they were 'of the opinion that the use of axes in the cutting away of rigging was unjustifiable.' Lord Belfast later announced in the club room that in the event of any vessel on the larboard (port) tack attempting to cross him when on the starboard tack, he would cut that vessel in two. To which threat both Mr. Weld and Mr. Assheton-Smith replied by saying that they would never race against his Lordship again.
Anthony Heckstall-Smith, SACRED COWES
(Allen Wingate 1955)

It was so old a ship — who knows, who knows?
And yet so beautiful, I watched in vain
To see the mast burst open with a rose
And the whole deck put on its leaves again.
James Elroy Flecker, THE OLD SHIP

It is as hard to describe the fascination of the sea as to explain the beauty of a woman, for, to each man, either it is self-evident, or no argument can help him to see it. Men love the sea in various ways and in different degrees. To one, perhaps the largeness and boundless freedom of blue water may appeal so strongly the he grudges every day spent in even the most beautiful anchorage unless he has made a long sea passage to reach it; another delights most in intricate pilotage; while a third enjoys the handling of gear and sailing for its own sake, irrespective of his surroundings. To each the boat is his idol — the concrete expression of his love and faith.

I never make even the most familiar landfall after days at sea without feeling that I know why men flocked to the Crusades, why volunteers filled the tiny ships to conquer and explore the New World, why men strive to reach the Poles or to penetrate the deserts of Tibet. Hope of gain or glory, duty, patriotism, have each had a share, but the sense of romance and adventure and the joy of personal achievement have been the main incentives to nearly all noble enterprises.

We who adventure upon the sea, however humbly, cannot but feel that we are more fortunate than ordinary people, and that we have something which we could not tell nor they understand. A love of the sea with some seems almost innate, to others it may come late in life; but no man who has loved the sea can forsake her, ever. It is true that there are some who 'take up yachting' just as they might golf or motoring, and give it up as lightly; but they have never been of the brotherhood of the sea. The initiation is often difficult. A young man, perhaps, may have no friend to advise him, or he may lack the time or the means. An older man, instead of starting at the beginning, may buy a large vessel before he has learnt enough to take some share in the handling and navigation; and no mere passenger can ever know romance.

Claude Worth, YACHT CRUISING
(J D Potter)

JOHN STEERS THE *GOBLIN* THROUGH THE NIGHT

Gosh! Those had been an awful few minutes. Poor old Susan! And then that reefing . . . Jolly lucky he had tied that life-line around himself when he went forrard. And everything had gone all right so far . . . The *Goblin* was still afloat . . She wasn't leaking . . . Nothing had carried away, as it so easily might . . . He just would not think of what they would have to do next. Enough for now to keep her sailing safely along with her sleeping crew.

Her sleeping crew . . . Just for a second after leaning on the tiller he let it go and took a hurried peep over those closed doors and down into the lighted cabin. He could just see Roger's feet rolled in blanket, and a lump of red-tanned sail that Susan had used to stop him from sliding about in his bunk. Titty was out of sight in the fore-cabin. And here was poor old Susan asleep in her corner of the cockpit. All three of them were asleep. He was back at the tiller, leaning on it again. He took another look at the compass card under that dim yellow glow, wedged himself against the cockpit coaming with a foot against the opposite seat, looked up at the part of the sky that was full of stars, and a little ashamedly admitted to himself that he was happy.

He had done his very best. And anyhow, here, at night, far out in the North Sea, what could he do other than what he was doing? If anybody could have seen his face in the faint glimmer from the compass window, he would have seen that there was a grin on it. John was alone in the dark with his ship, and everybody else was asleep. He, for that night, was the Master of the *Goblin,* and even the lurches of the cockpit beneath him as the *Goblin* rushed through the dark filled him with a serious kind of joy. He and the *Goblin* together. On and on. On and on. Years and years hence, when he was grown, up, he would have a ship of his own and sail her out into wider seas than this. But he would always and always remember this night when for the first time ship and crew were in his charge, his alone.

So . . . and back . . . and back . . . lean and sway with this triumphant motion. Good little ship. Good little ship. He put a hand over the edge of the coaming and patted the damp deck in the darkness.

Arthur Ransome, WE DIDN'T MEAN TO GO TO SEA (Jonathan Cape)

BLUE WATER

THE ONE-HUNDREDTH-AND-SEVENTH PSALM

They that go down to the sea in ships, that do business in great waters;
These see the works of the Lord, and his wonders in the deep.
For he commandeth, and raiseth the stormy wind, which lifteth up the waves thereof,
They mount up to the heaven, they go down again to the depths: their soul is melted because of trouble.
They reel to and fro, and stagger like a drunken man, and are at their wit's end.
Then they cry unto the Lord in their trouble, and he bringeth them out of their distresses.
He maketh the storm a calm, so that the waves thereof are still.
Then are they glad because they be quiet; so he bringeth them unto their desired haven.

MISCHIEF GOES SOUTH

It is astonishing how quickly a southward bound yacht, even though it is not a flyer, reaches the warmer weather for which the crew long. Sweaters and shirts are shed, shorts and bathing bags appear, and the sun-starved northerner's passion for getting his body well tanned by the sun is given full rein. But perfect comfort must not be expected by folks who go a-pleasuring. After a few more degrees of southing the sun-worshippers are wearing dark glasses, rigging awnings over the cockpit, and taking refuge in the shade of the cabin where they do nothing but complain of the heat.

When we had outrun the Portuguese trades a westerly wind carried us along until in about lat 35° we were caught up in the strong embrace of the true north-east trades. With a wind which never fell below force 4 (about 16 knots) and more often reached force 5 or 6 sailing was exhilarating. We lowered the mainsail and stowed the boom, hoisted the twin staysails and let her go. The sky overhead with little fleecy clouds sailing across was a pale reflection of the sparkling blue sea flecked with foam and dancing spray. Rolling became continuous and sometimes heavy as the pursuing waves surged by, lifting the counter with a friendly shove forwards and slightly sideways, before hissing past the rail and depositing a dollop of water on deck by way of salute. Steering was easy,

for there was no fear of a gybe. Sheets had scarcely to be touched, and perhaps best of all with this rig the gear subject to chafe was reduced to a minimum. *Mischief* seemed to enjoy sailing before a wind that blew true and steady as the wind of a bellows, as much as did her crew. She frequently showed her pleasure by some very lively rolling. This rhythmic rolling, inseparable from down-wind sailing, becomes a nuisance, particularly at meal times, when a man needs two pairs of hands, or when any work has to be done on deck. Every few minutes the ship would glide gently into what would become a crescendo of rolling, each successive roll becoming livelier and longer until the dislodging of the helmsman from his seat or a loud crash from the galley, announced that she had had her bit of fun. Then she would sail demurely along until tempted by the laughing waves to do it again. One could almost hear her humming to herself:

Roll me over, in the clover,
Roll me over, lay me down, and do it again.

H W Tilman, ADVENTURES UNDER SAIL
(Gollancz)

He it is who hath appointed for you the stars, that ye guide yourselves thereby in the darknesses of land and sea; he hath made the signs distinct for a people which hath knowledge.
KORAN

A YACHT DISMASTED

I lay and listened to the slight change in the boat that follows a new hand on the helm. How long ought we to continue on this tack? Should we make a long leg of it and then one across to the outer Gabbard lightship and one up to Smith's Knoll? Or should we take short tacks, back and forth up the direct line between the West Hinder and Smith's Knoll? I thought three long tacks. It would be easier on navigation. I was beginning to worry about that. It's hard to concentrate on figures when the world is standing on its head, and I'm not fond of figures. Some of these liner boys would be horrified if they had to navigate the way we have to — wet and cold on a chart that's never still.

And then I was listening to the slams as she hit the seas. For a time they had been much less, as though the wind had lessened. But I knew the easing of the motion had been due to the fact that we had cleared the Hinder bank and the seas had become more regular. But now the tide had turned. It was running North. Wind against tide — the seas were getting steeper, breaking more often. I clambered out of my bunk, pushed open the hatch doors. Bob was at the helm. I can see him now — a tall, military-looking figure in yellow oilskins, his glasses misted with spray, his head bare and his neck muffled in a towel. 'Is she getting heavy on the helm?'

'Carrying a bit of weather helm, but nothing excessive. She's going very well.'

'You don't think she'd sail better if we changed to Number Two jib?'

'No, she's all right at the moment. Might be worth considering later if the wind gets up any more. But not to worry now.'

I went back to my bunk, lying there and feeling with every nerve the movement of the boat, trying to make up my mind whether to order the change. I wasn't thinking of the boat being too heavily pressed by the weight of canvas or that she was in danger. That never occurred to me. And the way we were going I was quite prepared to blow out the genoa if it would win us the race. No, all I was thinking about was whether she would go faster under the Number Two. It is a fact that in heavyish weather boats often lose time by hanging on to big canvas too long. *Mary Deare* I knew from experience slowed up as soon as the lee rail was under and the deck awash. I had proved this time and again, and the signal was invariably a heaviness on the helm.

About a quarter of an hour later my nerves came suddenly alert to the heavy slam of a wave and what I thought was an ugly additional sound. Did I imagine this, or was it premonition? I don't know. All I can remember is that I was wide awake and every nerve tense to the movement of the boat. I began to want very much to order the change down. I tried to balance my knowledge of the feel of the boat against Bob's experience. He was at the helm and I was well aware that what sounds like heavy weather down below is often an exhilarating sail for those in the cockpit. And so I hung between sleeping and waking again, listening, waiting — discouraged as much as anything by the effort it was going to cost to struggle into my oilskins and go for'ard into the wet and the wind to change the sail. I was only just recovering from a bout of 'flu.

Slam! And another sound. A sound like a sharp crack, merged with the slam. And then a sudden quietness. No rushing of water, no surging roar of speed, and the boat rolling.

The hatch banged open. 'That's your mast gone.' It was David's voice — quiet, but very clear and pitched a shade high.
Hammond Innes, SEA AND ISLANDS
(Collins 1967)

One Ship sails East, one ship sails West
By the self-same wind that blows.
But it isn't the gales but the set of the sails
Which determine the way she goes.
Anonymous

PURSUITS IN CALM

And the Winds having fallen from us so that the Sayles did naught but hang without Life so that the Tackles swayed with the sway of our Shippe and the cordage set up a Moaning and a Crekeing that was over piteous: and in the Sky was not so much as even One Cloud nor yet a small Cloud and there was only the Sun which was sette there that Man should ever be beneath him. And those of Our Companie who were of the Sea they knew that it was of Small Avail to bewail and to cry and shout for the Winds for these are of Mighty God and His giving and do come to all men not of their asking but of His Gift. Then were we wont to sit about ourselves in the Great Cabin in two or in four or in many of us and make discourse of Seas and of Divers Places and of Mountains and Strange Beastes and of the Good and the Evil of the case. Great store set we all by such Discourse in that when the Chance of the Day seemed ill with us yet were we in great part Content.
John Cartwright (1527) *A VOYAGE TO THE SOUTH INDIES*

Calms pass, like everything else at sea . . . the breeze when it does come in can be of unparallelled sweetness.
Michael Richey, ROVING COMMISSIONS (RCC 1980)

THE BRETON FISHERMAN'S PRAYER

Dear God! My boat is so very small — and thy sea so very wide. Have mercy!

THE SINGLEHANDERS SPEAK

Living in total isolation from the human community requires its own techniques. The dangers are lethargy, boredom and depression. It would be easy to pretend that the experience was at all times enjoyable and rewarding, that one never felt pangs of loneliness or acute boredom, or dejection. But that was not the case . . . The greatest single trial, because of the frustration, was the prolonged periods of calm, when the days seemed to telescope into a long meaningless twilight punctuated by periods of rest. One was grateful to turn in, feeling that surely there must be a breath when one awoke. Each day would start with the same heavy feeling, the same silence. A more balanced man would perhaps, knowing there was nothing he could do, stay below with a good book. I found reading impossible in these circumstances. In these times one saw oneself under a microscope, now always with pleasure.

There were of course moments of intense beauty and of wonderment. One of the rewards for solitude is the extent to which one becomes involved in the environment. This awareness seems blunted in company. The sea becomes not just the medium of travel, but the habitat. In a small sailing boat, too, silent and so close to the water, one sees things no steamship man would get near.
Michael Richey, JOURNAL OF THE INSTITUTE OF NAVIGATION (1969)

I have no fear of being alone at sea. Being at sea means being on a sailing boat, and once aboard a sailing boat I am at home . . . The race itself was no ordeal for me. It corresponded to the kind of life I most want to lead. And I really believe that I was capable, both physically and morally, of sailing on for many more days after reaching Newport.
Eric Tabarly

It is getting dark, and she is bounding along on a broad reach throwing up cascades of water on either bow as she dips into the backs of the waves every few moments. I have turned the hood so that its open side faces forward, and I stand after a hot supper with a full belly and a glass of wine in my hand, revelling in the way she goes. This is what I came for.
Lt Col 'Blondie' Hasler

In these conditions life on *Griffin* is wonderful. She is efficient, she is no automaton. It takes understanding, calmness and a sense of humour to guide her. In other words, together, in this race, *Griffin* and I create a world that is all I could wish for in life. The sadness I feel, and the emptiness, is that I cannot find such a direction ashore.
David Blagden, VERY WILLING GRIFFIN
(Heinemann/Peter Davies)

Whenever life seems to be in danger of getting on top on me, I have a way out. I go to sea. All I need to do is get in a boat and sail, and within hours, the whole land-based load will have left me. The sea has never yet let me down. For this reason, I suppose, I have never been frightened by it. I have been wet and cold and miserable and often seasick. I have longed for a storm to go away or a leak to stop dripping or for a particularly arduous voyage to end. But white-faced fear or panic — never.
David Palmer, THE ATLANTIC CHALLENGE (The Bodley Head)

THE PILOT OF THE *PINTA*

I gave her the double-reefed mainsail and whole jib instead, and set her on her course. Then I went below and threw myself upon the cabin floor in great pain. How long I lay there I could not tell, for I became delirious. When I came to, as I thought, from my swoon, I realized that the sloop was plunging into a heavy sea, and looking out of the companionway, to my amazement I saw a tall man at the helm. His rigid hand, grasping the spokes of the wheel, held them as in a vice. One may imagine my astonishment. His rig was that of a foreign sailor, and the large red cap he wore was cockbilled over his left ear, and all was set off with shaggy black whiskers. He would have been taken for a pirate in any part of the world. While I gazed upon his threatening aspect I forgot the storm, and wondered if he had come to cut my throat. This he seemed to divine. 'Senor,' said he, doffing his cap, 'I have come to do you no harm.' And a smile, the faintest in the world, but still a smile, played on his face, which seemed not unkind when he spoke. 'I have come to do you no harm. I have sailed free,' he said, 'but was never worse than a *contrabandista*. I am one of Columbus's crew,' he continued. 'I am the pilot of the *Pinta* come to aid you. Lie quiet, senor captain,' he added, 'and I will guide your ship to-night. You have a *calentura*, but you will be all right to-morrow.' I thought what a very devil he was to carry sail. Again, as he read my mind, he exclaimed: 'Yonder is the *Pinta* ahead: we must overtake her. Give her sail; give her sail! *Vele, Vele, muy vele!'* Biting off a large quid of black twist, he said: 'You did wrong, captain, to mix cheese with plums. White cheese is never safe unless you know whence it comes. *Quien sabe,* it may have been from *leche de Capra* and becoming capricious — '

'Avast, there!' I cried. 'I have no mind for moralizing.'

Captain Joshua Slocum, SAILING ALONE ROUND THE WORLD

I like my dog, I like my horses and I like the girls but I don't like everybody. I like being at sea and when I am I don't want to see the bloody land at all. The only thing I cannot understand about this race is why they are all in such a god-damned hurry to get to the other end.

Lt Col Jack Odling-Smee, Commodore of the Royal Western YC on the Single-handed Transatlantic Race

. . . So this was the great adventure, I thought disconsolately. Gales that went on for ever, wet long johns, soggy food that was impossible to cook, damp books that fell apart in your hands and, worst of all, no one to complain to.

Clare Francis, COME HELL OR HIGH WATER (Pelham Books)

SIR PATRICK SPENS SENT TO SEA BY THE KING

'Mak ready, Mak ready, my merry men a'!
Our gude ship sails the morn' —
'Now ever alack, my master dear,
I fear a deadly storm.

'I saw the new moon late yestreen
Wi' the auld moon in her arm;
And if we gang to sea, master,
I fear we'll come to harm'

They hadna sailed a league, a league,
A league but barely three,
When the lift grew dark, and the wind blew loud,
And gurly grew the sea.

The ankers brak, and the topmast lap,
It was sic a deadly storm;
And the waves cam owre the broken ship
Till a' her sides were torn.

from THE BALLAD OF SIR PATRICK SPENS, (Anon)

There be three things which are too wonderful for me, yea, four which I know not: the way of an eagle in the air; the way of a serpent upon a rock; the way of a ship in the midst of the sea; and the way of a man with a maid.
PROVERBS, XXX

At night came a hurricane, the sea was mountains rolling,
As Barney Buntline slued his quid and spake to Billy Bowline:
'A strong nor'wester's blowing, Bill: Hark, can't ye hear it roar now?'
Lor' love me, how I pities them unhappy folks ashore now,
As comfortably you and I upon the deck are lying,
Lord knows what tiles and chimney pots about their ears are flying'.
Dibdin

LOSS

Few sailors can behold the ship in which they have sailed sinking before their eyes without the same emotion of distress and pity almost which the spectacle of a drowning man excites in them. She has grown a familiar name, a familiar object; thus far she has borne them in safety; she has been rudely beaten, and yet has done her duty; but the tempest has broken her down at last; all the beauty is shorn from her; she is weary with the long and dreadful struggle with the vast forces that Nature arrayed against her; she sinks, a desolate, abandoned thing in mid-ocean, carrying with her a thousand memories, which surge up in the heart with the pain of a strong man's tears.
William Clark Russell, THE WRECK OF THE GROSVENOR

TYPHOON

The motion of the ship was extravagant. Her lurches had an appalling helplessness: she pitched as if taking a header into the void, and seemed to find a wall to hit every time. When she rolled, she fell on her side headlong, and she would be righted by such a demolishing blow that Jukes felt her reeling as a clubbed man reels before he collapses.

A dull conviction seized upon Jukes that there was nothing to be done. If the steering gear did not give way, if the immense volumes of water did not bust the deck in or smash one of the hatches, if the engines did not give up, if way could be kept on the ship against this terrific wind, and she did not bury herself in one of these awful seas, of whose white crests alone, topping high above the bows, he could now and then get a sickening glimpse — then there was a chance of her coming out of it.

The seas in the dark seemed to rush from all sides to keep her back where she might perish. There was hate in the way she was handled, and a ferocity in the blows that fell. She was like a living creature thrown to the rage of a mob: hustled terribly, struck at, borne up, flung down, leaped upon. Captain MacWhirr and Jukes kept hold of each other, deafened by the noise, gagged by the wind; and the great physical tumult beating about their bodies, brought, like an unbridled display of passion, a profound trouble to their souls. One of these wild and appalling shrieks that are heard at times passing mysteriously overhead in the steady roar of a hurricane, swooped, as if borne on wings, upon the ship, and Jukes tried to outscream it.

'Will she live through this?'

The cry was wrenched out of his breast. It was as unintentional as the birth of a thought in the head, and he heard nothing of it himself. It all became extinct at once — thought, volition, effort — and of his cry the inaudible vibration added to the tempest waves of the air. He expected nothing from it. Nothing at all. For indeed what answer could be made? But after a while he heard with amazement the frail and resisting voice in his ear, the dwarf sound, unconquered in the giant tumult. 'She may!'

Joseph Conrad, TYPHOON

THE MUTINY OF THE *BOUNTY*, IN THE SOUTH SEAS

TUESDAY, the 28th April 1789, just before sunrising, while I was yet asleep, Mr. Christian, with the master-at-arms, gunner's mate, and Thomas Burkett, seaman, came into my cabin, and seizing me, tied my hands with a cord behind my back, threatening me with instant death if I spoke or made the least noise: I, however, called as loud as I could, in hopes of assistance; but they had already secured the officers who were not of their party, by placing centinels at their doors. There were only three men at my cabin door beside the four within; Christian had only a cutlass in his hand, the others had muskets and bayonets. I was hauled out of bed and forced on deck in my shirt, suffering great pain from the tightness with which they had tied my hands. I demanded the reason of such violence, but received no answer, than abuse for not holding my tongue. The master, the gunner, the surgeon, Mr. Elphinstone, master's mate, and Nelson were kept confined below; and the fore hatchway was guarded by centinels. The boatswain and carpenter, and also the clerk, Mr. Samuel, were allowed to come upon deck, where they saw me standing abaft the mizen-mast, with my hands tied behind my back, under a guard, with Christian at their head. The boatswain was ordered to hoist the launch out, with a threat, if he did not do it instantly, to take care of himself.

The master, by this time, had sent to request that he might come on deck, which was permitted; but he was soon ordered back again to his cabin.

I continued my endeavours to turn the tide of affairs, when Christian changed the cutlass which he had in his hand for a bayonet that was brought to him, and holding me with a strong grip by the cord that tied my hands, he with many oaths threatened to kill me immediately if I would not be quiet: the villains round me had their pieces cocked and bayonets fixed. Particular people were called on to go into the boat and were hurried to the side; whence I concluded that with these people I was to be set adrift: I therefore made another effort to bring about a change, but with no other effect than to be threatened with having my brains blown out.

The boatswain and seaman, who were to go in the boat, were allowed to collect twine, canvas, lines, sails, cordage, an eight and twenty gallon cask of water, and Mr. Samuel got 150 lbs. of bread, with a small quantity of rum and wine, also a quadrant and compass; but he was forbidden on pain of death to touch either map, ephemeris, book of astronomical observations, sextant, time-keeper, or any of my surveys or drawings.

The officers were next called upon deck, and forced over the side into the boat, while I was kept apart from everyone, abaft the mizen-mast; Christian, armed with a bayonet, holding me by the bandage that secured my hands.

Much altercation took place among the mutinous crew during the whole business: some swore 'I'll be damned if he does not find his way home, if he gets anything with him'; and when the carpenter's chest was carryed away, 'Damn my eyes, he will have a vessel built in a month.' While others laughed at the helpless situation of the boat, being very deep, and so little room for those who were in her. As for Christian, he seemed as if meditating destruction on himself and everyone else.

Capt William Bligh, 1789

COME CHEER UP MY LADS

Come cheer up my lads, 'tis to glory we steer,
To add something new to this wonderful year;
To honour we call you, not press you like slaves,
For who are so free as the sons of the waves?

Heart of Oak are our ships, Heart of Oak are our men,
We always are ready,
Steady, boys, steady,
We'll fight and we'll conquer again and again.

We ne'er meet our foes but we wish them to stay,
They never see us but they wish us away;
If they run, why, we follow, and run them ashore,

For if they won't fight us, we cannot do more.
Heart of Oak, etc.
David Garrick

GOD AND THE SAILOR WE ALIKE ADORE

God and the Sailor we alike adore
But only when in danger, not before:
The danger o'er, both are alike requited,
God is forgotten and the sailor slighted.
John Owen

DRAKE'S DRUM

Drake he's in his hammock an' a thousand mile away,
(Capten, art tha sleepin' there below?),
Slung atween the round shot in Nombre Dios Bay,
An' dreamin' arl the time o' Plymouth Hoe.
Yarnder lumes the Island, yarnder lie the ships,
Wi' sailor lads a dancin' heel-an'-toe,
An' the shore-lights flashing', an' the night-tide dashin',
He sees et arl so plainly as he saw et long ago.

Drake he was a Devon man, an' ruled the Devon seas,
(Capten, art tha sleepin' there below?)
Rovin' tho' his death fell, he went wi' heart at ease,
An' dreamin' arl the time o' Plymouth Hoe.
'Take my drum to England, hang et by the shore,
Strike et when your powder's runnin' low;
If the Dons sight Devon, I'll quit the port o' Heaven,
An' drum them up the Channel as we drummed them long ago.'

Drake he's in his hammock till the great Armadas come,
(Capten, art tha sleepin' there below?),
Slung atween the round shot, listenin' for the drum,
An' dreamin' arl the time o' Plymouth Hoe.
Call him on the deep sea, call him up the Sound,
Call him when ye sail to meet the foe;
Where the old trade's plyin' an' the old flag flyin'
They shall find him ware an' wakin', as they found him long ago!
Sir Henry Newbolt

Rest after toil, port after stormie seas;
Death after life; these things doe greatly please.

THE LEADSMAN'S SONG

For England, when with favouring gale,
Our gallant ship up Channel steered
And scudding, under easy sail,
The high blue western lands appeared.
To heave the lead the seaman sprang,
And to the pilot cheerly sang,
'By the deep — Nine,'

And bearing up to gain the port
Some well-known object kept in view,
An abbey tower, a ruined fort,
A beacon to the vessel true.
While oft the lead the seaman flung,
And to the pilot cheerly sung,
'By the mark — Seven.'

And at the much-loved shore we near,
With transport we behold the roof
Where dwelt a friend or partner dear,
Of faith and love and matchless proof.
The lead once more the seaman flung
And to the watchful pilot sung
'Quarter less — Five.'

Now to her berth the ship draws nigh,
With slackened sails she feels the tide,
Stand clear the cable is the cry,
The anchor's gone, we safely ride.
The watch is set and through the night,
We hear the seaman with delight
Proclaim — 'All's Well.'
Traditional

THE NAVY PRAYER

O Eternal Lord God, Who alone spreadest out the heavens, and rulest the raging of the sea; Who hast compassed the waters with bounds until day and night come to an end; Be pleased to receive into Thy Almighty and most gracious protection the persons of us Thy servants, and the Fleet in which we serve. Preserve us from the dangers of the sea, and from the violence of the enemy, that we may be a safeguard unto our most gracious sovereign Lord King George and his Dominions, and a security for such as pass on the seas upon their lawfull occasions; that the inhabitants of our Island may in peace and quietness serve Thee our God, and that we may return in safety to enjoy the blessings of the land with the fruits of our labours; and

with a thankfull remembrance of Thy mercies to praise and glorifie Thy holy Name.
Attributed to
Bishop Sanderson,
circa 1650

RULE, BRITANNIA

When Britain first, at Heaven's command,
Arose from out the azure main,
This was the charter of her land,
And guardian angels sung this strain:
'Rule, Britannia, rule the waves;
Britons never will be slaves.'

The nations, not so blest as thee
Must, in their turns, to tyrants fall;

While thou shalt flourish great and free,
The dread and envy of them all.
'Rule', etc.

Still more majestic shalt thou rise,
More dreadful from each foreign stroke;
As the loud blast that tears the skies
Serves but to root thy native oak.
'Rule', etc.

Thee haughty tyrants ne'er shall tame;
All their attempts to bend thee down
Will but arouse thy generous flame,
But work their woe, and thy renown.
'Rule', etc.

To thee belongs the rural reign;
Thy cities shall with commerce shine;
All thine shall be the subject main;
And every shore it circles, thine.
'Rule', etc.

The Muses, still with freedom found,
Shall to thy happy coast repair:
Blest isle! with matchless beauty crowned,
And manly hearts to guard the fair:
'Rule, Britannia, rule the waves,
Britons never will be slaves.'
James Thomson

Ships that pass 4

The unsung tugboat

'Do it *properly*'
Tugmaster Roy Horace Short, MBE

A tug is always the bridesmaid. The great ship steams on towards the deep water, the open sea and the far harbours; the tug turns aside, back to the berth or the next brief job. You don't hear a lot about tugs, except as walk-on actors in coastal dramas; even then, the glamour falls brighter on the lifeboats which save people than on the tugs which only save ships.

Tugs, though, have their own appeal. Any small child can see it: the compact, chugging shape, with the high bridge and low flat afterdeck, the great towing-hooks, and the snub rubbing-band lined all around with solid fendering, speak of concentrated power: to tow, or shove, or shoulder greater ships aside. It is a muscular shape. 'Like a clenched fist', I suggested to Captain Short of the *Calshot,* as we walked past the row of tugs in the Empress Dock. 'Like a tuna fish?' he suggested, then more firmly, 'No. Like a shire horse. A Suffolk Punch'.

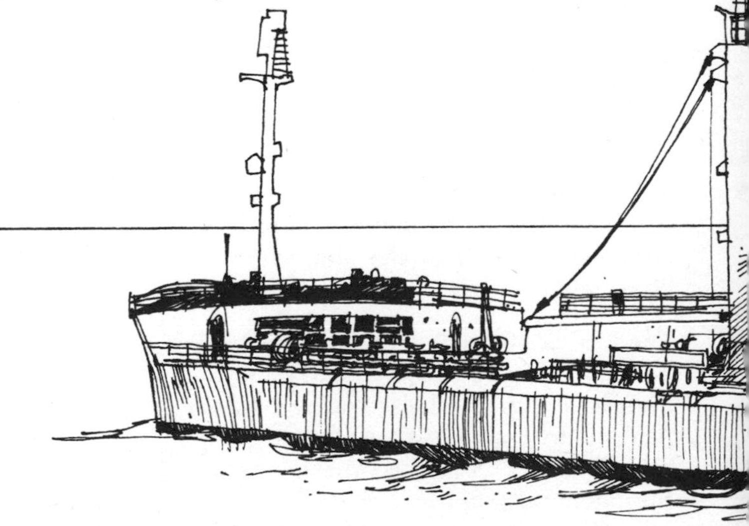

Calshot belongs to the Red Funnel Group. The towage business of Southampton is divided between them and the Alexandra Towing Company. Alexandra are bigger, nationally; 'but we' say Red Funnel 'are the home team'. They have run Cowes ferries since 1861, tugs since 1885. The record book for 1912 is still on the office shelf, and for 10 April it reads:

'TITANIC out of No, 44 New Dock — £25.4s.Od'. Her tugs were *Neptune, Hector, Hercules, Ajax, Vulcan,* and *Albert Edward.*

That first and last undocking of *SS Titanic* was only one job in a busy day: the *Prinz Eitel Friedrich* was tendering-off passengers outside the harbour, the *Tagus* sailed, the *Orsonia* docked. For the towing trade, those were palmy days — ships growing larger, with none of the efficient bow-thrust propellers that today enable huge ferries to dock and sail alone; air transport unthought-of on any scale. Even in 1964, when *Calshot* was built, it was considered worthwhile to make her 'a tug-tender', designed to ferry in passengers from big liners at anchor in Cowes Roads. In the age of the airport bus, her two stately saloons get little use: when the *Oriana* was kept out of Southampton docks by a strike, Red Funnel felt a certain nostalgia, as well as financial, satisfaction in sending *Calshot* out to tender the passengers ashore.

Even without such breaks, her place in the fleet is assured by her power — 1800hp in two Crossley engines — and her ability to go offshore. When the emergency calls come ('generally out of the blue on a Friday night') the Towage Manager Tony Coslett-Derby can send her out to salvage, to oil-spills and strandings, as readily as her 1980 sister *Clausentum*. The two roles blend with unexpected elegance: on the stylish art nouveau engraved mirror by the main saloon stair, is the later adornment of a plaque 'to commemorate the successful salving of SS *Christos Bitas*, Irish Sea, October 1978'. *Calshot* is, as Derby puts it, 'a tug with glamour'.

Tugmen are a hybrid. They belong, not to the National Union of Seamen, but to the Transport & General, or AUEW for engineers. Until the last few years, even the master of a tug needed no paper qualifications at all. 'They start as boys and work up', says Derby. 'A narrow world'. The mate or master will have grown up in the trade, learning from experience what strains his boat can take, how to spare the wires from the deadly snatching as a great ship rolls, when to take the drastic decision to trip the wire and get out. A tug can be pulled right over. In this narrow, skilful, unappreciated world men live in the trade and sometimes choose to return to it in death. Three times recently, Derby has been asked to take out the ashes of a late tug seaman and, with a Seaman's Mission chaplain, consign them reverently to the Solent. He pushed across a photograph: ashes being scattered over the snub black fendering. 'One of our masters'.

Calshot lay waiting by the old banana berth in the Empress Dock. Waiting is a great occupation of the modern tug; it seemed ironic that the Townsend ferry should slip by, neat and tugless with her modern propeller system, while beyond the dock wall *Calshot* and *Clausentum, Culver* and *Chale,* stood by patiently, their crews catching up on the painting and scrubbing between rain-showers. *Calshot's* boy mended a broom; the seamen scrubbed down the red funnel. A bitter wind fluttered their oilskins and hair, and ruffled the ragwort between the flags of the quiet dock.

In his cabin Captain Short pulled out his certificate: Roy Horace Short, MBE. Anticipating the new regulations, he took the tug-master's course at Warsash. It did not, he indicated with a greying eyebrow, teach him anything new. At ten, he was fishing with his father off Lowestoft; in the war, serving in the Navy; in 1946, coxswain of a fire-boat; seven years later, Able Seaman on his first tug. And in that world he chose to stay; when he retires it will be with 30 years' Red Funnel service behind him.

And with a medal. In the small cabin, one ear to the radio and one indulgent eye on his engineers, who were trying to mend the kettle, he told me how he came to win the MBE, on a winter night 12 years ago.

It was 29 October, 1979: south of the Isle of Wight, the tanker *Pacific Glory* and the *Allegro* collided. Short was on *Culver,* the first standby. At

2300, he switched off his bunk-light; seconds later, the radio called 'Ship on fire, under way right away'.

A nasty sight met the tug south of St Catherine's Point. *Pacific Glory* had ruptured her fuel pipes in the collision 'must have. A hell of an explosion, people killed, the whole bridge gone'. It was a mass of flames. Culver's job was not rescue — there was nobody left aboard — but it may be even harder to risk your life when there is no human life to save. 'Well I was concerned for the oil, and the pollution'. He had no firemen aboard, but *Culver* is a fire-fighting tug, and Roy Short had been coxswain of a fire-boat 30 years before. 'I took the *Culver* round the bow, and my heart did stop. There was a gushing hole, the oil was burning, you could see into the tanks . . . smoke and flames coming out through the side. So we got the foam on, and I laid the tug at an angle so the smoke blew away from us . . .' And incredibly, he nudged the *Culver* in to within three or four feet of the inferno, and played foam into the hole. 'We were doing all right. We were. Then I suddenly see the next tank. Glowing red — those plates were an inch thick — dull red. Then cherry red, then white. Then I start to back her away just as all the burning oil and flames come out'. He stopped for a moment and looked at his hands. 'The water around us was burning, so I spun the tug around, with the wash o'the water to keep the flames away from us'. As the tide took the fire away, he returned again and again to the side of the burning, melting ship, his tug covered in foam, 'the telegraphs hot, hot in my hands'. He dreamed of it for months. 'Dull red, cherry red, then white. Back off, spin her round, come back with the foam'.

Very few tug seamen get decorations. It was luck that the *Culver's* battle was witnessed by a fair-minded naval officer. 'C in C Portsmouth, I did hear, in one of his navy ships. Apparently he put my name in and, I'm just saying what I heard, he said "he had never seen a ship manoeuvred with such precision and bravery", sort of thing'. Later, the Queen Mother gave him the medal, and said 'Ah, a night to remember, I think, when the *Pacific Glory* caught fire'.

As we talked, the sharp rain stopped, and the mate got the men painting again. The VHF radio from the office crackled briefly to remind *Calshot* of her main duty of the day: undocking the P & O liner *Canberra* and sending her on her way. Not that a reminder was needed: passenger liners are a treat. The older crewmen, over cups of tea in the mess, had told me of the great days now gone: of hectic moments with the *Ile de France* on the wire, of the last voyage of the old *Queen Mary*, of the *France* ('A terrible one, terrible. Never had steerage way of her own until she had so much speed up she nearly ran over her front tugs'). They had remembered the time they towed the *Reina del Mar* out, bound for Jersey, with Captain Short in a borrowed blonde glamour wig 'which I took off with a bow to the passengers'. Towing out a ship full of people, its rail lined with bright headscarves and waving children, has the edge over most of the work tugs get now. 'Tankers. A great big damn black sheet of iron. You can't blow kisses to one bored deckhand, waiting only to drop the wire and forget you. Passengers wave at you. It's good'. And they watch you out of sight.

We dropped the lines by the banana warehouse, and chugged past the sister tugs to the dock entrance. On the long afterdeck, the men and the boy laid out the towing line, 35 fathoms of heavy cable fit to pull 40 tons. The wire runs from its hook by way of a length of stretchy rope cable to absorb the snatching strain; through a gob-iron between two bollard's at the stern, and only then up to the towed ship. Without the guiding bollards the tug could slew sideways and wrap its own bridge up in the wire. Does this ever happen? 'Ah' say the tugmen affirmatively, without detail. In operation, the tug is a tool of the pilot, and obeys. 'But nobody, nobody but me is responsible for the safety of the tug. If I need to trip my line', said the Captain, 'I order it'. A tug once overturned, dragged down on her beam ends until it was too late to trip; the wire stuck fast, lying tortuously sideways across the hook. 'You have to know your boat exactly'.

With Benny the mate on the wheel, the skipper leaning out of the bridge window, and the men sorting cable on deck, we turned up towards the job. A south-westerly wind whipped up a few crests of foam; ahead, two tugs handled a troopship across our path. Southampton city to starboard, fields and shipyards to port; against the smoky dock cranes ahead, *Canberra* loomed white as a gigantic ghost, as graceful as a yacht.

We were 20 minutes early for sailing time, and I had expected a period of jilling-about in the choppy water, circling around the moored yachts perhaps — standing idly by. Two Alexandra tugs booked to haul the stern out were doing just that, but Captain Short preferred, to my delight, a uniquely tuggish form of waiting. With a spin of the wheel, Benny nuzzled the heavy black rubber bow into the liner's side, put the engine in very slow ahead, and leaned on the wheel as the tug leaned, balanced and restful, on the ship. The effect was of a patient dog leaning its nose against a door. The crew gazed up; the passengers waved down across the whiteness. 'See? Much better than a black old tanker'.

After ten minutes' nestling, the pilot crackled orders, a black seaman tossed down a messenger-line, and the heavy cable sagged across in the water, then rose as *Calshot* eased herself off, holding gently against the weight of the wire's catenary fall without pulling on the ship. It was ballet; a routine job polished by decades of practice. *Canberra* lay nailed to her berth by the weight of wind alone, the whole of her length a great white sail. On a curt word from the pilot, the tugs moved up to full power, geared down to their greatest pull;more heads appeared along the rail as the whole of *Calshot* churned and vibrated under us. 'Feel the power', said Short happily, and Benny inched the wheel to stop the turbulent wash of the tug from pushing the liner back. The bow inched outward from the dock. For a long moment, despite the struggling power that rattled our teeth, the tug seemed herself to be hanging, a tiny helpless toy on the wire; then she began to gain, and the pilot informed the vibrating air that the ship's engines would go ahead shortly.

Cautiously, Short kept the pull on the outer side, away from the dock, upwind. The pilot ordered him across to the port bow. 'He won't want us there, noooo', muttered he tugmaster, anguished, but a tug is a hireling, and Benny, blank-faced, moved across the white bow towards the wall, and tidied his churning wash away from the ship's keel. 'Right ahead now', said the pilot quickly, amid an eruption of relieved laughter. Benny said something, but not loudly.

Fairhead buoy to starboard, Gymp Elbow to port; *Calshot* pulled faster, the ship astern took on more power. The engineer remembered 'muck in the fuel line once, towing ahead like this. You know the big bulbous bows those tankers got? . . . oh, very nasty, we didn't half concentrate on getting the engines going'. A ship could run over a disabled tug now; the helpless hulk at the dock wall becomes, at nine knots, a juggernaut.

Up to Royal Pier, still towing. Halfway to Dock Head, the wireless barked, and the cry was loosed: 'LEGGO!' During the 15 seconds when the liner's seamen didn't leggo, I realized the understatement of the engineer's 'very nasty'. The wire slackened, the *Canberra* bore down close; the tug was still uncomfortably tethered as it dodged aside. When they did let go, the cable had not hit the water before little *Calshot* was shooting away clear, her winch twirling up the slack, dancing in the liner's wake. 'Slow b......s'.

Canberra steamed southward, between yachts and ferries, past Coronation and Hook, Calshot and the Brambles, to pass Spithead with the failing sun and leave St Catherine's light astern; to sail to Vigo, Madeira, Tenerife. *Calshot* chugged gently past city and fields and shipyards, to turn back in at Dock Head and make for her berth. Always the bridesmaid. 'Kippers for tea', said the Captain. 'I like kippers'.

He likes tugs, too. Thinking suddenly of Tony Derby's snapshot of the chaplain and the urn of ashes, I asked whether he would want to be scattered one day from this deck. 'Oh yes. Oh definitely. But lean well outboard when you do it, Benny, for God's sake. I'd hate to end up on the rubbing-band. Do it *properly*'.

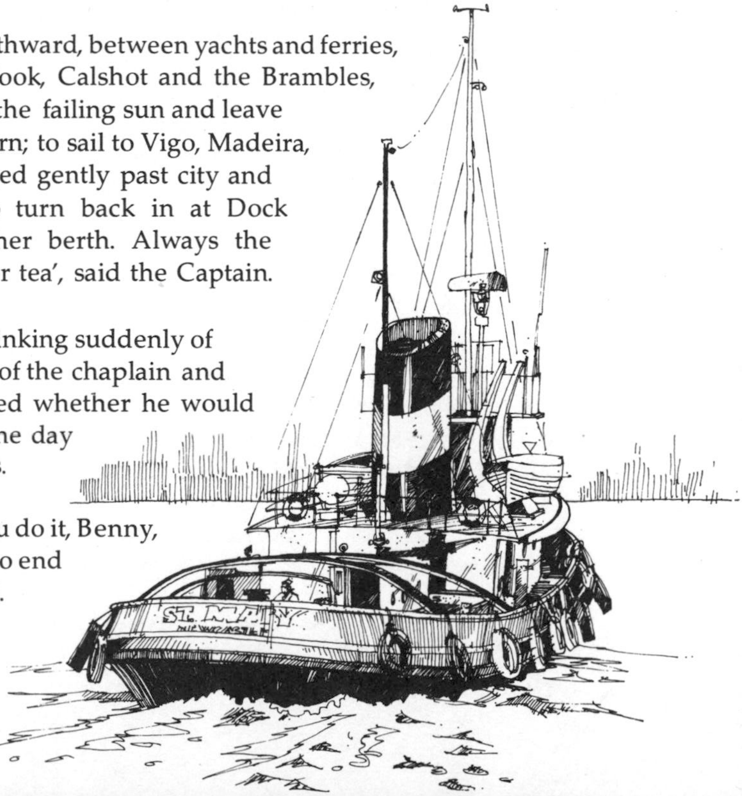

The lower deck

— 40 ways to keep children happy afloat

You are ready for anything. You have full set of charts, dozens of flares, a liferaft, spare batteries for everything; food, drink, dry clothes, wire-cutters to free a fallen mast and every almanac in print. You have heavy warps to trail, oil-bags, waterproof matches, a courtesy flag for every European nation including Monaco; you have heard the weather forecast and filled the water-tanks . . .

But if you have forgotten the shrimping net or omitted to pack Teddy Bear's Sun-Hat, all may yet be lost, and the voyage dissolve in tears before you are across the harbour bar. Children and yachts are not one of nature's effortless combinations. Both demand a genius for compromise and improvisation; but children like mess where ships like neatness; children like running and the largest yacht is smaller than the meanest garden. Children like other children; skippers can only take so many at once without climbing up the mast. Still, with a bit of low cunning and a good deal of foresight, you can sail with your children from birth to sail-handling age with no more horrors than attach to any family holiday. Indeed, as many battered grey sailing parents will tell you, there can even be pleasure in it. At least you always know where they are.

From a team of these veteran sailing families, closely questioned by your authors, we offer the following ways to keep kids happy.

Babies are a special case. If you are lucky, they will actually lie in their special case, or carrycot, all day long; dozing as the wind rocks them and waking occasionally for a suck at whatever is on offer. (Breast is best; the gimballed Milton bottle-sterilizer is, as yet, in its own infancy). If you are not lucky, they will need to be entertained for at least eight hours a day.

A supported baby chair is essential. Plastic ones for less than a tenner may be fitted with a lanyard, and a series of cleats unobtrusively fitted in various corners above and below decks, so that the upright and harnessed baby may be always in view, regarding you and your gyrations with a beady and attentive eye.

A device called a Wobble Globe — a clear plastic sphere mounted on a rubber stalk and sucker, containing coloured balls — may be fixed to any smooth GRP surface, and bashed freely by the baby without snagging any lines on its smooth surface; we had ours for a whole season on the cockpit side, where it drew crowds of onlookers in marinas, convinced that it was the latest advanced satellite device from Brookes & Gatehouse.

Our son's bunk-cushions were backed with velcro, matched to velcro-covered battens on the leeboard. At six months his fiercest delight was to rip them off with a terrible tearing sound at 6 am, and stick them back to repeat the process indefinitely. It used up time.

Raisins and shreds of dried coconut and banana are popular, rarely cause any choking, and take an enormously long time to eat off the plastic chair's tray while you struggle to heat the rest of the meal in the galley.

Hang mobiles and bells and pull-knob musical boxes on every available knob or cleat below decks. For a brief, valuable time they will distract the baby from pulling at any of the other interesting fittings you would rather he left alone.

Tiny, unwaterworthy plastic gimmicky dinghies (as sold on seafronts at resort towns) may be a worry to the lifeboat service, but they do make brilliant paddling pools for the smallest cockpit floor. When your baby finally outgrows the biggest ship's bucket, he can have his bath in it, too.

This relatively simple stage of management is soon over. The other suggestions relate to slightly older, or much older, yachting children. What stage your own have reached depends on them, and on whether a touch of seasickness causes them to regress a year or two in their tastes or advance to the torpid Athaeneum stage with premature haste. Here we go:

Katharine Thornhill, marking a decade of sailing on the family boats, tells me categorically that the single most important thing from the start has been 'My bed'. It has to be your absolutely own bed, she continued, no messing around with other people having turns in it or stowing fenders in it all day; it is your castle and your kingdom and your refuge. You can keep your dolls in it, stick up pictures with Blu-Tak, and keep a stock of books. Her sister Mary has been known to take things even further; she has spent a 48-hour rough sea passage entirely secluded behind her leecloths like the elderly Queen Victoria, eating biscuits, fiddling with toys, and sleeping.

Another favourite occupation is jumping up and down on deck shouting songs. Make sure your child knows enough songs.

Take a series of smaller craft to tow astern. Behind the tender, up to a dozen assorted toy barges, ducks, washing-up liquid bottles etc may be trailed in line, mesmerizing the watching child. If your tow exceeds a few feet, you could always add a small dan-buoy with warning red flag on it, like an Irish fishing boat.

Or tow a fishing line and catch mackerel. Gauge first whether the excitement of it all is going to outweigh the squeamish distaste of your most sensitive child for the killing.

Draw faces on fenders and tow them astern, laying bets as to whose face lasts longest in the wash. This may, felt pen being what it is, result in your printing silly faces on the sides of white boats next to you in harbour that night. Decide whether this is worthwhile.

'The front of the boat', said the above-mentioned Katharine's father, 'is always for some reason very special'. It is the nicest place to be, perched or squatting by the pulpit, watching the water rush by. Make sure that your lifelines run right forward; there is no point having such an attractive spot if nobody under 12 is ever to be allowed up there.

'Swinging like Tarzan from all the handholds' was a frequently quoted pastime. Since they will do this whatever you say, you might as well make sure the handholds are up to it.

When in harbour, stock up on baby crabs etc, to keep in a bucket of sand and stones and seawater the next day in the cockpit. With luck, this may assuage the longing for pets which will otherwise manifest itself in stowaway kittens, dear little earwigs in matchboxes, etc being smuggled aboard at the start of the voyage.

You cannot have too many books aboard. Colouring books, dot-to-dot drawing books, magic water-painting books, story books, and totally blank books to draw in. Above all, totally new and unsuspected books, to be brought out only in an emergency of terrible boredom.

An extra child friend is the single best toy. Someone to show off the boat to and boss over sail-handling. If you have any spare room at all, invite one occasionally.

Next to that (especially for small children) an extra adult is very valuable. A good uncle will generate endless amusement, and read *Little Black Sambo* with a better grace than the jaded parent can manage.

Most of the above suggest that the weather is at least fine enough to be on deck, and that you are not stuck on an anchorage in a gale, safe enough but unable to land for two days. The following are suggestions for small-area amusements to be pursued below decks. All require some prudent stocking-up beforehand, though:

A tape cassette machine is excellent; not only to prevent your having to sing *'Old Macdonald Had a Farm'* too often personally, but for older children to devise, produce, and script their own radio programmes, including tin-saucepan sound effects. Take extra batteries.

Oddly enough, several children seem to have taken to the gentle business of embroidery on board boats. Highly decorative patches for jeans and smocks can be cobbled out of canvas and coloured wool. If you spend a long time becalmed, your whole family could turn up in L'Abervrach looking like genuine Gitanes.

Very, very, time-consuming cooking is good for older children. Try stuffing prunes with peanut butter, or picking the meat from undersized crabs.

I hesitate to pass on a child's recommendation for collage, because of her father's explosive snort when he heard her mention it. Perhaps we should just say' all right, collage, only nowhere near the chart locker' . . .

The same goes for rub-down transfers. Beware lest your Thames buoys get replaced by E.T.

Snap, Happy Families, Scrabble, Monopoly . . . surely you have these already, for the adults?

A decent mirror and a set of greasepaints (with some crepe hair) makes — in the absolutely last resort — for an hour's absorbed giggling and an impromptu theatrical performance in the fo'c's'le archway. Keep the existence of said greasepaints a deadly secret until everything else has failed and the gale is still keeping you aboard at anchor.

Nearly all this last group of amusements imply that the children are not particularly concerned with the boat, except as a rather confined playing-space. But in fact, most bright children are captivated by the idea of sailing; so long as the reality is made to match up to their expectations of fun and security, this is a good time to lay down the foundations of a real and enduring interest in the sea. So — greasepaint and cassette machines for the moment forgotten, along with the rest of shore life — try using the great resources of the sea and seamanship to entertain them and yourself:

There is always baggy-wrinkle. Store up tatters of rope and allow the children to make yards and yards of baggy-wrinkle in traditional style. The slight snag is that you will then have to let them festoon your shiny new stainless rigging with it until you look like an 1870's tunnyman fresh in from the Azores.

The art of knots is a good one; from two years old onwards, there is always a knot that your hands can tie. Small children can learn half-knots and grannies and figures-of-eight; older children master bowlines and sheepshanks; older still, Turks' Heads, ornamental mats, rope fenders, and the rest of *Ashley's Book of Knots.* Take plenty of spare cordage. Try and get some fender-lines whipped while you are at it.

Children need their own dinghy; a small rubber inflatable that will not damage anyone's topsides. Used with discretion in sheltered waters (and with another, faster, rescue dinghy available to the watching parent) the dinghy should be rowed, properly, *without* a long painter to the moored yacht. Nobody, (says K Thornhill) can row with a rope dangling off the front of their dinghy; the more real independence the child has, the safer it will be in the end.

You cannot beat a complicated rig, with children of eight and above. Use lots of sails; a yawl would be good, or a ketch with a gaff or two and some fiddly little topsails. One can tinker with rigging all day in identical conditions. On one boat — a standard Bermudan sloop — the owners craftily instituted 'the children's sail'. It was a brightly coloured,-somewhat clapped-out old cruising 'chute a size too small; whenever the weather was light enough to use it, it didn't really matter where the children hoisted it, or which way up. Some highly original sail-plans were devised by this means.

It is never too soon to learn about navigation. A spare chart for plotting imaginary voyages; a main chart encased in a plastic envelope, to be marked up with chinagraph pencil by your child; some dividers (perhaps not your best ones) for endlessly measuring off distances; a parallel rule, with all give endless constructive amusement.

Nor is there any point keeping the only hand bearing-compass to yourself. If you cannot face the sight of little fumbling fingers holding the main one out over the side, spend a couple of pounds at a boat jumble sale on an old one with bubble in it; so long as the card still swings.

Steering is fun, so long as there is something visible to point at. Nobody under eight is going to be much cop at holding a compass course, though a grid compass might help. Even over eight, if you ask for a compass course, for heaven's sake write it on a piece of paper and Blu-Tak it above the instrument. Even the occasional 30-year-old has been known to forget whether it was 280° or 350°, especially under engine.

Nail a coin to the mast, like Columbus, for the first to spot land. All right then, stick it to the mast with the ever-useful Blu-Tak.

One father devised a brilliant game called 'Buoy Bingo'. He always planned his passages meticulously in any case; and as he planned one crossing, it occurred to him to note down every likely buoy or beacon which might be seen (this was the Thames estuary), with its markings, and to draw it in a square of his 'bingo' board. He then photocopied the board, issued one to each of three children, and offered a 50 pence prize to the one who scored highest. As well as ticking off the square, the players had to write in it the exact log reading at the time of spotting the buoy, so that he could verify the likelihood of their telling the truth. Not only did two of them tie with a full house, but all three saw more buoys than he ever did on that trip.

Invent your own weather rhymes.

Teach the children about the shapes of clouds; include types in your bingo or scavenger games; let them fill in the isobars on the weather map. Desist from this game, perhaps, when the weather pattern is actually beginning to worry you seriously . . .

Try and find mnemonics for learning all the flags too, eg: Yellow means quarantine; sick people go yellow . . .

One family instituted 'tests'. Children were examined, twice a season, on their knowledge of boats and seamanship; when you passed the first test, you got your hat badge; at the second test, you got your whistle; at the top level, your sailing knife, This, apparently, did not put any of the family off the whole business, but led to fierce ambition and a lifelong mania for getting things right. If your family is up to this, try it.

Turn to the chapter on Flag-Upmanship and try dressing overall, making a paying-off pennant, and devising new ways to dip your ensign with dramatic effect. Dip it to every single thing you pass, including oil rigs. Fly regional courtesy flags of your own devising for every single county you pass going down-Channel. Let the little blighters design and sew their own huge house flag and run it up in marinas.

And that makes 40. Used with discretion, they may help you put off, or avoid entirely, the terrible day when you have either to take a portable television, or not take the children. Good luck!

Well whipped ropes' ends

Advice has a quality which renders it easier to give than to take, in a similar way to that in which the thought of whipping the end of a frayed rope is far less effort than hunting for the whipping twine. That is why John Iriving came up with such an apt title for his chapter in the original 'Week-End Book' when he called his collection of tips, wrinkles and cautions, 'Well Whipped Ropes' Ends' As he described it.

'Armchair advice is so like a patent medicine — much advertised but seldom taken.' Allow us to place a selection of his nostrums before you, and swallow them if you will.

The best cruising yacht is a conglomeration of compromise, so is cruising — and sailing too.

Efficiency, effectiveness, speed, seaworthiness and a 'happy ship' depend upon the ability to strike a mean.

Do not refer to your 'cock boat' as a yacht when buying stores, it influences the addition of the bill.

And as she is not armoured, there is very little harm in saying that you are 'on' her when the captious critic would have you to be 'in' her.

What of the wierdness of the complaint that a merchant officer isn't much use in a small ship, and this from someone to whom the Horn is just geography and 'Typhoon' is a long short story.

It is on a par with, 'Four things shalt thou not see aboard a yacht for its comfort — a cow, a wheelbarrow, an umbrella and a naval officer.'

As to the size of boat — some say there is no fixed rule, but there is — a foot of waterline for every year of a man's age.

ON YACHTS

If you have a ship and she seems to be almost what you want, keep her. There may be a better ship, there is *certainly* a worse one.

She may starve you, but she probably won't drown you: at least she hasn't done so yet.

Cruising comfort is increased by reducing luxuries, not by increasing them.

The more gadgets you accumulate the less sea time you put in. The less gadgets you adopt, the less there is to think about.

And the less there is to think about and worry about, the freer you are, and the happier.

And the essentials of a good ship are a tight hull, good gear, a reliable engine — and a sane cabin.

And the sane cabin: size doesn't matter, what does is a dry bed and a tight deckhead.

Beware a well painted and well varnished yacht for sale: paint and enamel on a 'she' afloat can serve the same purpose as paint and enamel on a 'she' ashore.

When buying: trust all men, yea, even princes — and then cut the cards yourself.

ON FITTING OUT

Paint may cover a multitude of sins — but murder will out. Don't try to varnish after tea — unless you want a milk-white bloom over all.

Gear which falls from aloft is usually harder than the head it falls upon.

When working aloft remember the old Navy motto — 'One hand for yourself — and one for the King.' (That's why a seaman is a 'hand' — in the singular).

ON GOING TO SEA

When preparing for a cruise, hope for the best and prepare for the worst-and then, probably there will be no worst.

A well fed ship is a happy ship Don't live on cold food all the time — you can do that anywhere, why come to sea to do it.

When the weather sets in cold and wet, and the glass is on the downward run, nothing is more valuable than hot food and drink.

And the worse the weather, the hotter the food and drink and the more of it.

For a good stout heart is the child of a well-filled belly.

All these things bear in mind when catering — and then have some to spare.

When the day planned for the start arrives — START even if you have to put back again, for the ice must be broken. Nelson said, 'Harbour rots good ships and good men,' and he was very right.

Don't be deterred by the wind in the harbour. It is seldom as bad outside as it sounds inside. At least go out and look at it.

This does not imply that senseless risk should be taken for fear of armchair critics on the club veranda. 'When I was your age, my lad, I'd have pulled down three reefs and seen it out!' That sort of nonsense does all harm and no good. Any fool can walk blindly into trouble 'outside'; it is the wise man who knows when to keep clear of it.

A night under a weather shore at open anchor is better than a night in port. For a night in harbour is half a day and a whole tide wasted and that may mean an advance of 40 miles thrown away at the least.

ON NAVIGATION

There were three Graces and Three Muses and there were three L's for the Deep Sea sailor Lead, Latitude and Lookout, or Lead, Log and Lookout. These still hold good and in addition,the small ship man must have three C's Chart Compass and Confidence and the greatest of these is Confidence.

The man who can sail the Thames Estuary in safety and with confidence should at once seek Ostende and Dunkirk (if his ship is suitable) and, thereafter, the Earth's compass will have no bounds for he has become a navigator — and all because of the gift of confidence.

Screw down every hatch while sailing out of harbour. It is more pleasant to remember to open them out again (if the seas are smooth) than to spend an hour with a mop through forgetting to close them.

When in doubt reef, indeed, reef the first time it crosses your mind — it is easier to shake out a reef than put one in a hurry.

On a lengthy passage, start regular watches as soon as the navigator is satisfied that he has a good departure.

Four-hour watches are quite long enough, and with two in a watch, hourly spells at the tiller will achieve results which will gratify the navigator.

When only one is on deck at a time at night, it should be the rule of the ship that he wears a harness — with the other end clipped on!

And a word of watches. Prompt relief is the essence of a happy ship. You may feel that you haven't had enough sleep — but the man you relieve has had none at all yet. And he won't bless you for being late.

So long as there is a fair wind, keep her going at it. Nelson's fame rests as much upon the fact that he never neglected a fair wind as upon anything else.

Sailing in heavy weather may be a test of a seaman's nerve, but drifting in the lightest of airs is a test of his skill and temper.

Sail full and bye in a seaway, start your sheets and let her fall off half a point and even more, but keep her sailing.

Luff to a breaking wave crest, start your sheets a little if need be at a crest, then bear away again on the down slope.

The navigator might also remember that at the end of a long, dirty, weather thrash to windward, his position will probably be nearer the wind than his reckoning suggested. This will be partly due to the 'luffing' that has gone on.

In dirty weather, it is always a good idea to heave to for a meal. What is lost thereby in progress is gained in well-being.

Remember that Lord Nelson said, 'It is often easier to attack than to achieve.'